CONTENTS AT A GLANCE

TRAIN OF THOUGHTS

DESIGNING THE EFFECTIVE WEB EXPERIENCE

JOHN C. LENKER, JR.

www.trainofthoughts.com

New Riders

201 West 103rd Street
Indianapolis, Indiana 46290

TRAIN OF THOUGHTS—Designing the Effective Web Experience

International Standard Book Number: 0-7357-1174-7
Library of Congress Catalog Card Number: 2001092826
Printed in China
First Printing: May, 2002

06 05 04 03 02   7 6 5 4 3 2 1

Interpretation of the printing code: The rightmost double-digit number is the year of the book's printing; the rightmost single-digit number is the number of the book's printing. For example, the printing code 02-1 shows that the first printing of the book occurred in 2002.

PUBLISHER
DAVID DWYER

ASSOCIATE PUBLISHER
STEPHANIE WALL

EXECUTIVE EDITOR
STEVE WEISS

PRODUCT MARKETING MANAGER
KATHY MALMLOFF

MANAGING EDITOR
SARAH KEARNS

DEVELOPMENT EDITOR
BARBARA TERRY

PROJECT MANAGER
JENNIFER EBERHARDT

PROJECT EDITOR
LINDA SEIFERT

TECHNICAL EDITOR
JULIE DIRKSEN

COPY EDITOR
JOY DEAN LEE

PUBLICIST
SUSAN NIXON

CREATIVE DIRECTOR
JOHN LENKER

DESIGNER
BRAD RANDALL

PHOTOGRAPHER & DESIGN CONSULTANT
STEVE LASTAVICH

CASE STUDY WRITER
JENNIFER JESSE

PROOFREADER
ROBIN DRAKE

INDEXER
CHERYL LENSER

ACKNOWLEDGMENTS

THE BOOK TEAM

Barb Terry—Thanks for sticking your neck out, going to bat, and all but shedding blood for this project. I owe you so much. You're talented, kind, patient, and a genuinely caring person. I'll never forget what you've done for me.

Jennifer Eberhardt—Although you were the cleanup pitcher in this particular game, you came in, worked your heart out, and threw straight strikes. Thank you for adopting *Train of Thoughts*.

David Dwyer—Thanks for your vote of confidence in green-lighting this book. You helped get all the necessary people on board, and you provided much encouragement. There's a reason why everyone who works for you likes you.

Steve Weiss—Thanks for finding ways to make all the unique things we wanted to do with this book work. You not only kept things on track but also went the extra mile. I appreciate it.

Karen Whitehouse—Thanks for showing me the ropes in the beginning. I feel honored to work with someone who has helped so many great authors along the way.

Brad Randall—Thanks for putting more into this project over the last year than you got out of it financially. You're one of the true design craftsmen. What's more, you have the strongest work ethic and the most persistent integrity of any designer that I know. You have tremendous potential and a great career ahead of you. Thanks for helping to make the journey through my ideas more beautiful.

Steve Lastavich—Thanks for putting so much into the two thousand pictures you composed for this project that you practically broke your head, nearly got run over by a train, and were almost arrested in the process. You also are a true designer, and it shows in your photo compositions. Both your insight into the creative process and your design guidance were crucial to the success of this project.

Julie Dirksen—Thanks for fitting this project into your busy schedule. You have great insight, flare, and skill. Your comments helped me to really gauge the tone of my arguments.

Jennifer Jesse—Thanks for keeping tabs on so many details in the galleries and in the case studies. Many things would have fallen through the cracks if it weren't for you.

Scott Hamlin—Last, but not least. Thanks for inviting me to work with you on *Flash 5 Magic*, for recommending my book proposal to New Riders, and for encouraging me through the process. You're a wonderful person and a great friend.

Thanks also to Jim Conway, Robin Drake, Aren Howell, Joy Dean Lee, Cheryl Lenser, Linda Seifert, and everyone else at New Riders whom contributed to the success of this project.

FAMILY & FRIENDS

Jennifer Lynn Lenker—Wife, friend, poet, zookeeper. I know that work has taken precedence over many other priorities. Thanks for your love, support, and patience throughout the course of this project and throughout our many years together. You're a wonderful person, and I don't deserve you—but I'm glad we're together.

Adrianne, Zoë, and Noah—Although you're the most important design and development projects of my life, much of the time I suspect that it is you who are designing me! You kids are the best. I'm not quite sure how you all are turning out so well—your mother and I've put so much of our time into other projects that are much less important. The answer must be that you're all just plain terrific! Thanks for your understanding and for your undying affection.

Bonnie Lenker McGill—Mother, drill sergeant, and guide. You've always tried to help me even though I've relentlessly confounded your advice throughout my life. Thank you for your love, patience, and support as I've faced both successes and failures throughout the course of my life.

Thanks to those who've helped and encouraged my work:

Michael Allen, Jeff Anderson, Tony Axtel, Irvine Baxter, Jim Bickle, Andy Car, Page Carr, Scott Colehour, Keith Craig, Mike Drebenstedt, Jo-Anne Ebensteiner, Vince Freeman, Brian Gimotty, Diana Grasselli, Chas & Pat Groves, Camilla Grozian, Kent Hathaway, Darlene Heimerl, Scott Hoffman, Paul Howe, Jesse Imgrand, David Katz, Ingrid Krampe, Ken Kyle, Katherine Lambe, Sterling Ledet, Adam Lee, Dennis & Diane Lee, Matthew & Nikki Lee, Steve Lee, Angie Lenker, Fritz Lenker, Martin Lipshutz, Tom & Sammy Lyon, Jobe Maker, Vic Marotta, Andy Marshall, Jerry McGill, Jane Meyer, Keith Meyer, Brett & Jennifer Michlitsch, Chris Mourton, Mike & Nick Mourton, David Nanos, Dale Ogren, Vince Overton, Mark Patterson, Robert Peterson, David Plummer, Jerry Points, Andy Props, Eric Rautio, Eric Rawe, Keith Robertson, Trever Russell, Gregg Sampson, Joe & Amy Schuller, Joan Schultz, Linda "Bink" Semmer, Lester Shen, Carlos Sosa, Alec Syme, Mike Teller, Lance Thornswood, Jason Thorp, Bob Tuthill, Peter Tye, Brandon Williams, Marty Yde, Charles Youel, Jason Zeaman, and Robert Zielinski.

A special thanks to those not on the book team who spent time reviewing various drafts of my manuscript including Michael Allen, Paul Bieganski, Richard Harris, Brett Michlitsch, Byron Reeves, and Linda Weinman. Your comments were extremely valuable.

Finally, to Truth, I say thanks.

I dedicate this book to the memory of my father,
JOHN C. LENKER (1941-1994).

In his life he both dreamed big dreams and worked hard to realize those dreams. From a cook in a small-town pizza joint, to a captain in the Marine Corps, to the president of Green Giant, Europe; he pursued excellence in everything that he did. He's the example that has always inspired me to strive to do the same.

CONTRIBUTORS

TECHNICAL EDITOR
JULIE DIRKSEN

Julie currently serves Allen Interactions—a computer-based training company—as an instructional interactivity designer and project manager. Ms. Dirksen has also worked as a project manager with WisdomTools, an online training company created from the Research and Development Division of Indiana University's Center for Excellence in Education, developing internationally implemented collaborative web and Lotus Notes training environments. Ms. Dirksen also has several years' experience working in corporate training.

Ms. Dirksen holds an M.S. degree in instructional systems technology from Indiana University, with an emphasis on human-computer interaction. She is also adjunct faculty at the Minneapolis College of Art and Design, teaching courses in project management and instructional design.

CASE STUDY WRITER
JENNIFER JESSE

Jennifer is an interactive media and graphic design consultant with a passion to provide her clients with visually and mentally engaging media. Her keen interest and talents in usability, visual design, communication, and technology have provided opportunities ranging from interactive producer to lead designer, where she has led initiatives on numerous training, entertainment, and promotional projects.

Over the past five years, she worked on projects for numerous Fortune 500 companies as well as the US Air Force. Her work has been featured in *Flash 5 Magic* and *Flash 5 Cartoons and Games*. Her collaboration with Allen Interactions has sparked a relentless pursuit to blend human psychology and usability factors with innovative design and technology.

Originally from Detroit, she holds a BFA from Wayne State University, graduating with top honors. Jennifer currently resides in Minneapolis and enjoys design, computers, photography, travel, cooking, and biking. Her work can be viewed at http://www.jenniferjesse.com.

PHOTOGRAPHER
STEVE LASTAVICH

DESIGNER
BRAD RANDALL

Steve is a freelance interactive designer and consultant. He specializes in visualization—helping organizations bring the true meaning of their messages out in their designs. Steve has applied his talents in projects for major corporations, including:

Allen Interactions, DaimlerChrysler, IBM, Lincoln Financial Group, Marvin Windows & Doors, Minneapolis College of Art and Design, Minnesota Historical Society, Target Stores, and the U.S. Department of the Interior.

Steve has a B.A. from Minneapolis College of Art and Design (MCAD) where he majored in interactive and graphic design. He also holds a Bachelor of Individualized Studies from the University of Minnesota, which emphasized marketing and organizational psychology.

Steve has won numerous awards including, *HOW* magazine—Interactive Design Annual 2000, Best of Show and CMYK Interactive 2000—Best of Show, as well as numerous scholarships .

Acknowledgments:
> Rebecca Alm at Minneapolis College of Art and Design (MCAD)
> Don Meyer, executive director at the Minnesota Transportation Museum, and his volunteer staff, including John Wellman
> Gina Sorci, my assistant
> Melanie, Mic, and Chuck, and the rest of the folks at ProColor
> My mother and father
> My 1971 Nikkomat 35mm with a 1x, 2x, 4x macro system and a 180-300 telephoto lens

Brad is a freelance graphic designer based in Minneapolis. His interests and capabilities also include illustration, furniture design, and industrial design. He has passion for appreciating and creating meaningful and affordable utilitarian design accessible to everyone.

Brad received a BFA from the Minneapolis College of Art and Design (MCAD), where he garnered top honors. He was awarded the Wanda Gag Merit Scholarship, the Yamamoto Moss Merit Scholarship, and the Van Derlip Award. Since graduating, he has done work for 3M, Martin/Williams, Uno, and invioni.

In his time away from the mouse and keyboard, Brad enjoys seeing, creating, reading, Frisbee golf, good food, and good company.

For more information about Brad Randall and to view an online sample of his portfolio visit http://www.trainofthoughts.com.

Acknowledgments:
> Jan Jancourt
> Catherine Russell
> Stephen and Carol Randall

FOREWORD: DR. MICHAEL ALLEN

This book isn't politically correct. It's just plain correct.

At least for the moment.

If ever there were an example of ready, fire, aim, it's the Web. What an unexpected spurt of growth it had—from an indispensable form of document sharing among governmental and university research organizations, to the ubiquitous backbone of contemporary communications and commerce it has become almost overnight!

It isn't right to cry out "Who could see it coming?" however. Many visions of the future have included descriptions of universal, instantaneous access to information. Every Star Trek fan knew that someday we'd just ask the computer for any information or analysis we needed, with most results politely returned in just a moment—often without a delay in the rhythm of conversation.

What we didn't see was how fast the future would arrive, and we weren't prepared for it on a broad scale. Of course, as Yogi Berra said, "The future isn't what it used to be." If this book were politically correct, it would continue to portray the future and the Web as we saw them years ago. And it would not be correct.

After years in its cocoon, the Internet's metamorphosis produced something of a giant moth. Suddenly, the Web was everywhere, overtaking postal services and forcing telephone systems to embrace it or fall to the wayside. Computer operating systems needed optimization for access, computer applications needed to become Web-compatible, and people—well, people needed to learn new applications, new behaviors, new jargon, and adapt. To be in fashion, corporations needed to provide new services, staff differently, compete differently, market and sell differently whether they knew why or not. No one would say the impact of the Internet has been anything less than profound, although to find an unanimously upheld evaluation might be more than difficult. At the very least, the moth ate holes in many long-lived if not stodgy structures.

Has its effect been good or bad? It's too soon to tell. There has been some good, some bad. The fact is, we're not ready for the Web yet. Sure, many of us have been working on interactive applications, tools for their development, and principles of design for decades. But with the sudden advent of an omnipresent Web, legions of designers and developers have undertaken the challenge of designing Web sites. These people are smart, energetic, and talented. They are at home with technology, cool design, and creativity. They are off and running, but they don't know where they are going. Many become lost and drop out before getting their Web applications launched. Others regrettably unveil Web applications that do their owners in or succeed only in causing a radical reconsideration of the scope and nature of the task at hand.

What's wrong? Simple. Energy and good intentions do not a good Web site make.

The models emulated by so many are close derivatives of models appropriate for print publications. They are flat, non-interactive, uninteresting, boring. They are content-centric, imperfect in design, and of doubtful value on most viewers' screens. As John says, "Because many experience designers view design for the Web as an extension of print design, much of the multimedia that's produced for the Web is perceptually ineffective." Indeed.

This book is correct. At least for the moment.

There is a tremendous amount to be learned as we experiment with the Web and explore new uses and new designs. We will know more, probably much more, about good design in the future. But what John shares in this book is unfortunately the needlessly uncommon wisdom of today. In Web design, the "just do it" philosophy hasn't worked out so well.

What should be known more widely is that much current design is bad—dreadfully bad. John is not hesitant to point out wide ranging

weaknesses from the rampant tendency to force feed content down the throats of Web guests to the details of design aesthetics that destroy many effective long-lasting relationships between people and Web services.

Until Web sites are people-focused and experience-focused, instead of being content-focused; innumerable misperceptions about what can be achieved through the Web will constrain its second metamorphosis in which it will become something beautiful, pleasant, and indeed welcome. The technology is here, although it could easily be much better, and the opportunity is here too as millions have affordable, convenient access, but there has been too much focus on the technology and the message rather than on the true purpose of the experience and desired outcomes.

Train of Thoughts provides a clear destination. People have rightly criticized the inefficiency of Web experiences and their poor user interfaces. They are there and they are horrific. But correcting inefficiencies and user interfaces doesn't get us where we really want to be. We need not to be in a place of doing things right as much as one where we're doing the right things.

John properly sees the Web as a purveyor of personal experiences that meet our needs not only efficiently but effectively. Without mincing words, John decries concerted efforts to reach efficiency in senseless, worthless experiences—the "ditches of mediocrity." We can do better. It is known how to do better. We must do better.

When the Web is done right, we learn, we buy, we experience, we laugh, we grow, we return with enthusiasm because our time is well-spent. We feel connected with others through the technology, not separated and isolated. We feel appreciated because our individual values and preferences are honored. We are glad to live in the time of the Web.

This book is correct. At least for the moment.

John is clear about not only where we need to go, but also how we can get there. As our experience grows, we will undoubtedly find better ways to produce the experiences and outcomes we seek. But processes that work have been devised, applied, and tested. Why not spend a little time learning how to save a lot of time?

As have many others, I spent a lot of time teaching students an essentially linear method of application design that we now know to have very objectionable flaws. As we worked to remedy the flaws, we evolved our processes into much better approaches which are iterative and far more effective. Those many people who have not been acquainted with more effective approaches will find this book enlightening—maybe invaluable. Experience teaches us much, but unless that experience is shared, its value is minute.

When John first joined Allen Interactions Inc. he brought with him an enormous creative talent that we were happy to tap. In exchange, we did our best to share with him our experience in the design and development of interactive applications that "enhance the human mind and spirit" (our mission statement). As all teachers hope, the student has become the teacher. John has absorbed and synthesized outcomes from his wide-ranging experiences and shared very useful and often very pragmatic advice. The case studies and galleries alone will make your time with the book beneficial. Most of all, we hope you will join the campaign for Web designs that are not only tolerable but also enriching to our lives in a complex world.

Michael W. Allen

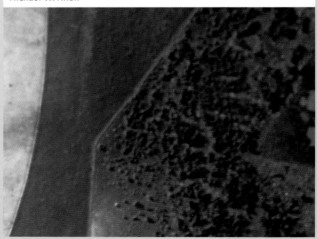

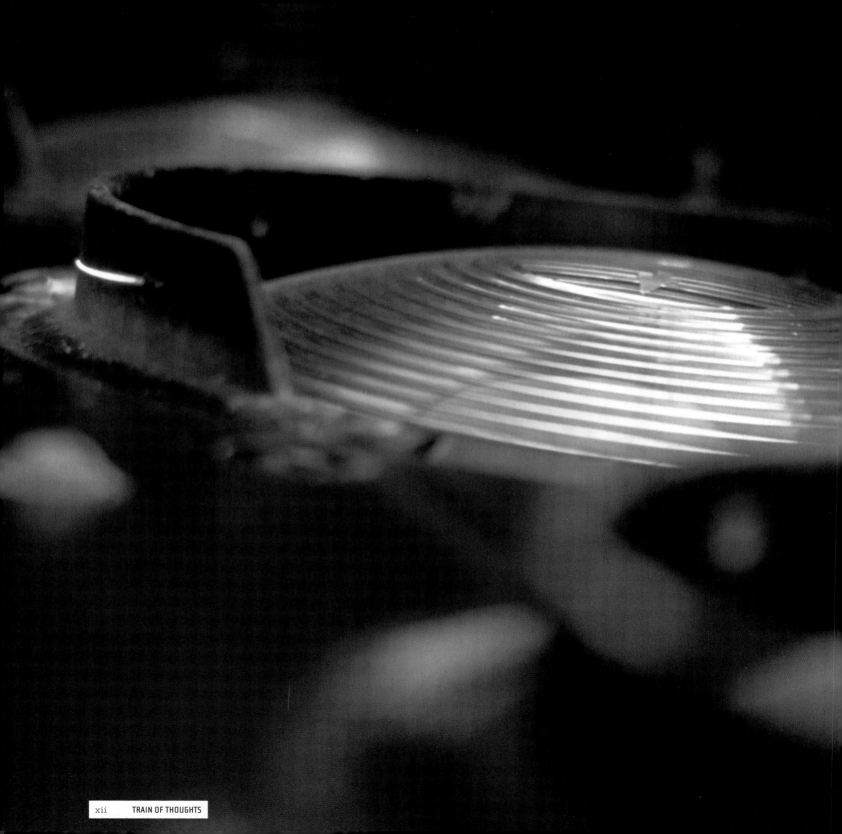

CONTENTS
TABLES OF NOTION SUMMARIES

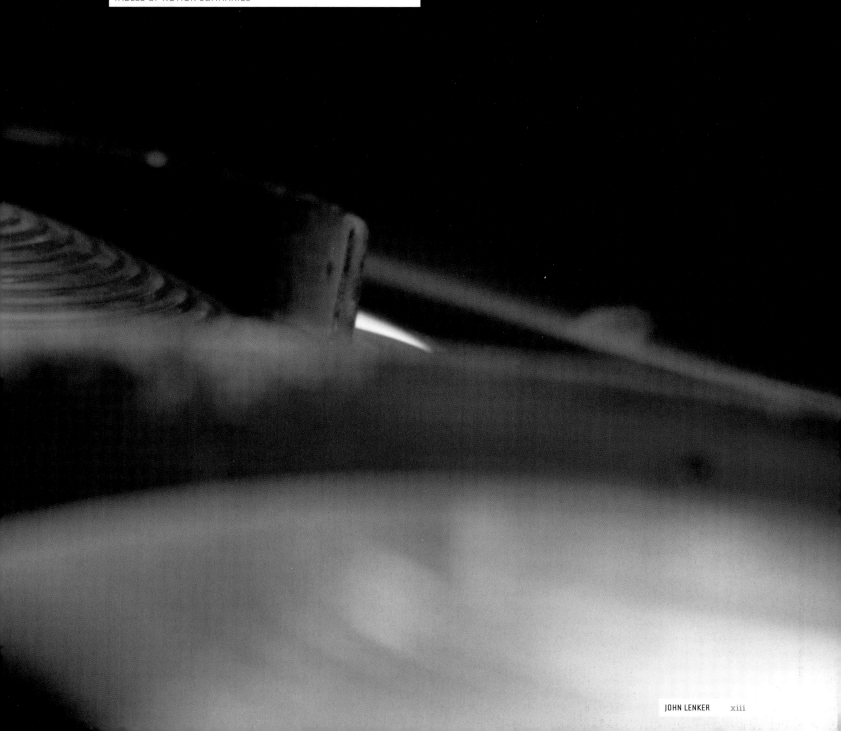

INTRODUCTION TO PART ONE

CHAPTER 01

CHAPTER 02

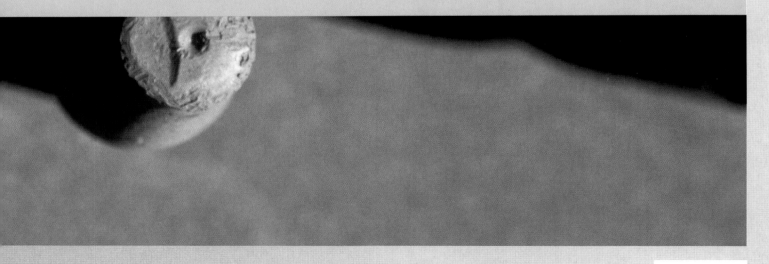

CHAPTER 03

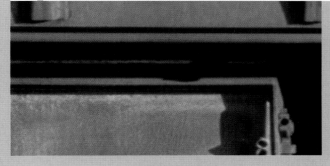

CHAPTER 04

CHAPTER 05

CHAPTER 06

INTRODUCTION TO PART TWO

△ = Planning

◆ = Execution

● = Evaluation

CHAPTER 07

CHAPTER 08

and self-pa ed manner. Those people who ld opportunities gain exposur

CHAPTER 09

CHAPTER 10

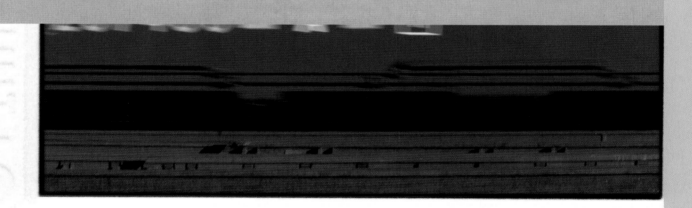

PART ONE

UNDERSTANDING WEB EXPERIENCE DESIGN

INTRODUCTION
To Part One

i1.00 Initial experience design standards have been tenacious even though they're inadequate.

It's been years since private organizations as well as the general public began to interact with and through the Web on a widespread and regular basis. Many of us have come to depend on it, and the numbers of us who are benefiting from it continue to grow both exponentially and internationally.

Still, Web enterprises are clinging to design standards that were largely based on the needs, limitations, and shortsightedness of computer scientists working in government and in major universities decades ago. It's hard to blame the inadequacies of these standards on those who first developed them, however. After all, who could have predicted that the Internet would transform from a contingency communications network for the U.S. Defense Department and a research tool for universities into both a communications system for the public as well as a central component of popular culture? Who could have known that it would morph from being a platform to view and share electronic versions of paper-based documents to a medium that distributes interactive multimedia? Who would have thought the Web would someday be populated with intelligent systems that were capable of simulating relationships with people?

Maybe Arthur C. Clarke and Gene Roddenberry did, but that's about it.

i1.00.02
Nielsen seems to disregard people's consumptive, social, and emotional needs and focuses almost exclusively on their practical needs.

i1.00.01 Enter the 'usability' experts.

Notwithstanding those who unwittingly stumbled upon the seeds of an information revolution, it's hard to understand why, even to this day, well-known usability gurus continue to toe the party line. The foundation of usability as a field has traditionally been based on the laudable desire to make software applications, such as word processors, easier for people to *use*—this largely through the practice of what is known as "user testing." Unfortunately, these principles have been overextended and have often been applied to the Web in inappropriate ways.

More than being conglomerations of mere *interfaces* for tools such as car dashboards or microwave ovens—which are *Human Factor* concerns and which the field of usability largely emulates—the Web as a medium has come to primarily be a vehicle for human communication and interaction. It, therefore, should be treated as such, and new Web design standards should be developed that support this more sophisticated role.

Meanwhile, usability principles continue to be overgeneralized and misapplied, and people continue to be stifled and confused as they're forced to interact with online resources that more often than not provide ineffective online experiences.

i1.00.02 The movement toward accepting usability as the de facto governing philosophy for Web experience design has largely been driven by Dr. Jakob Nielsen.

As the cofounder of the Nielsen Norman Group, Dr. Nielsen has been one of the chief advocates of tenaciously adhering to Web experience design standards that are based on a confluence of traditional usability principles and initial Web design standards. These standards and principles are insufficient on their own to guide experience design because they ignore the needs of the whole person and therefore weren't conceived with people's broad consumptive, social, and emotional needs in mind.

Nielsen's rationale for this narrow focus doesn't seem to be that these standards make for engaging Web experiences but rather that people have become too familiar with *his* interpretation of these standards and, therefore, anything that doesn't comply with them is by default confusing, ineffective, and wrong.

Surprisingly, the other primary member of the Nielsen Norman Group is the notable Dr. Donald Norman. Dr. Norman has often written very eloquently about broader cognitive, social, and emotional issues. It therefore puzzles me why Dr. Nielsen takes such a narrow stance on experience design issues when Dr. Norman places such importance on these broader issues in his writing.

i1.00.03 Hopes for the Web have been dashed.

In the late 1990s, expectations for the Web were soaring. In recent years, however, these expectations have come crashing to the ground as Web enterprises have widely failed to meet their objectives. As a result, many of these enterprises are no more.

While some usability gurus may contend that Web enterprises have failed because not enough people have followed established Web usability principles, I believe that the Web has probably struggled as much, if not more, because it's filled with ineffective content that's been formulated by organizations that haven't acquired proper online communication skills.

The reality is that people have grown weary of our misguided efforts to communicate with them online and have, in many cases, turned their attention back to more traditional channels and mediums. People expect online resources to be simple to access—yes, but they also expect them to be extremely interesting, imaginative, engaging, and appropriate. The public instinctively knows that something better is coming and that it's only a matter of time and a matter of which innovators will lead the way. We've spent too much time trying to make our Web enterprises more *usable*. It's time that we move on to the more challenging task of making them truly *valuable*.

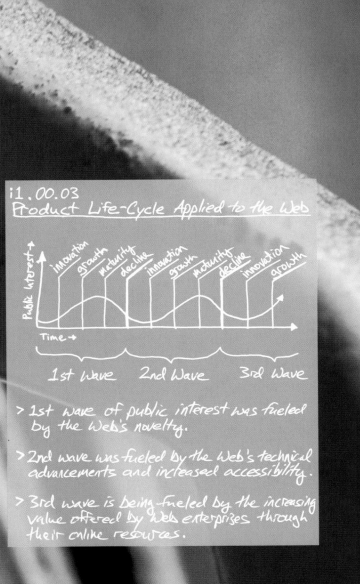

i1.00.03
Product Life-Cycle Applied to the Web

> 1st wave of public interest was fueled by the Web's novelty.

> 2nd wave was fueled by the Web's technical advancements and increased accessibility.

> 3rd wave is being fueled by the increasing value offered by Web enterprises through their online resources.

Note:

I refer to these white boxes as "notions," and try to present a clearly-defined thought within each of their boundaries. I've numbered them for easy reference:

Chapter ┬   Notion ┬

$\boxed{i1}$. $\boxed{00}$. $\boxed{04}$

     Series

The scale on the left is intended to indicate your progress through the book as well as help you gauge how long that a chapter or section is. The longer dashes indicate a page-spread where a new series of notions begins.

i1.00.04 My purpose in writing this book is neither to dismiss all usability standards carte blanche nor to endorse the notion that creativity is the answer to designing effective Web experiences. Instead, the aim of this book is to acknowledge the evolution of Web experience design as a form and the World Wide Web as a medium. My contention is that this form must offer more than mere simplicity and practicality to be an effective mass-communications medium. It must also offer easily comprehensible messages, emotional and social relevance, as well as aesthetic gratification.

My aim in Part I of this book is to present a cogent argument for a holistic and innovative online communications philosophy which I refer to as *notion-flow philosophy*. This philosophy roughly breaks down into three areas:

1. Chapters One and Two deal primarily with issues related to *psychology*.
2. Chapters Three and Four deal primarily with *understandability*.
3. Chapters Five and Six deal primarily with what I view as the proper application of *creativity*.

My aim in Part II is to provide guidance for those who wish to apply this philosophy to their real-world Web experience design projects by putting it to work within the context of an effective process.

i1.00.05 Warning: This book was not written to acquiesce to the status quo of established industry "best practices."

It's intended to shake things up and to get those who have any role in a Web enterprise to reevaluate what constitutes effective Web experiences—perhaps in ways that they never have before.

Although there's currently a tremendous backlash working its way through the experience design community against the role that usability standards play in experience design, there are yet many who want the online community to maintain a "business-as-usual" mentality. Some members of that community will likely disagree with the philosophy I present, but I believe that there are many more who will open their minds and benefit from the principles that are presented herein. If this happens—if only in a small way—I feel that my efforts in writing this book will have been worthwhile.

i1.00.06 Disclaimer: I'm neither a psychologist nor a social scientist. I have, however, worked closely with those who are. In particular, I've benefited most significantly from working with educational psychologist Dr. Michael Allen, who led learning technology research and development at The Ohio State University, led design and development of PLATO Learning Management and authoring systems for PLATO, founded Authorware Inc., merged his company with others to form Macromedia Inc., and founded Allen Interactions Inc., a leading e-learning consulting and development firm. I consider my tenure under his guidance as an interactivity designer, creative director, and studio executive to be the series of life-events that sparked my thinking on this subject. My warmest thanks to Dr. Allen.

My perspectives have also been shaped through the confluence of experiences I've had as an artist, musician, writer, media producer, technology consultant, creative director, and experience design specialist which have spanned from the late 1980s to today. In addition to these experiences, I've also spent countless hours both studying and pondering the issues that face Web enterprises.

As I've worked on projects for numerous Global 2000 companies, I've tried to listen and keep my eyes open. This has lead to a conviction that many of the problems facing those who create online resources could be solved if they had a better understanding of the need to synthesize principles related to the fields of psychology, understandability, and creativity. What you're about to read is the result of the inspiration that has grown out of these convictions.

I'm not writing as a "know it all." No one in this field knows it all. Instead, I'm writing as a dedicated student and practitioner of this medium who has a vision and a dream for a Web that fulfills a greater potential than we had ever thought possible. I hope you enjoy your journey through these thoughts, concepts, and ideas as much as I enjoyed writing them.

CHAPTER 01

Society has unwittingly fallen into a machine-centered orientation to life, one that emphasizes the needs of technology over those of people. [This forces] people into a supporting role, one for which we are most unsuited. [...]

The same analytical methods that work so well for mechanical things do not apply to people. [...] As a result, the technology that is intended to aid human cognition and enjoyment more often interferes and confuses than aids and clarifies.

—Dr. Donald Norman, *Things That Make Us Smart*

'Users' Versus People—
Understanding What Motivates Online Behavior

The people who interact with your Web enterprise through its online resources aren't users; that would make you—the person or organization responsible for the existence of these resources—a pusher. They're people and you function more like a facilitator. People don't *merely* use the information that they access; they perceive it, absorb it, try to comprehend it, are affected by it, and then decide how to respond to it.

With this guiding notion in mind, the intent of this chapter is to persuade you to stop listening to those Web usability consultants who recommend that you dull-down your online resources and focus solely on the practical aspects of experience design. These one-track-minded consultants are as much hypnotists as anything else. They've basically succeeded in mesmerizing the online community by cultivating the false notion that people are mechanically minded robots whose *sole* motivations are to experience their online world as expediently and as practically as possible.

While there are certainly *many* valid practical considerations when designing online resources, under the guise of "usability standards," practicality *itself* is currently being taken to an extreme.

01.00.02

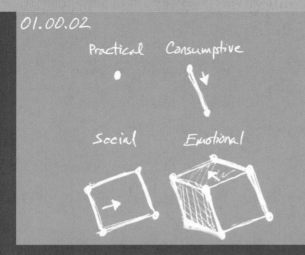

Practical   Consumptive

Social   Emotional

01.00.02 Journeying along a well-conceived experiential pathway *is* what makes interacting with a Web enterprise compelling. Because people are multidimensional, an effective Web experience is successful on many different levels. Consequently, *paving* this "experiential pathway" involves employing varied sets of principles that address our multidimensionality. This holistic design perspective should draw from and synthesize principles that are related to *psychology*, *understandability*[1], and *creativity*.

Up until now, however, consultants who are more technically minded have confused experience design with usability design. Usability traditionally relates to a "user's" ability to navigate through and find information quickly on the Web, and grapples with some, but not all issues relevant to understandability as I've framed it in this text. Although usability *does* try to help people avoid the detrimental emotions that accompany frustration, for the most part usability ignores broader issues related to the psychology of emotion, the cognition of perception and learning, as well as the very *real* human need for aesthetic gratification.

01.00.01 Practicality is not an underlying human motivation. Instead, people seek fulfillment through consumption, as well as through social interaction and emotional experiences. The Web *can* help us be more practical people, yes; but more importantly it has the capacity to help us become *better* people—to enhance our minds and our lives—to help us better understand each other, the world, and ourselves.

Although the *appropriate* application of practicality in the design of Web experiences *can* contribute to fulfilling our true human needs and desires, designing our online resources to be practical for the *sake* of being practical is a misguided and dangerously flawed idea. And most certainly—elevating practicality *above* all other design considerations goes far beyond necessity.

[1] When the ideas that we communicate through our online messages are understandable, they're easy for people to attend to, comprehend, and remember.

01.00.03 As arguably the most influential Web usability consultant, Jakob Nielsen has, through a narrow set of heuristics, succeeded in convincing Web enterprises to base their experience design policies on a single facet of people's experiential needs.

Dr. Nielsen has derived his heuristics—which are speculative formulations—largely from informal, context-specific Web usability testing. The conclusions drawn from years of conducting this testing have then been extrapolated by Nielsen and others to apply to all cases. The problem with this approach is that usability testing is geared toward determining the flaws in a specific interface through educated intuition rather than through empirical scientific testing.

Nielsen would himself likely be the first to admit that most Web usability testing lacks the rigor of scientific research. This makes the credence given to his Web usability heuristics as scientifically-proven fact all the more puzzling. It's frustrating for many Web experience designers who are trying to build inspiring online resources when they're blocked in their efforts by Nielsen's heuristics—which are accepted as absolute truths, when they're in fact only based on Nielsen's observations. The heuristics of Nielsen and others have taken on a glow of sanctified commandments—Thou Shalt Not Use Flash!—rather than being regarded as the potentially helpful but highly subjective design suggestions that they really are.

Usability experts rightly feel that if a person can't interact with an online resource easily, then that resource has likely failed. However the passionate conviction that makes them good advocates of interface logistics can sometimes blind them to the core purposes of an online resource. The most logistically predictable experience may not be the most engaging or the most persuasive or the most compelling one. Usability needs to support other design considerations, not replace them. A logistically appropriate, "practical" online resource that isn't at all compelling is just as big a failure as one that's compelling yet impractical.

Many of the design considerations that have traditionally fallen under the moniker of "usability" are important and should be considered when designing online resources. Some of Dr. Nielsen's observations can, when appropriately applied in a given situation, be quite helpful. Usability, however, is only one voice in the democracy of experience design, and therefore should only get one vote. There are many other types of observations, both subjective and scientific, that must be taken into account when settling on a particular experience design strategy for a given situation and needs (see Chapter Seven).

01.00.04 Poor usability isn't the primary reason why Web enterprises have experienced widespread failure.

They've experienced failure because the organizations behind these Web enterprises haven't understood and fulfilled the needs of the people in the online marketplace holistically. By the online market's rejection of the 1990s crop of dot-coms, people have made it clear that they're no longer willing to subject themselves to bland, incomprehensible, poorly stylized, *marginally valuable*, OR difficult-to-use online resources. There are two reasons for this.

The first reason is that other forms of media such as TV, movies, and interactive games have trained people to have increasingly sophisticated expectations in terms of the emotional and aesthetic dynamics of the media that they consume. These media do a really great job of reaching people deeply on social and emotional levels.

The second reason is that conventional sources of needs fulfillment are beginning to combine the inherent social and emotional powers of live people and environments with progressive implementations of technology. The combined benefit in many cases provides a more compelling value proposition than their online competitors can offer.

We've reached the point where people expect to be treated as well online as they're treated in physical consumptive settings. In light of this, we must stop expending all of our resources designing online experiences that, at best, try to be sensitive to navigational frustration and, at worst, ignore the broader body of people's experiential needs as a whole.

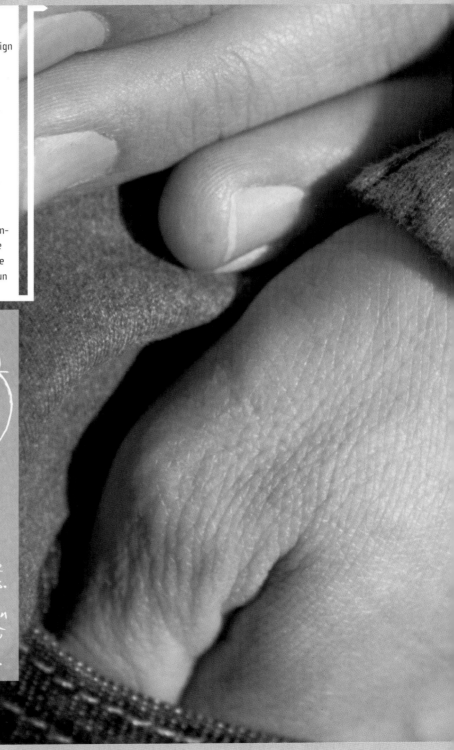

01.00.05 The core of an effective Web experience is NOT *user*-centered design but *person*-centered design.

Therefore, we must design every aspect of an online resource to align with a person's natural human needs and desires. Although one of our human desires is to avoid the frustrations of inefficiency and impediment, we also have very deep and primal needs to maintain a positive social and emotional relationship with our environment. When given a choice, people usually choose options that engender the most positive feeling (Reeves and Nass, *The Media Equation*).

In light of this fact, it's essential that in addition to designing our online resources to be efficient, we design them—whether austere or flamboyant—to be compelling as well. In a sense, the role of an experience design team is to pave the way for people to enjoy themselves as they make unimpeded progress in their quest for consumption, meaning, enjoyment, or—whatever. And although people are often most interested in the direct route, it's important that we don't barricade the scenic route for those who feel that "half the fun is in getting there."

01.00.05

A → B 1. The Direct Route

2. The Chaotic Route

3. The Scenic Route

1. Many usability consultants claim that the direct route is always the best.

2. They often assume that the alternative to the direct route is the route of chaos.

3. A non-direct route (scenic route) can often times be appreciated, however, as long as it's contributing to the meaning and value of the experience.

01.00.06 As consumers of online experiences are becoming more sophisticated and demanding, understanding and applying psychological and sociological principles in the design of online resources is becoming increasingly critical.

Psychologists and sociologists are becoming increasingly interested in *why* people go online and *how* they engage emotionally with Web enterprises. Some of the factors that these studies consider are whether people:

> are aroused by an online resource and find it interesting
> feel understood by a Web enterprise
> identify areas of personal interest
> make sense of the content
> remember the ideas being presented
> are invoked to respond to online messages
> find a Web enterprise cumulatively helpful and engaging over time

Online resources that are designed to address these factors will be successful not only in helping people *find* what they're looking for, but also in helping them attend to, understand, and relate emotionally to the content that these Web enterprises have to offer. Furthermore, when online resources meet basic human needs for consumptive, social, and emotional relevance, people will be more motivated to interact with them. Helping *people* be successful in this way will maximize a Web enterprise's chances of being successful in the online marketplace.

01.01 People Go Online to Consume

> A researcher is writing a report for work and needs to gather appropriate information.
> An accountant just met a big deadline and wants to "get mindless" playing a game for a while.
> A teenager wants to customize his own tennis shoes or find a really "cool" new skateboard.
> That same teenager wants to find a great place to wear those tennis shoes or ride that skateboard (http://www.3rdlair.com).
> A couple wants to find a more progressive pediatrician.
> That same couple wants to find a reliable financial advisor that can help them plan for their children's education.

We don't always think about it this way, but these examples all relate to various forms of consumption. When we think about what we can "get out of" the Web, these are the types of things that typically come to mind. We're consumers of information, entertainment, products, and services. It seems really simple—cut-and-dried and very practical. But how cut-and-dried is it really? Is the role of an effective online resource to provide the most expedient, most practical way to get people from point A to point B? If you listen to some usability consultants, you get that distinct impression. They represent the group of experts who try to understand *what* people want while ignoring *why* people want.

01.01.01 The fact is, expediency and practicality are not sufficient to meet our consumptive needs in either the physical world or the mediated world of the Web.

The success or failure of any organization in the physical world hinges not only on how well it meets tangible needs but also on how well it anticipates and meets the more subjective and intangible aspects of the need. Retail businesses invest heavily in the look and feel of their stores because people are affected emotionally by the tone and tambour of the environments where they shop. This affects their purchasing decisions. Good restaurants pay careful attention to the flavor of their food, the ambiance of their dining rooms, and the personality of their wait-staff. These factors affect where people choose to dine.

Those who design Web experiences must understand that considerations such as these are equally important on the Web. Understanding *how* people most enjoy their consumption ("Would you like that medium or rare?") is an important key in designing effective Web experiences ("Well done, actually; but frankly, I'd rather be waited on by someone who doesn't smell funny.").

01.01.02 We consume information to build knowledge and attain deeper understanding.

How does this process happen? If we don't understand how people learn, how can we have a positive impact on the quality of the information that we're publishing online? How will we know how to best combine words, photos, illustrations, audio, video, simulation, animation, and/or interactivity to best get an idea across? Some feel that these considerations are only relevant to online learning and training resources. This is certainly not the case. Almost *everything* we consume on the Web has a learning curve associated with it whereby we gather, reinforce, or restructure our knowledge in order to make decisions related to our further consumption. This can happen before, during, or after the consumption itself.

> We learn about the car *before* we buy it.
> We learn how to be good at the game *while* playing it.
> We realize the value of a product or service *after* we've tested it.

Conveying ideas and making them memorable to people through an online resource is an art. There's a lot to take into account in order to do a good job. Not only are there different types of learning, but there are different stages of learning. There are also many principles of human perception, motivation, and cognition to consider as well. These topics will be covered in detail in Chapters Two through Six.

01.01.04 We consume goods to meet a multitude of tangible and intangible needs.

This is the type of consumption that is easiest to understand because it's...well...tangible. People want widgets so they interact with your Web enterprise to buy them—or is it that they interact with your *competitor*'s Web enterprise to buy them?

Those in sales say that people base their purchasing decisions on price, quality, or service. This is only partly true. In reality, people buy based on their *perception* of the price, quality, and/or service that they *believe* constitutes an overall better value proposition than that which is offered by a competitor. In light of this, it's clear that as much thought needs to be put into the appropriate *presentation* of the price, quality, and service message as possible. This should be blatantly obvious to those with sales, marketing, or advertising backgrounds. In the future—if it's not already—it really needs to be obvious to those involved in Web experience design as well.

01.01.03 We consume diversions such as entertainment to give our minds a break from the burnout that comes from thinking too much about one thing day in and day out.

This "one thing" tends to be our primary occupation. Diversion takes us away from worry and responsibility and lets us think freely without much concern as to consequence. We generally don't have much at stake when we seek diversion. But who wants to spend time in boring, dulled-down diversions?

The answer is—not many of us, and there's an important reason why. Things that are boring aren't relaxing because paying attention becomes a struggle, and that's hard work!

In light of this, the degree to which we're drawn into and engrossed by our diversion experiences is a strong indicator of the value of the time spent engaged in those experiences. If we have trouble "getting into it," the diversion has not achieved its goal. Since the degree to which we're consumed by our consumption of diversion is so important, Web enterprises that employ these diversions need to understand how, when, and why they should be provided.

This amounts to understanding how to anticipate the emotional state of a person at the time of interaction. Is that person worried, sad, happy, glad, etc.? In light of our insight into his or her state of mind, what can we do to benefit it?

CASE STUDY 1A

Express Fashion

Address: http://www.expressfashion.com
Client: The Limited, Inc.—Express
Experience Designers: Ten/Resource

Expressfashion.com is not a Web "site;" it is a Web Experience.

Expressfashion.com, as part of The Limited, Inc. retail clothing store group, is the Web presence for Express stores. The marketing focus behind Express is geared to the modern woman—a brand loyalist who is fashion-forward and techno-savvy. For the redevelopment of their design, the goal was to allow customers to LIVE the high-energy, fashion-forward brand, not just shop it. According to their outstanding and "high-energy" design team:

"The design of the site is critical in connecting the total brand picture. It captures the electricity of the brand through the visuals, the motion, and the music, and then it offers interactive tools that create a virile energy that gets people spreading the word and talking about fashion and EXPRESS. The fact that people have included Expressfashion.com as a must see site on their own personal web pages seems to say it all."

The creative team at Ten/Resource worked hard to develop creative, interactive ways for customers to become part of the Express experience. Through consumer research, they found that increased interaction and engagement with a Web enterprise will create a deeper emotional connection to a brand. The team designed Expressfashion.com to capture the emotion of the Express brand online through the use of motion, music, and interactivity. Features include the Groove Music Box, offering six music samples from the retail store, customized menu configuration, and QuickTime runway videos.

Read our interview with Ten/Resource online at:
http://www.trainofthoughts.com

01.01.05 We consume services to ease our burdens.

How we value services is different from how we value products in that there tends to be a greater degree to which we value the relationships that accompany the benefit that services provide. Because of this, a purchasing decision is based as much on the intangibles of factors such as personality, values, and integrity as it is on the more tangible aspects of the service. A person isn't just purchasing a completed tax return, but the security, comfort, and flexibility of a reliable advisor who wants what's best for him or her. A widget can't do that. Only a person can.

When selling a service online, it's essential that the intangibles be addressed. It's often said, "People buy from people." This is true. What's more, when given a choice, people will buy from people they like and believe will help them by making helpful recommendations. Web enterprises that sell services need to understand the cognitive and emotional triggers that cause people to put confidence in others and then design their interactions to incorporate these triggers. For an in-depth look at what these triggers are, read *The Media Equation* by Byron Reeves and Clifford Nass.

01.02 People Go Online for Social Reasons

It was once said, "We read to know that we're not alone." I believe that this is the primary social motivation that draws people online. We want to know that we're not alone. Before the Internet, an individual was but an indistinguishable drop in the sea of humanity. It was rare that a sole individual would ever be noticed, let alone have a voice that could be heard across the continents. What's more, social mores have caused many people to feel socially stifled. Most people have had very few opportunities to express their most real and uninhibited thoughts, perspectives, and feelings within their existing social network because of fear of misunderstanding or outright rejection. Because of the Internet, this is not the case today.

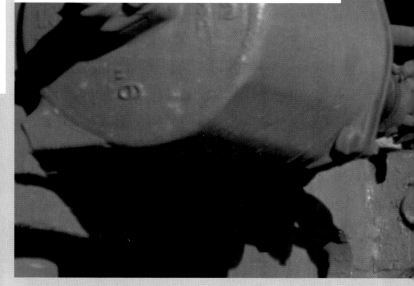

01.02.01 We go online to fulfill the social desire to find people, places, and things with which we can identify.

The reason is that we as people have a strong internal need to reinforce our sense of self. We feel drawn to things that we can identify with because it makes us feel like we're okay and that somehow we fit into the bigger picture. In their book *The Media Equation*, Byron Reeves and Clifford Nass state:

"People like to interact with personalities that resemble their own. In psychology, this is known as the 'law of similarity-attraction.' Despite the folk wisdom that opposites attract, there is strong empirical support for attraction based on similarity."

In his book *A Cognitive Psychology of Mass Communication*, Richard Harris sheds further light:

"The emotional involvement that we have [interacting with media] depends in part on how much we *identify* with the character (i.e., mentally compare ourselves to and imagine ourselves to be the lead character]. It is easier to identify with characters with whom we have more in common.

"When we have the ability to understand and feel what another feels, we experience empathy. Empathy may be seen as emotional identification, and it is a very important factor in the enjoyment of [our consumption of] media."

The desire we have to identify with others has *intellectual*, *ideological*, and *emotional* dimensions.

01.02.02 We seek intellectual identification in a quest to answer these questions: "Is there anyone out there who thinks the way I do? Am I intellectually alone?"

The intellect has to do with our rational mind, our self-directed thinking. This is the part of our mind that seeks to define reality. It wants to know what the facts are by reasoning with the evidence. Part of how we develop our intellect is by absorbing the ideas of others and by reflecting upon and restructuring what we understand those ideas to be. By doing this we channel the original thinking of others through our own experiential filters and reformulate our perception of their thoughts into our own knowledge structures. This process happens throughout our lives as we observe our parents, our friends, our teachers, and even the media.

Our exposure to the input of others is what stimulates our thinking the most. Until the Internet came along, however, we were very restricted in terms of the times, places, and ways that we were able to expose ourselves to the thinking of people outside our everyday circles. Even though books and other printed literature have always been available to us in modern times, discovering material that has deep personal significance was often a lengthy and frustrating process. Most of us often didn't have a clue as to what material to look for in pursuit of expanding our intellectual identity or where to look for it, if in fact we had an inkling as to what our undiscovered interests were. In many instances, our success with finding these influences has been the result of chance. Consequently, society has by and large taken the role of choosing when and how our intellectual frameworks were to be cultivated by default:

> We went to school at a certain time and learned what the school board decided we should learn.
> We watched the programming on TV that the networks decided we should watch and when they decided we should watch it.
> We learned the values that our parents wanted us to believe.

Although we chose some of our own friends and would sometimes have "deep" conversations, those discussions were limited to the combined knowledge of people who were from similar circles and who had similar experiences. This is not the case today.

The Web has given people the opportunity to dig deep into their thoughts and interests at any time, any place, and in an almost limitless fashion—and this within the safe confines of anonymity, which the Web affords them. Even a very young person—and this most certainly can be a danger—can take the initiative to learn about advanced topics in a self-directed and self-paced manner. Those people who learn to take advantage of these unlimited opportunities gain exposure to some of the greatest thinking on any subject.

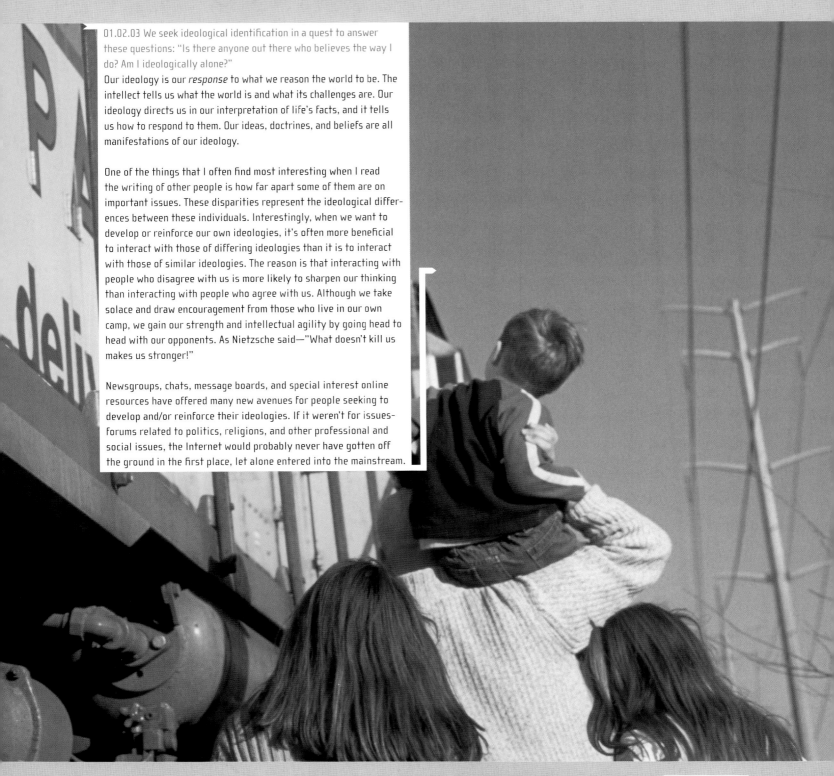

01.02.03 We seek ideological identification in a quest to answer these questions: "Is there anyone out there who believes the way I do? Am I ideologically alone?"

Our ideology is our *response* to what we reason the world to be. The intellect tells us what the world is and what its challenges are. Our ideology directs us in our interpretation of life's facts, and it tells us how to respond to them. Our ideas, doctrines, and beliefs are all manifestations of our ideology.

One of the things that I often find most interesting when I read the writing of other people is how far apart some of them are on important issues. These disparities represent the ideological differences between these individuals. Interestingly, when we want to develop or reinforce our own ideologies, it's often more beneficial to interact with those of differing ideologies than it is to interact with those of similar ideologies. The reason is that interacting with people who disagree with us is more likely to sharpen our thinking than interacting with people who agree with us. Although we take solace and draw encouragement from those who live in our own camp, we gain our strength and intellectual agility by going head to head with our opponents. As Nietzsche said—"What doesn't kill us makes us stronger!"

Newsgroups, chats, message boards, and special interest online resources have offered many new avenues for people seeking to develop and/or reinforce their ideologies. If it weren't for issues-forums related to politics, religions, and other professional and social issues, the Internet would probably never have gotten off the ground in the first place, let alone entered into the mainstream.

01.02.04 We seek emotional identification in a quest to answer these questions: "Is there anyone out there who feels the way I do? Am I emotionally alone?"

Emotion is our spontaneous, involuntary combination of *physiologi*cal and cognitive responses that are automatically activated when we're confronted with a stimulus. When we're seeking to emotionally identify with others, what we're seeking is the people "out there" who are similarly affected by what they think about or believe in.

When Princess Diana died on August 31, 1997, thousands of people flocked online to chat about and deal with their emotions related to her death. Many people had developed a parasocial relationship with her and felt as if they had lost a member of their own family. The Web provided an outlet for emotions that, at least in non-Western European cultures, would not have been fully received or understood.

The Internet offered an alternative way for people to seek out others with whom they could emotionally identify and with whom they could go through the grieving process in ways that circumvented the disinterested social mores of non-Western European cultures. In this sense, the Internet was offering a social outlet and a release that otherwise would not have been possible for these individuals. A Web enterprise that succeeds in helping its patrons relate to itself and to each other on an emotional level in this way goes a long way toward winning their loyalty.

01.02.05 We seek social interaction and acceptance in a quest to answer this question: "How will the world embrace my intellectual, ideological, and emotional uniqueness?"

We all seek acceptance. Acceptance occurs as a result of being embraced by those with whom we identify. People don't generally care if someone outside their group doesn't care for them, but if the people inside their group don't care for them, this becomes a really big problem. This is further complicated by a dynamic known as *group-think*.

Group-think is the process by which a group of people come to a common equilibrium that tends to represent a moderate overall averaging of opinions among its members. The problem is that the outliers of the group—those who don't fit within the norm—can often feel unable to express their true feelings for fear of social rejection and isolation. Not surprisingly, we all have a sense of being on the outside of the norm in some area of our lives. These are the areas that we are most likely to repress our feelings in. The need to release these feelings is something that applies to everybody.

One of the motivations that people have in going online is to find opportunities where they can identify with others while at the same time maintain their own sense of identity. Specifically, because of the inherent anonymity of the Internet, people are willing to take more risks in terms of expressing their true inner feelings within the membership of an online community. The cost of social faux pas seems low enough to the average person that they're willing to accept social failure more often than in "real life." What's often gained in the online community is a sense of social interaction and acceptance that's unmatched in unmediated social equivalents.

01.03 People Go Online for Emotional Reasons

When a person's mind opens to an experience, it's like a floodgate opens—a river of meaning begins to flow into the mind. This meaning appeals not only to our cognitive sensibilities (how we think about things) but also to our emotional sensibilities (how we *feel* about things). In *A Cognitive Psychology of Mass Communication*, Dr. Richard Harris describes emotion:

"There are two components of emotion, the physiological, and the cognitive. When we are aroused, there are certain changes in our bodies, such as increased heart rate, sweating, and changes in electrodermal (skin) measures. We also *think* about our feelings and attribute causes and interpretations to them. The emotions we feel are a product of both our bodily state and our cognitive appraisal of that state."

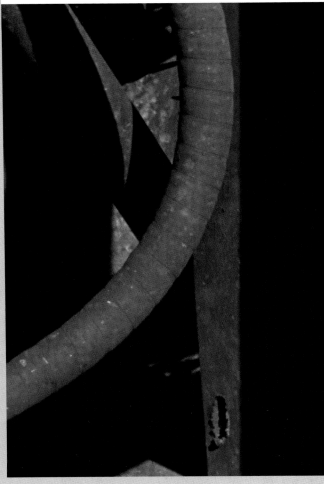

01.03.01 It's impossible to design effective Web experiences without taking human emotion into consideration.

Emotion is a big part of who we are and how we interpret the world around us. If an organization makes an online resource easy to navigate, an individual *might* have a good experience. If an organization makes their Web enterprise easy to relate to, however, the way is cleared for an individual to have an even greater experience because he or she is able to participate emotionally with the Web enterprise. Dr. Harris continues:

"Emotions are an integral part of the appreciation of media. [...] What we feel while watching or listening is a central part of the whole [experience]. If the emotional aspect is absent, we miss an important dimension of the experience."

In *The Media Equation*, Reeves and Nass state:

"Media have evolved to capitalize on fundamental human responses to them. [...] By trial and error, people who design media are gradually discovering the intricacies of how media work [on the human psyche.]"

It's inevitable that Web enterprises will come to embrace emotional design sensibilities such as those that have evolved in television and in other media industries. In the case of the Web, however, it shouldn't have to come through as much "trial and error" as has been the case with traditional media. There are well-established psychological principles in television, radio, and print mediums that, according to Dr. Richard Harris, "apply equally well to all media." Dr. Harris concludes:

"Our relationship with the media is [...] profound. [This] is precisely because it meets some of our deepest psychological needs and contributes naturally to our ongoing psychological development."

01.03.02 The Web is a vehicle for emotional fulfillment.
The Web *can* help us complete tasks more efficiently, but what is perhaps of even *greater* significance is that it can make us feel more complete emotionally. We look to the Web to help us find this emotional completion in many ways:

> We're empty and seek fulfillment.
> We're overburdened and seek enjoyment.
> We're under stimulated and seek intensity.
> We're underwhelmed with our own lives and seek catharsis.
> We feel ordinary and seek to experience the emotions of a life that's more dramatic.

01.03.03 We seek to fill an emotional void on the Web.
All people who go online are seeking the same thing—every single one of us. Perhaps you're thinking, "That's not true! With all the possibilities on the Web, how can we possibly know what an individual person is seeking?" It's true that there are variations in the primary needs, but there's a commonality in the secondary need.

All people seeking a restaurant to spend an evening at, for example, are seeking the same secondary fulfillment. They may *feel like* eating steak, or they may be *in the mood for* good conversation—two very tangible and distinguishable desires. They do, none-the-less, have the same secondary desire—the emotional fulfillment that accompanies the process of satisfying these primary needs. Although many Web enterprises may represent restaurants that offer the same tangible opportunities for consumptive or social fulfillment—which are primary—the ones that speak to the "feel like" and "in the mood for" components of the need will generate the greatest response.

The reason is that people go online to find more than mere tangible items like information about places that serve great steak or that provide environments conducive to good conversation. They go online to build emotional confidence that the choices that they're making will lead to the fulfillment that they believe these tangible choices will bring them. It's not merely a practical hunger that they're trying to satisfy but an emotional hunger as well. They wonder, "If I choose this restaurant, will I have a good time?"

When considering Web experience design, it's the quality of our effort to identify, amplify, and satisfy these emotional hungers that will ultimately lead people to choose our Web enterprises in the search to fill their primary needs.

01.03.04 We seek enjoyment on the Web.

These days, life is very stressful. We work our minds as hard in the information age as our forefathers worked their bodies in the industrial age. Our brains are very active analyzing, experimenting, problem solving, and reflecting (trying to make sense of things) all day long. It's important to understand that, although our computers are great "business tools," when we go online our computers play more than just a business role. They suddenly become windows by which we travel through time and space to take in the experiences that the universe has to offer.

Although we may have practical tasks to perform, there's a part of us that wants to transform these tasks into opportunities to have fun. We want to find, tap into, and pursue interests that are more than just practical, even if they are, well—practical. When we talk about the "entertainment value" of an online resource, we're talking about the degree to which a Web enterprise makes routine operations rise above the level of the mundane—even if the *purpose* of the Web enterprise is not necessarily to entertain.

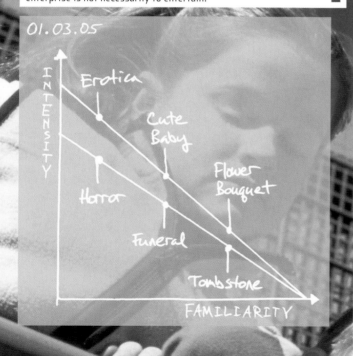

01.03.05 We seek intensity on the Web.

How much we enjoy a Web experience depends on the *degree* to which we find it arousing. Is it just "good," or is it "really, really good?" Is it merely "bad," or is it "terrible"? Reeves and Nass use the word "valence" to refer to the judgment we make about something being either good or bad. "Arousal" is used to indicate the level of intensity that we attribute to the valence. They state: "Valence and arousal are essentially biological." Taken together, they're the "two basic dimensions of emotion." Reeves and Nass offer these examples:

"Flowers, a cute baby, and erotica all have positive *valence*, but they have distinctly different levels of *arousal*: Erotica ranks highest and flowers, lowest. Similarly, a funeral procession and mutilated bodies are both negative, but only [mutilated bodies] will produce significant arousal."

"As things get arousing, they also are more likely to be either good or bad. Neutrality, it turns out, is not a big part of excitement. It is also difficult to find material that is extremely good or bad and totally un-arousing—it's hard to be blasé about highly valenced material."

Reeves and Nass have done an exceptional job explaining *how* we get excited. What's even more significant is their reason for *why* getting people excited is important. When we get excited about an experience we have, we pay closer attention and tend to remember the details of that experience more than we would if the experience had been blasé. In a nutshell, excitement can be used as an effective memory aid. Isn't this one of the chief aims of any online marketing or communications initiative—to make a message as memorable as possible? As it turns out, designing our online resource to be emotionally engaging isn't a luxury—it's a necessity. Of course, people in sales and advertising have known this for many years, as Reeves and Nass plainly state in their book:

"The basis for the success of websites, in addition to their usability and efficiency, is often the potential to arouse. This may require changes in the ways that websites are evaluated."

This is something that both usability and experience design specialists need to understand.

SPOTLIGHT ON:

DR. BYRON REEVES

Dr. Byron Reeves, a professor in the Department of Communications who conducts psychological studies at Stanford University, is one of the most frequently quoted authorities regarding the psychological effects that various media have on people. Together with collaborating researcher Dr. Clifford Nass (also of Stanford), he wrote *The Media Equation*, which documents their extensive scientific studies.

Their book has provided some of the most intriguing revelations regarding human-computer interaction published to date. Their studies have ranged from gauging people's sense of social connection through media, to measuring how their level of enjoyment influences long-term memory. The following are his answers to some questions I posed based upon the ideas presented in this chapter:

Lenker: How is the Web's role growing in the way people are forming their social, emotional, and intellectual identities?

Reeves: The most important development since the Web's inception is the fact that it is now able to carry symbol systems that are capable of influencing social and emotional responses. Now that bandwidth limitations are not so constrained, the utilization of multimedia elements, rather than mere words alone, is having a significant effect on people's ability to find emotional and social significance online.

Lenker: Why are people so interested in interacting with Web media?

Reeves: Shopping, for example, is inherently a social experience. More than mere economic transactions, it involves social transactions. The cues that *people* add to a transaction are tremendous. When we use Web media to introduce a greater manifestation of these very human social cues, people find more enjoyment in and put more confidence in the online resources.

Lenker: What will contribute the most to making Web enterprises of the future more successful than those of the late 1990s?

Reeves: I actually think that it won't so much be a matter of making interfaces better, although that in itself is important, but it will be a matter of making content more effective for people.

Lenker: How do you respond to critics who say that trying to make online resources behave socially and emotionally will always result in experiences that are bogged down in excessive dialogue?

Reeves: The thing that these critics don't realize is that just because social and emotional cues are incorporated in a virtual interaction with an online resource, that doesn't mean that these cues need to be intrusive. These critics are in reality probably reacting to examples they've seen where experience designers try to make their Web enterprises social in an excessive or inappropriate way. Trying to "yuk it up" too much, or being a little too clever with dialogue, are examples of this. Being successful at incorporating social cues isn't about doing *everything* that can be done, but doing what's appropriate. This can be measured through researching feedback from representatives from the target population.

The key to success is in how we design and program these systems to behave. We shouldn't design them to "run off at the mouth." We want to be as appropriate in an interaction as would be expected in real life. The point is that when we decide that we're going to attend to social features, what we're doing is deciding to have more of a tangible presence for the purpose of gaining more social control over people's impression. Just as in real life, this is something that must be worked at and refined over time.

Lenker: Can an online resource still succeed if social cues [...]

Read the entire interview online at:
http://www.trainofthoughts.com

Learn more about Dr. Byron Reeves at:
http://www.stanford.edu/%7Ereeves/

Buy *The Media Equation* today at:
http://www.trainofthoughts.com

01.03.06 We seek catharsis on the Web.

It's important to understand that one major way people seek emotional satisfaction when they go online is through a notion taken from psychodynamic theory known as *catharsis*.

Catharsis is the emotional release of tension that we feel when we watch others (in media or otherwise) experience or express something that we ourselves are inhibited from feeling or expressing in real life. Closely associated with this notion is the notion of *vicarious* release, whereby we live out our own fantasies through the lives of others. We live vicariously through those we know; like our children, for example, when we push them in sports to achieve goals that we ourselves were not able to achieve. We can also live vicariously through fictionalized characters such as those in fantasy role-playing games such as EverQuest. In both cases, we have the opportunity to experience catharsis if the stimulus that we're experiencing is sufficient to draw our minds into the illusion and trap us there. Richard Harris writes in *A Cognitive Psychology of Mass Communication:*

"Many emotions are enjoyable to experience vicariously. Many TV sitcoms show people in embarrassing situations that are really only funny when happening to someone else. TV characters may do things we would like to do but have moral or ethical proscriptions against."

01.03.07 We seek drama on the Web.

Sigmund Freud said, "We are so made that we can derive intense enjoyment only from a contrast and very little from a state of things." What Freud is saying is that for people to get excited about something, it has to rise above the drone of everyday life.

For most people, life seems typical, drab, and sometimes downright boring. The cure for this sense of the mundane is *drama*. The mechanism that is the vehicle for the range of emotions that we experience through catharsis is known as *dramatization*. We're fascinated by the intrigues of the seedier side of life—thus the popularity of romance fiction and reality entertainment. Often people go online to add a more interactive dimension to the drama they experience through television or films. The Web offers organizations the ability to allow people to choose the aspects of a storyline that they want to dramatize. Krome Barratt writes in *Logic & Design in Art, Science & Mathematics:*

"Dramatization is the process of making an experience more exciting, vivid, emotionally stirring, and memorable. [Dramatization is] achieved by emphasizing some aspect of an experience at the expense of others. Selection, abstraction and hierarchy are of its essence, and these to be reordered, grouped and juxtaposed to maximum effect. [...] Drama is a meeting and rivalry of human antithesis. In counterpoint, two contrasting themes which share a common space-time scale discuss, compete, debate, argue, fight for their point of view."

01.03.08 Sterilizing Web experiences is a seriously flawed experience design strategy.

If the only way people can experience intense enjoyment is through rising above the drone of everyday life, how can it make sense to ask Web enterprises to standardize on a design status quo that strips out every component that can lead to emotional fulfillment?

When we sterilize the material that our Web enterprises present, it puts MORE burdens on the people interacting with them, not fewer. Is this a practical approach to designing Web experiences? Hardly. As I mentioned in 01.01.03, it's actually quite difficult to pay attention to things that bore us to death! People want more out of their con-sumptive, social, and emotional exploration on the Web than merely getting it over with. They want to find satisfaction *throughout* the experience, not merely as a *result* of the experience. This notion seems so intuitive; how has our industry gotten so far off track?

01.04 Grappling with Our Misdirection

The bottom line in developing effective Web experiences is that practical considerations are just *one* of the several categories of considerations that must be employed in the design of online resources that properly address a visitor's consumptive, social, and emotional needs. Sure, we want people to know where to type in their credit card numbers when transacting with our Web enterprises. I don't argue points such as this. But before they're going to care about where to enter in their credit card numbers, we're going to have to somehow help them care about what it is we're trying to sell them! In light of this, why is it that many usability consultants give preferential and sometimes *exclusive* consideration to the practical aspects of experience design and then condemn those of us who attempt to design more holistic experiences?

One explanation lies in the word *attempt*. Historically, most who have attempted to go beyond mere practicality with Web experience design have failed. The fact is that amateurs design most online resources, and we're ALL amateurs when we start. The industry has only been viable since about 1995, for heaven's sake! Many organizations simply haven't attained enough insight to do a proper job of designing effective Web experiences yet. Many, in fact, have innocently or naively created online resources that appeal to their own, unrefined sense of aesthetics. As a result, the experiences they design use media and interactivity inappropriately to emphasize the wrong types of things.

The practical result is that their online resources are hard to navigate, take forever to download, and in the end haven't succeeded in using media or interactivity to add much value to a person's overall experience. We've all been guilty of this, but this is no time to give up on our ideals. It's time to apply ourselves as serious students of the arts and sciences whose disciplines we employ in our pursuit of crafting appropriate, elegant, and effective Web-based interactive multimedia. We can do better than we have done in the past. We've learned and are learning from our mistakes. The purpose of this book is to aid in that learning process. ;-)

01.04.01 Our industry *will* evolve just like every other industry has before us—through the natural selection of a free-market economy. Do bad television shows, commercials, films, or video games ever get produced? The answer is yes—but they don't last long because they prove to be ineffective. More successful efforts rise to the top and extinguish the others. And although certain projects will always stand out as both positive and negative examples, eventually all efforts will settle into an overall equilibrium where quality is more homogenized. It will be the same with Web enterprises. Let's just make sure that that homogenized equilibrium isn't as boring as usability standards are currently constraining it to be.

In light of this, it seems inappropriate for usability consultants to tell designers to stop using rich media and interactivity based on the fact that others have used it and have failed. Can you imagine where the entertainment industry would be if, for example, sci-fi movies were never allowed to evolve into a legitimate art form simply because some early attempts weren't very convincing?

No; usability consultants shouldn't be pressuring Web enterprises to quit trying to make online experiences more dynamic, engaging, and therefore more meaningful. Instead, these experts should instead be drawing upon their own experience with and wisdom regarding the studies of perception, cognition, emotion, persuasion, and the philosophy of aesthetics (if any) to show Web enterprises how to properly employ the more elegant aspects of experience design.

The laws of natural selection do apply to the Web just as they do to real life; and the fact is that natural selection favors the strong and the beautiful. The Web enterprises that see it this way will be the ones that will not only survive, but thrive.

01.04.02 We must stay on the road of progress and out of the ditches of mediocrity.

My gripe with those who condemn the use of sophisticated media and interactivity on the Web is that they offer nothing better than a fleshless skeleton as an alternative. They're in effect pressuring the industry to exchange one set of mediocrity for another—to drive from the ditch on one side of the road right smack-dab into the other!

The Web development world is oversaturated with consultants who are experts at efficiently *getting* people to relevant content but are amateurs at helping people either relate to or make sense out of that content. Why is this? For every usability expert advocating sterile, stifling Web experience design, there are at least as many credible design and interactivity experts advocating experiences that reach deeper inside people. It's an injustice on the part of usability experts when they group design and interactivity experts with the amateur crowd and blanketly condemn all attempts to employ high-concept media or sophisticated interactivity.

We can do better than we have done—and we will. Not because we *limit* the scope of our work, but because we *refine* the quality of our understanding. We must therefore do the hard work that's necessary to hone our abilities to represent our ideas on the Web with passion, meaning, elegance, and clarity.

01.04.03 We must qualify our experience design recommendations with appropriate analysis.

To put it simply, good design is good design no matter what it consists of—be it simple or elaborate. The same can be said for bad design. But what makes a design good versus bad? What are the criteria? The purpose of this book is to explore these questions.

In order to judge the quality or value of an experience design, we must be at least somewhat familiar with the various disciplines that are employed to formulate that design. In our exploration of these disciplines, it's important that we keep an open mind. The important thing to remember is that there's no one solution to every problem. Our solutions should be *situationally appropriate*.

Is HTML text better than rendered-graphic text? Are full-color animated images preferable to monochromatic stick figures? The answer is—it depends on the situation. What's the purpose of the online resource? Who are the primary audience sets and subsets? What's the nature of the content? How engaging is the content on its own? How difficult is the subject for the average person to comprehend?

The answers to these types of questions have a lot to do not only with determining how content elements relate to one another, but also with how the content chunks themselves are put together.

CASE STUDY 1B

BMW Films

Address: http://www.bmwfilms.com
Client: BMW
Experience Designers: Fallon Worldwide

The Ultimate Online Movie Experience.

BMW, manufacturer of luxury/performance automobiles, has a global presence on the Web. One of their most emotionally engaging online resources, bmwfilms.com, entertains customers by showcasing various BMW automobiles in a five-part short film series titled "The Hire." They feature such high-profile stars as Madonna, Mickey Rourke, and Forest Whitaker, among others. Designed to create emotional identification with its audience members, the films, shot by various acclaimed film directors, seek to convey the performance, energy, and spirit of BMW.

The creative challenge for the design team at Fallon Worldwide, the creators of bmwfilms.com, was to promote the performance aspects of the automobile while improving the perceived brand image. The goal was to shift opinion of BMW from being a "yuppie car" to that of a phenomenally cool performance machine. They achieved this task by developing a series of films that put the car in various dramatic chase scenes. The driver, Clive Owen, is faced with unique situations where he must push his cars to the limit. High-speed chases, spinouts, and jumps coupled with pumping music and action storylines all work to create an emotional impact on the viewer. This sense of "cool" aids the brand image by entertaining viewers without a hard sell of the products. The design team remarks:

"We did this project because we believed that the excitement of the films, the emotional draw of the story lines, the talent of the directors, the passion of the driver (lead actor Clive Owen), the music, and the sheer thought that BMW would go to this extent to offer this type of experience, would be very provocative for our target audience."

Read our interview with Fallon Worldwide online at:
http://www.trainofthoughts.com

01.04.04 As Dr. Donald Norman says, humans are 'active, creative, social beings.'

Dr. Donald Norman of the Nielsen/Norman Group offers some good insights in his book, *Things That Make Us Smart*, that should give other usability consultants some food for thought:

"We humans are thinking, interpreting creatures. The mind tends to seek explanations, to interpret, to make suggestions. We are active, creative, social beings. We seek interaction with others. All of these natural tendencies are thwarted by the efforts of the engineering approach to efficiency. The danger is that things that cannot be measured play no role in scientific work and are judged to be of little importance."—Chapter One

"If we are to be able to use [digital media] easily and efficiently, the designers have to provide us with assistance, with an understandable, coherent structure. Design should be like telling a story. The design team should start by considering the task that the artifact is intended to serve and the people who will use it. To accomplish this, the design team must include expertise in human cognition, in social interaction, in the task that is to be supported, and in the technologies that will be used."—Chapter Four

"It is also the social side of technology that is least well supported. After all, the technologists are not social scientists or humanists; they are researchers and engineers. They can be excused for not understanding the social side of their handiwork. However, they [can't] be excused for not acknowledging their own lack of understanding and having some social experts join their team." —Chapter Eight

01.05 Summary

Yes—people *use* online resources, but we're more than mere "users" and are motivated by more than mere practical considerations. Far from it. As people, we have very complicated and interrelated, consumptive, social, and emotional motivations which we desire to somehow satisfy *through* more holistic online experiences.

> What do these motivations lead us to desire?
> How can we satisfy these desires through Web experience design?
> What are the broader cognitive, social, and emotional principles that we must consider?

Web enterprises must begin to grapple with and answer questions like these if they're ever to pave *experiential pathways* that are not only easy to follow but also are natural, meaningful, and enjoyable for people to journey along in pursuit of their goals.

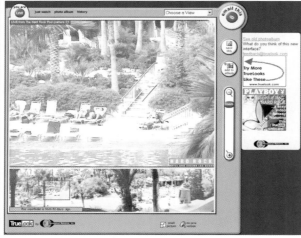

01.00.05 – http://www.hardrockhotel.com

To create an effective Web experience, the Hard Rock Hotel & Casino online entices potential guests with engaging casino games like blackjack and voyeuristic Web cams such as the "Live Bikini Cam."

01.01.01– http://www.emerils.com

Emerils.com captures the charismatic dining experience and "kicks it up a notch" with immediately accessible restaurant information, menu listings, photo tours, recipes, and an online store.

01.01.03 – http://www.center-of-the-world.com

Capturing the sultry essence of Wayne Wang's movie, "Center of the World," the online resource that supports the movie lures people into the seductive world of adult entertainment and creates a close approximation to a real interaction with an adult entertainer.

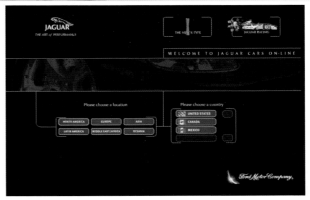

01.03.01 – http://www.jaguar.com

Jaguar.com brings the showroom experience to the Web, allowing people who may feel intimidated to enter a real showroom the chance to discover more information about the automobile, configure a dream car, and calculate the costs privately online.

01.01.05 – http://www.hermanmillerred.com

Hermanmillerred.com provides live customer assistance chat, allowing customers to ask specific questions, receive immediate feedback, and see recommended products within the chat window.

01.03.07 – http://www.mypetskeleton.com

The haunting music and dark, ghostly images create a dramatic impression while capturing the artistic style of Vincent Marcone's illustration portfolio at mypetskeleton.com.

CHAPTER 02

"The prime objective of our work with interactive multimedia is to get people to do the right things at the right times."
—Dr. Michael Allen

Affecting Outcomes—
Converting Motivation into Online Results

In Chapter One, we focused on *what* motivates people to go online. In this chapter, we'll explore *how* to tap into people's motivations and move them toward a desired outcome.

Our aim is to affect the people who interact with our Web enterprises. What effect are we after? We generally don't publish an online resource as an act of benevolence. We want something out of it. We don't want to *merely* assist and inform people; we want to influence their thinking and their behavior.

By influencing thinking we affect how people structure knowledge and develop attitudes and beliefs. By influencing behavior we affect how people decide to act upon their knowledge, attitudes, and beliefs. Whichever the case, what, how, and when we communicate with people online is really, really important if we want to make a genuine and lasting impact on their thinking, on their behavior, and on their lives.

02.00.01 The goal of experience design is to elevate a person's readiness to absorb and respond to our online messages.

Often the most favorable result of presenting an online message is a person's positive response. The point at which a person transitions from merely going through the material and chooses to enter into a dialogue with a Web enterprise is truly a defining moment psychologically. This being the case, the question becomes this:

How do we most effectively influence people to enter into what I call a *response interaction* with our Web enterprises?

Response interactions can range from disclosing personal information to engaging in e-commerce transactions. These are sensitive areas because they involve formations of relationships between people and Web enterprises. Because of widespread information abuse by unscrupulous entities, this is something most people don't enter into lightly. To understand how to influence people to respond to our online messages, we must first understand something about human nature.

02.00.02 Before people can be effectively influenced, they must first believe; to believe, they must first understand; to understand, they must first be effectively informed.

What's *your* strategy to effectively inform the people who interact with your Web enterprise? I'll give you a hint. It should have as much, if not more, to do with information *design* as it does with the trendy topic of the moment—information *architecture*.

To illustrate the distinction, the ways you cook up and dish out your online messages are even more important than the ways you list them on a menu. Information architecture has traditionally focused on helping people *access* the right information. Information design, on the other hand, focuses on helping people *understand* and *embrace* information once they've accessed it. Just as a library has great organizational schemes for its books, the library won't effectively inform anyone if the books are all lousy. The same can be said for an online resource.

02.00.03 Response interactions can best be achieved as the culmination of an *iterative* online learning process during which the things people learn continually build their confidence in and enthusiasm for the message.
This confidence and enthusiasm must increase until each person is willing to take action. This process can happen quickly—within mere seconds—or it could take minutes, hours, days, or even longer, depending on the nature of the call to action.

If we're going to be successful at creating these iterative learning experiences, we must understand the nature of the learning process. We must also understand that if the people interacting with our Web enterprises are in the process of learning, then we as creators of online resources are in the business of teaching. If we don't know how to teach, then there's little chance that anyone's going to learn anything valuable from us, let alone put any confidence in what we're purveying. Only the most determined people will press on when an online resource is ineffective at aiding comprehension.

Again, if we want to influence what people think, feel, and do, we must first effectively inform them. This involves being successful at relating to them, setting appropriate expectations, and then presenting ideas in ways that are meaningful to them as individuals. In other words, we must adapt our messages to conform to how they most efficiently and effectively learn.

02.00.04 We need to have a basic understanding of learning theory.
There are various learning theories that are widely accepted; the
best known are these[1]:

> Social Learning Theory—We learn behaviors by observing and
  then imitating others.
> Cultivation Theory—Repeated exposure to an influence gradually
  reshapes our thinking.
> Socialization Theory—Prolonged exposure to those in our daily
  lives shapes our view of the world and our role in it.
> Cognitive Constructionist Theory—When we're exposed to a
  new stimulus, we interpret meaning by filtering that stimulus
  through knowledge structures that we've already formed. This
  filtration process not only influences how we interpret the new
  stimulus, but also how we reevaluate our prior knowledge.

The learning theory most relevant to our discussion of aiding online
comprehension is the Cognitive Constructionist Theory. It directly
relates to how we *proactively* build our knowledge and it helps
us understand how the things that we see, hear, and read take on
meaning in our minds. This area is the one that Web enterprises
need the most help in. We need to understand how people think
about the messages we're confronting them with and how they
understand, assign meaning, and respond to these messages.

02.00.05 We need to understand the various ways people approach
learning: *accretion, tuning,* and *restructuring.*
If we're going to help people understand our messages and find
meaning in them, it's helpful to understand some of the ways that
they're wired to learn. According to Dr. Donald Norman, there are
three general kinds of learning—*accretion, tuning,* and *restructuring:*

> "Accretion is the accumulation of facts...adding to the stockpile
  of knowledge." The key to successful accretion is making associations with prior learning.
> Tuning is practice. It shapes "...knowledge structures in thou-
  sands of little ways so that the skill that in the early stages
  required conscious, reflective thought can now be carried out
  automatically, in a subconscious, experiential mode. Experiential
  thought is tuned thought."
> Restructuring is the reflective part of learning and is the most
  difficult. It's exploration, comparison, integration, and the
  formulation of proper conceptual structures. It's the part of
  learning where we try to "figure it all out."

The way I look at it, restructuring is the big payoff. In it are the
winds of revelation and the ambition of self-actualization. Time
spent restructuring knowledge is the most precious time we as
humans can spend when we're alone. It's prayer, it's meditation, and
it's problem solving. It's when we strive to make heads or tails of
things, when we hammer away at the walls of intellectual limitation
that keep our minds imprisoned. It's when we mine our consciousness to exhume the coals that are buried deep within our memories
and use the pressure of our thinking to form them into precious
gems. These are the treasures we don't hoard but gladly offer to
enlighten the world.

[1] Each of these is actually a category for several other theories that fall under it.
(Harris, 1999)

02.00.06 It's important to understand that helping people interpret, comprehend, and make desired conclusions regarding ideas involves more than exposing them to materials related to the subjects.

It involves guiding them into comprehension of our online messages. We must take people from the known into the unknown—making sure that each succeeding thought is comprehensible, rational, and memorable to the individual. We must also make sure that our thoughts are compounding—that they build upon one another so that those learning from us have a sense of continuity and of making progress in their understanding of our ideas.

When we're successful at doing this effectively, the quality of a person's comprehension isn't left to mere chance. We don't just start throwing information at people and hope that some of it sticks. This is the approach traditional education and training takes and its results are mediocre at best. The performance results of all participants generally forms a normal (Bell) curve with some people passing and some people failing. If businesses opperated this way losses would always water down profits.

Instead, we must leverage technology to take a new approach with people so that no member in the group gets left behind intellectually. Instead of leaving comprehension to mere chance, we must flip our standard practices upside down so that we ensure that a person can build from the understanding that he or she currently has to the understanding that we would like that person to have. Notice that this is not a one size fits all apprach. Every person's pathway to comprehension can be different.

02.00.07 In guiding comprehension, we must understand the best ways to approach the psychomotor, cognitive, and affective domains of learning.

When we think about learning, there are a few categories that come to mind. We can learn physical *skills* such as typing, playing a musical instrument, or playing a sport. We can learn *knowledge* like facts, figures, or history. Finally, we can learn things related to *ideology* such as attitudes, values, or beliefs. In their 1996 book, *Multimedia Training,* Reynolds and Iwinski call these three areas *psychomotor*, *cognitive*, and *affective* domains, respectively. Typically the domains that we try to impact on the Web are the cognitive and affective domains.

Although the psychomotor domain isn't a big emphasis in digital media, there's still something we can glean from examining it. In the psychomotor domain, a common and effective way that people learn new skills is by first interacting with a knowledgeable mentor regarding the effective performance of the skill.

Think of a coach teaching a sport or a director teaching drama. The mentor doesn't merely give a lecture regarding effective performance but collaborates with the learner in order to find effective strategies for eliciting optimum performance. The basis for this collaboration will be the learner's prior knowledge and natural abilities. Learners who are considered to have talent are those who are, for one reason or another, *gifted* at successfully integrating the skills they're learning with their natural and above-average psychomotor abilities.

02.00.06
People's level of comprehension and therefore their performance is often left to chance.

Different People

F D C B A B C D F ←Grade

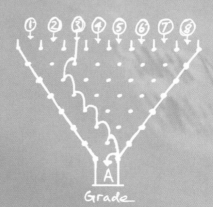

Instead, we must structure our interactions so that no matter "where a person's coming from," they are guided into comprehension of our online messages. The rationale? Different people learn differently.

A

Grade

02.00.08 To successfully instruct people in the cognitive and affective domains of learning, the methods of instruction should be similar to those employed in the psychomotor domain.

Rather than a cut-and-dried transfer or injection of knowledge into the learner's mind through an inflexible mechanism such as lecture, the instructor is most effective when an *interactive* process is employed. This occurs when the instructor and student collaborate to find the best strategy for producing meaningful insight in the learner's mind, and this is the essence of *cognitive constructionist theories*. The meaning that's formed in the learner's mind isn't an exact duplicate of the meaning that the instructor was conveying. It becomes something different in the mind of the learner based on how the new information mingles into the learner's existing knowledge structures.

In light of this, the purpose of testing shouldn't be to verify that an exact transfer of knowledge has occurred. Just because a person has temporarily memorized a fact doesn't mean that the person has attained any measure of meaningful or sustainable understanding. Instead, the purpose of testing should be to verify that the learner has gained sufficient grasp of the subject to reflect upon, compare, and evaluate several variations in meaning. This will equip the learner to attain deeper understanding through reflection as well as to relate to and interact with the perspectives, attitudes, and ideologies of others regarding the subject.

Interestingly—and most good teachers know this—the instructor who employs this more interactive process is just as likely to gain new insights into the subject as the learner is. These new insights are a result of the innovative reflection process that forces the instructor to invent new angles and new strategies for guiding that learner into comprehension. The reason for this is that in attempting to find new avenues to expand a student's conceptual framework, instructors inevitably both reinforce and expand their own conceptual framework in the process. If only all teachers would approach instruction this way, most learners would succeed.

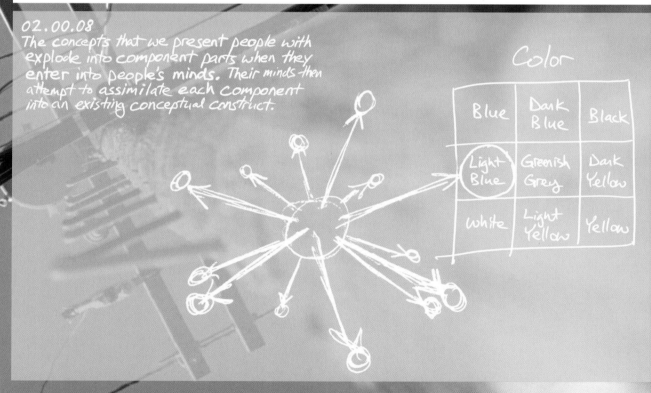

02.00.08
The concepts that we present people with explode into component parts when they enter into people's minds. Their minds then attempt to assimilate each component into an existing conceptual construct.

Color

Blue	Dark Blue	Black
Light Blue	Greenish Grey	Dark Yellow
White	Light Yellow	Yellow

When we inform people effectively, we *help* them to see the light. If we don't attempt to somehow assist them in their effort to attain comprehension of our ideas by interacting with them, we in effect leave them to struggle for interpretation on their own. People react to this in the same way that they do when approaching a very busy intersection. Just as people slow their vehicles down when coming to a busy intersection, they slow down their conscious thought when too much input is hitting them at one time. They're not quite sure what to do and are afraid of crashing.

It's the same when people approach a cluster of information. If we don't provide them with a clear place to latch onto the message and some guidance in how to see their way through it, the entire process of comprehension slows down. It's not that we want to try to inform people without presenting them with some challenges. If learning requires no cognitive effort, the lack of challenge will make the material seem boring, and we're more likely to lose their attention.

This doesn't mean, however, that we should throw people head over heels into the deep water of endless, formless information in the vacuums of an intangible Web enterprise. When we do this, what we're doing is forcing them to exert their minds in ways that are not ultimately profiting their comprehension needs. Those who struggle forward in these situations don't generally enjoy the labor that's involved in the sifting process. We're unlikely to get through to these people with our online messages, let alone gain their confidence.

If instead we first help people get their bearings and then allow them to engage in interactive learning that's challenging enough to hold their interest yet not so difficult as to discourage them, our Web enterprise will have gone a long way toward helping them to succeed with their online goals.

The key to helping people ease into information so that they can eventually see the light, is to first help them *see* that the information that they're about to interact with is going to be *light*—light enough to carry as they journey along their experiential pathway. This isn't to say that the information can't ever get *deep*—it should if necessary. The real trick at the beginning of an online interaction is to help people ease into more challenging information so that it doesn't appear to be overwhelmingly *heavy*.

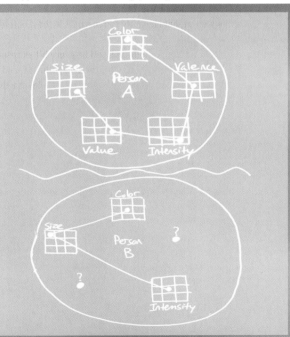

02.00.09
The components of a concept integrate into people's conceptual frameworks differently depending on the scope and nature of their prior knowledge.

The same presentation of a concept is ineffective in the mind of Person B because—based on personal factors which include prior knowledge, there isn't a sufficient conceptual framework within which the concept can be properly assimilated.

02.00.11 Now that we have a better understanding of the *learning process*, we can better understand the components of an effective *teaching process*.

In other words, we can better understand how to structure our online messages so that people truly get it and will in turn be more likely to get with it.

Because our ultimate goal is to inform, influence, and persuade, let's compare three prolific communication models that relate to persuading, educating, and selling (see figure). Again, our goal is to effectively inform those interacting with our Web enterprises so they're in the best possible position to respond to our online messages. My hope is that a strong link between effective online teaching and online persuasion can be clearly seen. My objective is that we can begin to define a strategic framework for building online messages that are likely to invoke people into response interactions.

02.00.10 The Web is a medium that can allow us to help more people than ever before in their pursuit of understanding.

Effective Web experiences can make the accretion and tuning process less ominous so that people can spend more time in reflective thought to answer the challenges that the world presents. Who will be the leaders in the online community that will take up the challenge to innovate the Web so that humanity can reach its highest potential?

The people who develop these solutions will be every bit as responsible for the discoveries that will cure cancer, end pollution, and shape our political and economic future as the people who use these systems to make these discoveries. Effective experience designs can be the very tools that accelerate people's insight and release their potential faster and more effectively than any other approach the world has ever known.

The reason is that *more* people can find comprehension of difficult ideas through *more* avenues and through *more* meaningful expressions than has ever before been possible. If we cut out the vast amounts of time spent trying to match needs with appropriate resources and then make those resources extremely effective, people will have more time to wrestle with and reflect upon the underlying problems that they're trying to solve.

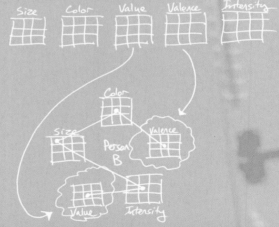

02.00.10
A good strategy to effectively inform person B from Figure 02.00.09 would be to use analogy and metaphor to build conceptual extensions from existing conceptual constructs so that the person can encode the unfamiliar aspects of the overall concept into long-term memory for later recall.

Figure 02.00.11

Aristotle's Three Elements of Persuasive Communication	Gagné's Nine Events of Learning	Shimp and Gresham's Eight Stages of Processing Advertising Messages
1. Ethos—Establish credibility with an audience. It answers the question "Why should I pay attention to your message?" It entices the audience to continue with the message.	1. Gain attention 2. Inform learner of objective	1. We're exposed to an ad 2. We attend to it
2. Pathos—Involve an audience emotionally with the message. It answers the question "Why should I care about your message?"	3. Stimulate recall of prior knowledge 4. Present the stimulus 5. Provide learning guidance	3. We comprehend the message 4. We evaluate the message 5. We encode that information into long-term memory
3. Logos—Deliver the key insight of the message. It answers the question "What should I do in response to your message?"	6. Elicit performance 7. Provide feedback 8. Assess performance 9. Enhance retention and transfer of learning	6. We retrieve that information 7. We decide among available options 8. We take action

CASE STUDY 2A

Centric Insecticide

Address: http://www.syngentacropprotection-us.com/
resources/index.asp?nav=I_Media

Client: Syngenta

Experience Designers: Martin/Williams

The Market Leader in Total Crop Protection.

Centric is an insecticide that's used to neutralize sucking and chewing insects such as aphids. Syngenta approached Martin/Williams to design a direct-response campaign, which included as its centerpiece an online info-marketing piece. The challenge was to develop an online resource that transformed what is often considered a rather "dry" subject, into a not only informative but also engaging and provoking experience. The goal was to invoke prospects to register with Syngenta so a sales representative could contact them for more information.

To help people tune into the message, a series of direct-mail postcards was sent to a highly targeted list of qualified prospects. On the postcard, a dramatic three-dimensional rendering of the aphid featured online was depicted. Recipients were promised an interesting interactive experience with this aphid as well as a premium in the form of a utility knife if they went online, learned about the product, and took a short quiz.

To increase emotional buy-in, the Martin/Williams team wanted to show growers an intimate portrayal of an aphid such as they'd never seen before. But these images and animations weren't merely frills. They played a major role in drawing the prospects into the substance of the message by helping them really visualize the process by which the insecticide neutralizes insects without causing any negative side effects to crops. These explanations involve anatomy and chemistry, and really lend themselves well to a multimedia presentation.

Read our interview with Martin/Williams online at:
http://www.trainofthoughts.com

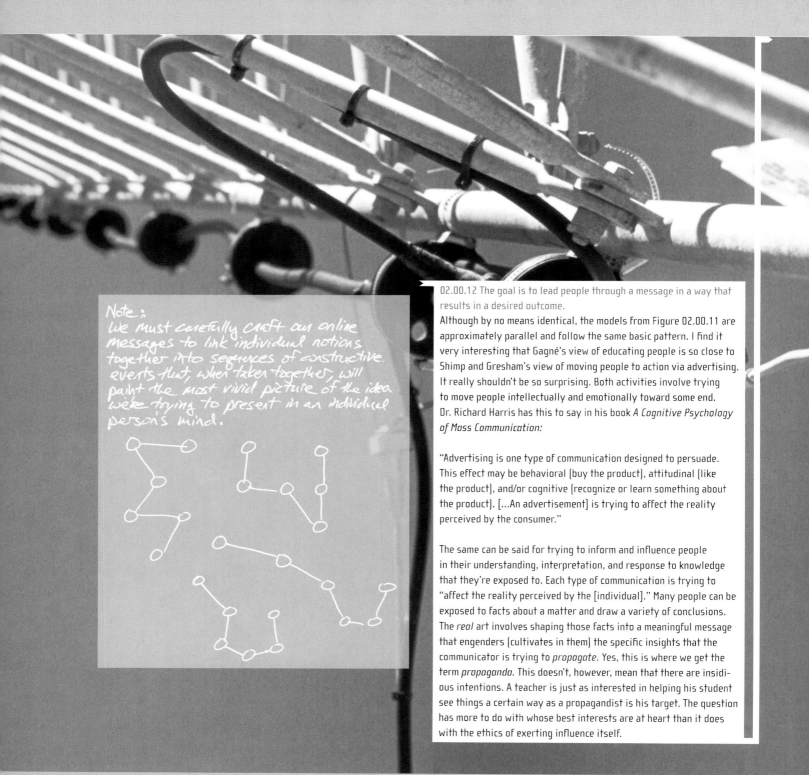

Note:
We must carefully craft our online messages to link individual notions together into sequences of constructive events that, when taken together, will paint the most vivid picture of the idea we're trying to present in an individual person's mind.

02.00.12 The goal is to lead people through a message in a way that results in a desired outcome.

Although by no means identical, the models from Figure 02.00.11 are approximately parallel and follow the same basic pattern. I find it very interesting that Gagné's view of educating people is so close to Shimp and Gresham's view of moving people to action via advertising. It really shouldn't be so surprising. Both activities involve trying to move people intellectually and emotionally toward some end. Dr. Richard Harris has this to say in his book *A Cognitive Psychology of Mass Communication*:

"Advertising is one type of communication designed to persuade. This effect may be behavioral (buy the product), attitudinal (like the product), and/or cognitive (recognize or learn something about the product). [...An advertisement] is trying to affect the reality perceived by the consumer."

The same can be said for trying to inform and influence people in their understanding, interpretation, and response to knowledge that they're exposed to. Each type of communication is trying to "affect the reality perceived by the [individual]." Many people can be exposed to facts about a matter and draw a variety of conclusions. The *real* art involves shaping those facts into a meaningful message that engenders (cultivates in them) the specific insights that the communicator is trying to *propagate*. Yes, this is where we get the term *propaganda.* This doesn't, however, mean that there are insidious intentions. A teacher is just as interested in helping his student see things a certain way as a propagandist is his target. The question has more to do with whose best interests are at heart than it does with the ethics of exerting influence itself.

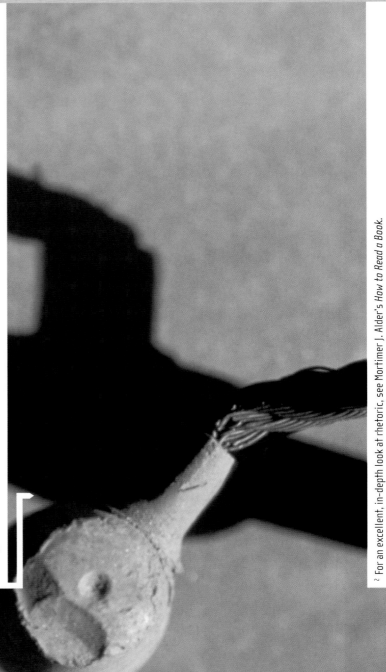

02.00.13 Aristotle's philosophy most closely follows the three-stage cognitive framework that we all carry around with us to interpret communications.

This is the framework that reminds us that the most meaningful information we encounter has a beginning, middle, and end. This framework is important because it triggers expectations regarding the work that each of these stages must accomplish in our minds in order for us to feel a sense of moving toward comprehension.

Aristotle's method is the formula for what is known as *rhetoric*[2]. Although the term *rhetoric* has undeservingly negative connotations today, it merely refers to the process through which we influence people. To paraphrase Aristotle's ideas, once people are exposed to our online messages, in order to guide them into comprehension and into a response interaction, we must

> Attract them
> Inform them
> Invoke them to take action

In examining these three stages in our online communication process, we'll see how crucial it is to understand and leverage certain fundamentals of human perception, emotion, and cognition. Far from being extravagant and peripheral, we'll see how structuring our messages to be aesthetically interesting, emotionally engaging, and easily comprehensible is both central and essential to an effective Web experience.

Specifically, we must try to understand *how* people notice, become interested in, comprehend, access, remember, and respond to the messages that they're confronted with on the Web. This will be the emphasis of Chapters Three through Six. Not surprisingly, I think you'll find that the *how* has more to do with making our messages more vivid and interesting than it does with making them more practical. Furthermore, I also believe that you'll find that the predictor of the success of an online message is the degree to which it taps into and leverages people's basic consumptive, social, and emotional motivations discussed in Chapter One.

[2] For an excellent, in-depth look at rhetoric, see Mortimer J. Alder's *How to Read a Book.*

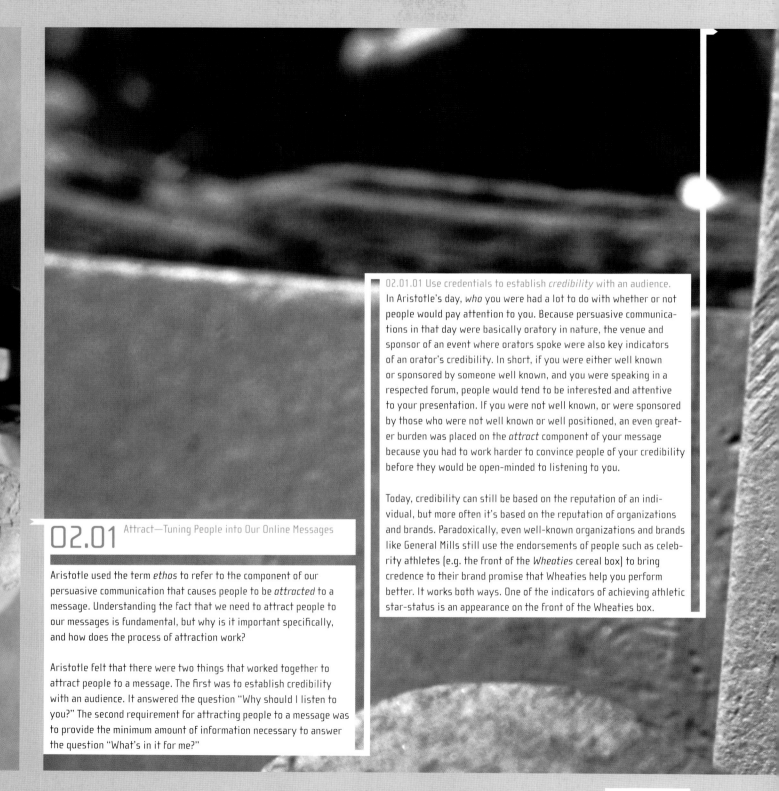

02.01   Attract—Tuning People into Our Online Messages

Aristotle used the term *ethos* to refer to the component of our persuasive communication that causes people to be *attracted* to a message. Understanding the fact that we need to attract people to our messages is fundamental, but why is it important specifically, and how does the process of attraction work?

Aristotle felt that there were two things that worked together to attract people to a message. The first was to establish credibility with an audience. It answered the question "Why should I listen to you?" The second requirement for attracting people to a message was to provide the minimum amount of information necessary to answer the question "What's in it for me?"

02.01.01 Use credentials to establish *credibility* with an audience. In Aristotle's day, *who* you were had a lot to do with whether or not people would pay attention to you. Because persuasive communications in that day were basically oratory in nature, the venue and sponsor of an event where orators spoke were also key indicators of an orator's credibility. In short, if you were either well known or sponsored by someone well known, and you were speaking in a respected forum, people would tend to be interested and attentive to your presentation. If you were not well known, or were sponsored by those who were not well known or well positioned, an even greater burden was placed on the *attract* component of your message because you had to work harder to convince people of your credibility before they would be open-minded to listening to you.

Today, credibility can still be based on the reputation of an individual, but more often it's based on the reputation of organizations and brands. Paradoxically, even well-known organizations and brands like General Mills still use the endorsements of people such as celebrity athletes (e.g. the front of the *Wheaties* cereal box) to bring credence to their brand promise that Wheaties help you perform better. It works both ways. One of the indicators of achieving athletic star-status is an appearance on the front of the Wheaties box.

02.01.02 The burden to persuade varies depending on the reputation of the person or organization making the presentation.

Here's an example that illustrates the variation in burden that's necessary to establish credibility with an online audience. We'll take a look at two companies selling potato chips on the Web—*Big Dog Food Products Inc.* and *Mom & Pop Chips Inc.*

People assume that if Big Dog Foods sells something, it must be good no matter what it is. One assumes that a firm with the stature and leverage of Big Dog will automatically filter out bad products in R&D. The same *cannot* be said for an unknown company like Mom & Pop Chips Inc. selling potato chips out of Boise, Idaho.

The messages on momandpopchips.com are going to have to work a lot harder to establish the reasons why people should go through the extra trouble of buying from a smaller player with a less-established track record. Big Dog's response to the "Why should I listen to you?" question can simply be

"Because we're Big Dog and everyone knows that we sell products that taste good."

In other words, their claim can be their established track record. Mom & Pop's answer will need to be more in depth:

"You should listen to us because we're experts at producing *organic* chips that not only taste good but also are good for you."

That may work for a while—until Big Dog slaps the word *Organic* on their packaging. Then Mom & Pop will have to go to some length in the *inform* and *invoke* stages of their rhetoric to develop an info-marketing message that educates people regarding what the word *organic* has historically meant versus what it has been distorted to mean by those in Big Dog's marketing department.

02.01.03 Superb execution can draw people to a message.
Beyond credentials, another key contributor to the ability of ancient orators to cause people to tune into their messages was the manner in which they delivered their orations. Orators who used dramatic body language and tone of voice were much more likely to attract and hold the attention of audiences. Orators were often celebrated, not because of their superior arguments, but because of the captivating quality of their refined delivery. Today the same thing needs to happen with the presentation of our online messages, but in a different, more diversified way.

Although celebrity status/established credentials is one way to get people to tune into a message, many of us who are not well known must use other methods to cause an audience to tune into our messages. Because we in the information age have grown accustomed to a high level of sensory stimulation in our communications mediums, attracting people needs to be much more than the tone of voice and gestures that were used in Aristotle's day. Furthermore, in the Internet age, people expect messages that they encounter to speak to them on more of an individual level.

02.01.04 Other factors attract people to and keep them exploring online resources.

As mentioned earlier, the credibility of a recognized person, organization, or brand has certain power to attract people and interest them in drawing deeper into an online experience—to go beyond the initial exposure to the online resource. Beyond the credibility/celebrity attraction, there are several other important forces that work to entice them deeper into our messages. Some of these include:

> Personal Interest—People who are genuinely interested in a subject such as physics, organic foods, horses, entertainment, fashion, etc. are predisposed to tune into messages related to these interests. They will tune in long enough to find out if there's anything new, unique, or that will in some way enhance the condition of their interest.
> General Interest—Subjects related to universal interests such as health, hard news, government, etc. have the power to attract all types of people as well.
> Specialized Information—According to Reeves and Nass, portraying media as being specialized " ... influences feelings about media as well as objective judgments about the [value of] the information that media present."
> Sensationalism—Gossip, the extraordinary, drama, the outrageous, all things shocking, and the unpredictable tend to have sheer stopping power. They break what I call *the pattern of the mundane* and tend to peak our curiosity.
> Cognitive Congruence/Incongruence—We are generally attracted to things that align with our own way of thinking or else set themselves up to be diametrically opposed to it. As Krome Barratt said in *Logic & Design In Art, Science & Mathematics*, "There is probably no surer way of holding the attention of a person than by projecting stimuli that identifies to a person's unique sense of self." This can range from notions that reinforce a person's ideals to notions that a person finds to be funny. When we encounter things that are incongruent to our way of thinking, we are often drawn to them because they can help us to reinforce our platforms and rehearse our rebuttals.
> Dramatic Involvement—Media such as games and interactive video have the ability not only to tune people into but also to draw people into an experience because these media make them feel like they're part of the action. Beyond these, situations that present conflict and resolution in general are attractive to most people and will both capture and hold their attention.
> Sensory Stimulation—Things that we consider to be beautiful, impressive displays, artfulness in execution, unique configurations, etc. all have the power to stop us and make us wonder.

02.01.05 It's important that we help people quickly establish the appropriateness of an online message when they first encounter an online resource.

If people must struggle at all with the appropriateness of information, it's likely that they will quickly move on to other possibilities. Dr. Ward Hanson elaborates:

"Web surfers [are] constantly making a judgment about the value of continuing a visit to a website or stopping. Two factors [are important]. First is the value of the current page. Second is the uncertainty about the value of pages not yet seen...[A strong] implication is the importance of guiding visitors to the relevant pages. [People] have limited tolerance for inappropriate material before abandoning their visit."

Although many usability consultants have similar *sounding* rhetoric, there's a very important difference. In many situations, usability consultants emphasis the aspect of the need for expediency that involves *accessing* content that has the *potential* of being appropriate. As I've said, there's no doubt that this is indeed important. The aspect that I'm emphasizing here, however, is the fact that content, once accessed, must effectively *communicate* its appropriateness. Typically, the proper approach to accomplishing this is not followed. We'll be exploring the proper approach throughout the remainder of Part One of this book.

02.01.06 Appropriateness is determined by answering the question: 'Is this good for me, bad for me, or just plain neutral?'

Reeves and Nass refer to these evaluations as *valence* decisions. The nature of this evaluation isn't reflective—we don't analyze and evaluate. Instead, the nature of this evaluation is experiential—it makes an instantaneous impression on our minds, and we react without reflecting before making a decision. We shoot first and ask questions later—or not.

The reason we do this is that we've learned by experience that the online resources that we like the most set off certain cognitive and/or emotional triggers. If these triggers aren't activated when we first try to engage a message online, we've learned, as Hanson pointed out, that it's a better risk to try another opportunity rather than dig for satisfaction in the current one. The key insight here is that this unconscious evaluation process has more to do with the *impression* that a message begins to form in our minds than it does with the *claim* that a message makes for itself.

We need to be successful in helping the people interacting with our online messages to quickly answer the appropriateness question in the affirmative if they're going to stick around long enough to be informed and invoked by our messages.

02.02 Inform—Drawing People into Our Online Messages

Informing people extends beyond merely providing them with useful information. It involves helping them to see—to attain a certain understanding. It's the stage of our communication in which it is most critical to tap into the prior knowledge that lives in people's existing conceptual frameworks. This has as much to do with appealing to people's emotion as it does their reason.

As mentioned in Figure 02.00.11, Aristotle's term *pathos* refers to the component of our rhetoric that causes people to be drawn into a message. The work of pathos is to involve people emotionally as it answers the question "Why should I care about your message?"

Depending on the nature of the message, this emotional involvement encompasses the full range of human emotions—from excitement to compassion to anger. To involve a person emotionally is to make a message become alive, real, and personal for that individual. It fosters empathy. It inspires. It taps into our basic motivations and unleashes the power of human will and determination, generating the momentum of passion necessary for results to occur.

02.02.01 We must tap into an audience's latent energy.

In Aristotle's day, when an orator successfully informed an audience, there was a transfer of energy from the orator to the audience. No longer was it necessary for the orator to kindle enthusiasm in the audience. When that orator had succeeded in making an emotional connection with the audience, that audience could reciprocate by fanning the orator's passions into flames.

The goal of informing an audience is to convince them of the relevance, importance, and timeliness of the message. It causes the audience to become open to the key insights that will be delivered in the *invoke* stage of the message. It makes them eager to hear the call to action so that they can respond.

According to Dr. Richard Harris, messages must " ... appeal to the affective (emotional) component of our attitudes. Influencing emotions is often the best first step to influencing beliefs and, ultimately, behavior."

02.02.02 Pathos is a vehicle for enhancing associative learning.

If we compile the steps from the other communication models in Figure 02.00.11 that correspond to the *inform* stage, we find that to be effective we must help an audience

> *Recall* prior knowledge
> *Comprehend* the message
> *Evaluate* the message
> *Encode* that information into long-term memory

The main thrust of the inform stage is that we're trying to take concepts that people are already familiar with and associate new thoughts and ideas to them so that people will relate to them better.

SPOTLIGHT ON:

DR. MICHAEL ALLEN

As can be seen in i1.00.06, not many people have been as professionally successful as Dr. Michael Allen. He received his Ph.D. in educational psychology from Ohio State University in 1971. There his research was sponsored at the National Science Foundation supported Learning Center for Biological Sciences. It led to one of the first Learning Management Systems, demonstrated the power of dynamic student-initiated testing, and explored measures of learner confidence as outcome variables.

As someone who's influenced many regarding the need to communicate effectively with people through interactive multimedia—particularly in the area of learning; I thought his comments on the material presented in this chapter would be both interesting and valuable. My interview with Dr. Allen follows:

Lenker: How has it come to be that so many Web enterprises spend millions creating online resources that don't communicate effectively with the people that interact with them?

Allen: It's not easy to communicate effectively in any medium. That's why the people who are successful are celebrated for their talents. But it's clearly possible to do better than most are doing now, and there isn't just one way to be successful. There are many.

I'll try to give you a concise answer in two parts:

First, organizations tend to have an agenda regarding what they want to "say" to their patrons versus trying to understand what patrons as individuals really need to "hear." Yes, it's important that we communicate ideas through our content online, but we don't want to inflict messages on people that they don't see the relevance in. It is especially detrimental when these messages stand in the way of people gaining expedient access to specific information that they came to attain. To serve their purposes and reach their own goals, Web enterprises need to avoid losing people's interest in the process of trying to convey their message. This requires meeting people's expectations while also delivering experiences that are interesting and which tantalize for more. It's not only what you say, but how you say it.

Second, many fail because they end up focusing on the technology through which content is delivered rather than on the user's experience. Just making the site do what you want it to do is still far more challenging than it should be, but that's another story. Our delivery technologies far supercede our development and authoring technologies, so developers justifiably feel gratified just by making things work reliably. When they can go further, they triumph in creating visual effects that unfortunately have as much likelihood

to detract from the user's experience as they do to enhance it. After all the challenges have been met to get something up and working, creators and investors see a lot of beauty in their accomplishments. Users may have a different perspective.

The sad part is that when content is given more careful attention, it's usually given the wrong type of attention. A premium is placed on creating "cool" visual effects that are, in most cases, more harmful to a person's online experience than they are helpful.

Lenker: What do you feel are the most important keys to guiding people into comprehension of our online messages?

Allen: It's most important to create an experience that patrons can relate to, enjoy, and find beneficial. When I interact with a Web site, I want my needs tended to first. If I'm looking for specific information, I don't want to suffer through a lot of other pitches, news releases, announcements, graphics downloads, and other items screaming for my attention. But if you're nice to me and make my experience both pleasant and productive, I may well want to stay around and chat; i.e. I might feel like hearing what's on your mind.

Lenker: In general terms, what's the best strategy to invoke people into a response interaction with our Web enterprises?

Allen: We are both intellectual and emotional beings. We are much more prone to action if both our reasoning and desires predict a positive outcome. If we want visitors to make quick decisions [...]

Read the entire interview online at: http://www.trainofthoughts.com

Learn more about Dr. Michael Allen at: http://www.alleni.com

Four-year-old Billy's first introduction to the concept of death comes—as with many families—from the demise of the family gold-fish. In order to help Billy understand that death is a natural process which is an extension of life, his mother relates it to a concept he's already familiar with:

"Billy, you know how at the end of the summer the leaves dry up, fall off the trees, and die? Well, it's the same with pet goldfish. After a while they die, too. The only difference is that they float up instead of fall down. Do you understand?"

As Billy grows up, the sight of leaves falling in autumn will remind him of his pet goldfish, Perky, that he had at age four. He's *encoded* the information about the death of his pet goldfish with what he had previously understood from observing nature. Although recalling his pet goldfish whenever he sees the golden leaves falling in autumn wasn't the intended outcome of his mother's analogy, it's become a side effect, nonetheless. Later, when Billy's grandfather dies, Billy's mother will help him recall the death of his goldfish and create a further association for him.

What do leaves falling in autumn, goldfish, and grandfathers have in common? Nothing, for anyone else except Billy. In his mind they all relate to lessons about death and dying.

The power that these types of associations have is that they relate what we already know or care about to something new that we *want* people to care about as well. The emotional component of this process is extremely powerful. What we need to do with our online messages is learn to tap into this inherent emotional power.

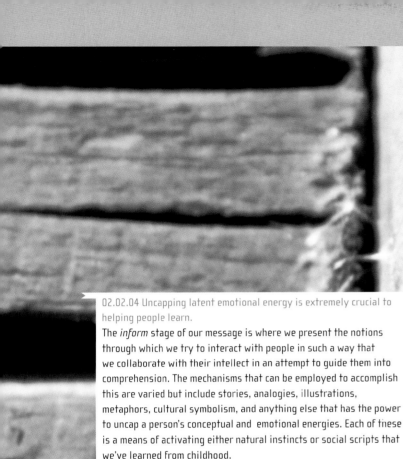

02.02.04 Uncapping latent emotional energy is extremely crucial to helping people learn.

The *inform* stage of our message is where we present the notions through which we try to interact with people in such a way that we collaborate with their intellect in an attempt to guide them into comprehension. The mechanisms that can be employed to accomplish this are varied but include stories, analogies, illustrations, metaphors, cultural symbolism, and anything else that has the power to uncap a person's conceptual and emotional energies. Each of these is a means of activating either natural instincts or social scripts that we've learned from childhood.

The ramifications of this are that when we're confronted with certain situations, our responses are somewhat predictable. This is why formula movies are often so successful. They're designed to present stimuli that illicit predictable responses from mass audiences within a culture. When presented with injustice and cruelty, we react with indignation. When confronted with the hardship and suffering of the very young or the very old, we react with pity and compassion. When confronted with behavior that violates social norms, we react with shock or curiosity. When confronted with the beautiful and seductive, we respond with desire.

02.02.05 The story form is a powerful learning device.

What's more, when confronted with the beginning of what we recognize to be a story form, we have an almost uncontrollable compulsion to experience the middle and end of that story. Dr. Harris writes about this in *A Cognitive Psychology of Mass Communication*:

"There is a very general [conceptual framework] for stories in Western culture (Kintsch, 1977). This narrative script is learned implicitly from the earliest days of young children hearing stories from their parents. Such stories are composed of episodes, each of which contains an *exposition*, *complication*, and *resolution*. That is, the characters and setting are introduced (exposition), some problem or obstacle develops (complication), and that problem or obstacle is somehow overcome (resolution). We grow up expecting stories to follow this general script."

Producers of television shows know this. That's why segments of the actual program are longer at the beginning of the story with few commercials. Once an audience is hooked, the segments of the program become increasingly shorter and the commercial interruptions become longer. The producers know that in later stages of a storyline, it's psychologically very difficult for an audience to move on without experiencing dramatic resolution. Even when there's a high degree of resentment for this practice, people succumb to their innate need for a sense of completion.

02.02.06 Using the story form can enhance our information-processing capabilities.

Dr. Byron Reeves found that children had a very well-developed conceptual framework for stories by the age of seven. Using this framework led to both better content recollection and retention, a reduction in processing effort, and greater attention span. By using a familiar framework, people can focus on the particulars of the message rather than the form.

In light of this, the story form is a very powerful tool for capturing and holding the attention of an audience. What's more, a really well-formulated story can be very effective in focusing people's thinking in a way that makes any other point of view seem less than optimal. This is where we get the term *rhetorical argument*. The point is that we structure our argument in such a way that there's only one logical answer—and that is the answer that the presenters had in mind. It's not that there are no other possible answers, but within the context of the structure of a given argument, an audience is left with no other choice. Stories empower this effect.

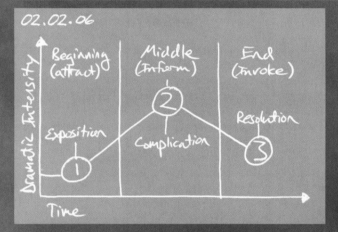

02.02.07 Especially when used as an analogy to cause an audience to understand a parallelism in real life, a story has done its job when it has caused an audience to *feel* something for the subject at hand. When stories are utilized effectively, it leaves people in a state in which they want to take some action or reform their attitudes and beliefs in some way.

Think of a religious sermon. The minister uses stories as analogies to lower an audience's guard and penetrate to the depths of their souls. He's told the story of the children starving in Africa and reminds them of the excessive luncheon that they've planned later in the afternoon. He has them right where he wants them. They're feeling guilty. They're feeling sorry and want a sense of relief so that they can eat their lunch in the peace that comes from having a clear conscience.

What will bring that sense of relief? Well, the minister is about to tell them in the *invoke* section of his sermon. He's about to deliver the key insight that will make the light bulb go on for them. They'll be told exactly what they should do, and they'll be glad to do it—even if it involves an offering plate. Whereas they would have scoffed if the minister had called them to this specific action at the beginning of the sermon, now that he's brought them through the emotional highs and lows necessary to trigger resonance, they're primed and ready to have a sense of dramatic resolution in their own lives.

We must do the same thing with our online messages. By drawing people in emotionally through the use of tools such as stories, analogies, and metaphors—whether textual, visual, or otherwise—we're putting them in the best possible position to respond to the online *invocation* that will follow.

02.03 Invoke—Persuading People to Buy into Our Online Messages and Take Action

As mentioned in Figure 02.00.11, Aristotle's term *logos* refers to the component of our messages that brings people to conviction and invokes them to take action. The work of the *invocation* is to bring people to the realization that a message is valid and is of personal importance. It must also call them to action as it answers the question "What should I do in response to your message?"

The strange thing about the messages that we typically encounter on the Web is that they seem almost schizophrenic in their call to action. These calls to action often aren't directed toward anyone in particular. They seem to be almost randomly fired at us. People have a very difficult time trying to figure out what they should do. This is a problem. Remember, the purpose of our online resource is usually to lead people through a process that begins by effectively informing them and ends by ultimately leading them through a successful response interaction. To be successful, this response interaction must address people's real motivations as well as meet real needs.

If we compile the steps from the other communication models that correspond to Aristotle's *logos*, with some simplification we're left with this list:

> Present the key insight
> Provide learning guidance
> Elicit performance
> Provide reinforcement/feedback

02.03.01 Everything that we communicate is intended to prepare people to receive the key insight.

If our messages have attracted people, caused them to tune in and be receptive to our ideas, we've had a great start. If we've made a message come alive and reach inside people, moving them emotionally and intellectually, we've positioned ourselves to succeed. But if we don't follow through by helping people attribute ultimate meaning to the message, our results will be haphazard at best.

An example of this point is the current antidrug campaign being targeted at teens, which focuses on the drug known as Ecstasy. The characters in the TV ads reflect the generation they're trying to persuade. The production values of the ads are high and the scripts are progressive. But to make an impression on these teens, the message must rise above the drone of the antismoking rhetoric that's commonplace. Otherwise the message would be filtered out of most teens' consciousness. So while the production values and the script attract their attention, the message must present something dramatic enough to make these kids stop and pay attention (see figure).

Figure 02.03.01

ATTRACT

Media: (Home video of youthful teen girl goofing around with friends at home)

Copy: Meet Becky. She's young, she's bright, she's talented, she's beautiful.

She's probably a lot like you.

ATTRACT

< This is the beginning of the story form script.

< This part creates social identification.

INFORM

Media: (Slow fade to black)

Copy: You know how you want to have the time of your life at your graduation party? You've heard how awesome they can be. Becky heard that, too. In fact, the night of her high school graduation party last spring, someone talked her in to trying Ecstasy for the first time—said it would be "awesome."

Media: (Close up of inscription on tombstone with flowers around it.)

Copy: And now Becky, who was my daughter…is dead.

Really awesome.

INFORM

< Here the ad taps into existing cognitive framework to access existing knowledge and values.
< An emotional bridge is being built here.

< Conflict is introduced. The juxtaposition of the carefree girl in the video having fun with the looming realization of what is likely to be revealed about the girl's fate is powerful. There's intense focus at this moment on the part of the audience.
< Conflict is resolved, except this is a tragedy.

INVOKE

Copy: Over three hundred teens die every year while using Ecstasy *for the first time.*

Please, don't be one of them.

INVOKE

< Key insight is presented.

< This is the call to action.

Figure 02.03.01 is the *approximate* transcription of a TV ad I saw in London in 2000. Although a pattern of anticipation is set up that casts the main character in a positive light, as the storyline unfolds, there's a powerful violation of expectation.

CASE STUDY 2B

Saab9x

Address: http://www.saab9x.com
Client: Saab
Experience Designers: Large Medium AB

A signpost to the future.

Swiss native Saab has been creating luxury automobiles since the 1940s. The brand intent maintains clear integrity while fusing form, function, and quality into every detail. The incredibly innovative Saab 9x sport coupe continues to portray every characteristic of the Saab line while suggesting a new aggressive, sporty attitude. Due to the inaccessibility of the car for the majority of customers, Saab sought a way to deliver a message about the 9x that would inspire interest and excitement. Enter Saab9x.com.

The design team at Large Medium developed an online resource to showcase the car while subtly communicating the future direction of the brand. The car was the main inspiration for the experience design. It projects a sense of boldness and sport, yet maintains the innovation, heritage, and quality of the current automobile line. Saab9x.com artfully tells the story of the Saab 9x through an anthology of media elements that present not only the final product but also a history of the car's development.

As the story unfolds, people are drawn closer into the experience with each succeeding notion. The use of subtle, fluid motion was not only key in attracting but also in directing attention from screen-space to screen-space. Each succeeding notion compounds the idea that the 9x is something special—something the world hasn't seen before. Perhaps the segment that makes this idea most clear is the one that documents the engineering team's story of the car's development. Various media elements are synthesized and presented in a scrolling timeline.

Saab9x.com has been well received and featured as Macromedia Site of the Day on October 12, 2001, and in Webspelan (Sweden's most prestigious e-business award)—Best Brand Campaign, Finalist.

Read our interview with Large Medium online at:
http://www.trainofthoughts.com

02.03.02 Stories that set up patterns of anticipation can be powerfully capitalized on in the *invoke* stage of our online communication. Hearing a shocking story as in Figure 02.03.01 about someone who suddenly died after using drugs only once can create a very powerful emotional connection—a powerful moment. It's at this moment that the key insight must be injected into a person's conceptual framework. For it to make a lasting impression, however, this key insight must be perceived by the audience as being profound and significant.

In the TV ad transcribed in Figure 02.03.01, the imagery, especially of Becky's sweet and youthful face, will be used as a rallying point for the rest of the information that will populate this knowledge structure. The result will be that audience members will have a modified cognitive script for the use of that particular drug. Instead of the script being this:

We get together > We dance > We have fun > We pop some Ecstasy > We sleep in the next morning.

The cognitive script is modified to become:

We get together > We dance > We have fun > We pop some Ecstasy > We sleep in *forever.*

02.03.03 The role of the key insight is not only to get people thinking but also to guide that thinking into a place of receptiveness for the recommended course of action.

To use the illustration from 02.01.02 regarding the need to establish credibility for Mom & Pop Chips Inc., we need to help people know what to make of all the information they've been receiving about the subject by presenting this message:

"Now you see that, just as it's foolish to spit into the wind, it's even more foolish to fill your body with the harmful chemicals that Big Dog potato chips are saturated with? We have empirical evidence from a meta-research analysis that shows that when lab rats are fed Big Dog chips, they have a 400 percent higher mortality rate than those that are fed Mom & Pop organic chips. You're a good parent, and we know that you certainly don't want to experiment with your children's health."

This is the final moment in this tongue-in-cheek endeavor to guide people into comprehension of this particular online messages. Mom & Pop's success here will be a key determinant of their success when eliciting performance.

02.03.04 The example of Big Dog versus Mom & Pop was designed to be silly, but the lesson it teaches is very serious.

The *inform* stage of communication uses stories, analogies, and metaphors to help people make associations between new information and prior knowledge. It in effect takes them on an emotional journey down roads they'd previously traveled and makes new information seem like it fits into the mental pictures that their memories paint. The purpose of presenting a final piece of new, *key* information in the *invoke* stage is to further elevate people's emotions and move them to the brink of decision.

The point of presenting a notion that both fits nicely into people's need to experience resolution, as well as their desire to be enlightened by something profound, is to give them a sense of satisfaction that something entirely new has been gained from the communication that has truly added to their existing knowledge structures in a valuable and inspiring way.

02.03.05 We must elicit performance from our audiences or else our communication has been in vain.

It's time to close the sale. If our goal is to ask people to enter into a response interaction with our Web enterprise by either filling out a registration form or by actually buying something, this is where we ask them to do so. This call to action can either be explicit or implicit. Using the serious example from Figure 02.03.01, we can see both explicit and implicit calls to action at work.

That call to action directed toward the target audience—teens—can be explicit, as in "Please don't be one of them (who tries Ecstasy)." But a different type of call to action is also being *implicitly* targeted to a secondary audience—parents of teens. In the anti-Ecstasy ad, parents weren't being explicitly targeted, but there was an implicit call to action there nonetheless. The writing between the lines read: "Hey parents, you had better talk to your teens about Ecstasy and make sure that they know how dangerous it is."

In our Mom & Pop chips example, there is a less serious call to action:

"Mom & Pop organic chips not only taste great, but they'll reduce your chances of dying from eating them by 400%! That's why we'd like to ask you to fill out this simple form and we'll send you a free sample. We know that you'll both taste and *feel* the difference a good Mom & Pop can make!"

02.03.06 Providing reinforcement and requesting feedback closes the loop on the current communication and opens the door for future online communication.

It's important to reinforce the vote of confidence that a person gives our Web enterprise when they choose to enter a response interaction. In the case of Mom & Pop chips, a person that responds is buying into their quality-of-taste and quality-of-health value promise. Reinforcement might be something like this:

"We'd like to thank you for your purchase. You've made a very wise decision—one that your family and your health insurance agent will thank you for."

If our interest in people is perceived to wane after we've gotten their money, it will not be looked upon very favorably. It's important that we acknowledge these people both immediately upon completing a response interaction as well as when they return to our systems in the future:

"John! Welcome back. We hope you enjoyed the sample of chips we sent you. We felt that you'd appreciate the barbecue flavor since you like spicy food. Did that flavor suit you? [Yes] or [No] ?"

As long as people have chosen to open the door to this type of response, this type of message can accomplish many things:

> It makes people feel appreciated and remembered. They have a sense of being understood—a sense of belonging and acceptance.
> It impresses the fact upon people's minds that the Web enterprise is making an effort to get to know them. The result will most likely be an improvement in the overall quality of both the messages they're exposed to while interacting with the online resource as well as the products they'll purchase online.
> It reinforces the positive impression they formed of the Web enterprise in the first place.
> It seems to care about their level of satisfaction after the fact and not just before the sale.

As we'll learn in Chapters Three and Four, it's very important to understand the nature of the systems that can provide these types of interactions with the people who interact with our online resources. Formulating messages that are both appropriate and meaningful is serious business nowadays. Organizations that know how to properly structure these messages through their online resource will be the most successful in the online marketplace.

02.03.07 The steps in our three-part communication model are iterative, not linear.

Once people are exposed to our online messages, the process of guiding them into comprehension is *rarely* linear. Instead, it's usually iterative. The reason is that the days of making speeches to mass audiences are over. The shotgun approach to communicating is too generalized for our online audiences. After all, we must keep in mind that the *real* power of the Web is in engaging people in one-to-one dialogues—or *interactions.* This is one of the keys to effective Web experiences. What I mean by saying that they're iterative is that they progressively help people zero in on comprehension of our messages. You can view this iterative process as a cycle that forms a spiral. The components are these:

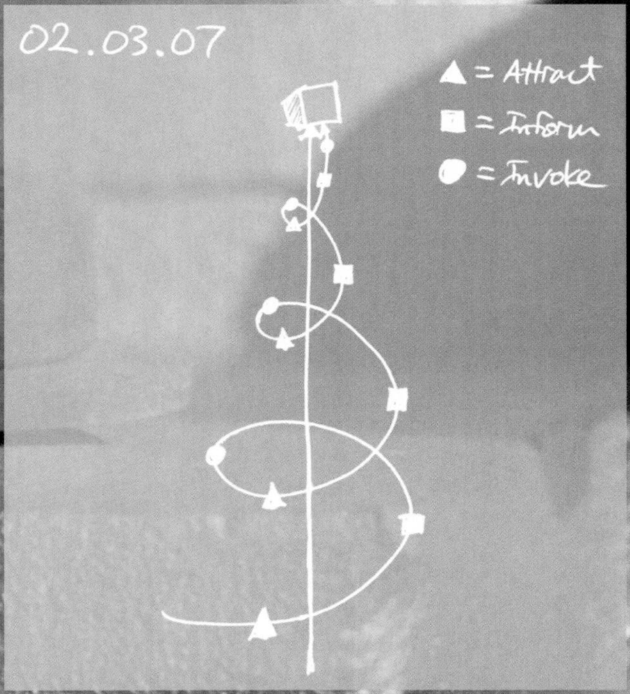

Attract > Inform > Invoke

I propose that the attract > inform > invoke cycle not only works at the top level of our overall message but also is nested into the component level of each stage:

> ATTRACT—When people are initially exposed to our online message, they need to be attracted to the content, informed as to the relevance of the message, and invoked to invest a few seconds interacting with the system at some level.

> INFORM—If people choose to go further with the overall message, they're again exposed to the next notion in the sequence and must make value judgments about the appropriateness of that stage of the message. We therefore must attract and inform them, as well as invoke them, to either extend the dialogue until they're satisfied or, if they're ready, to enter into a response interaction, whatever it may be.

> INVOKE—When we're trying to invoke people to take action in the last stage of our message, it's important that the pattern of anticipation that we've helped build is not violated at the end. To fulfill expectations, we must follow through with every facet of our message. In other words, people's social, emotional, and consumptive needs must continue to be met throughout the entire online message.

02.03.07

▲ = Attract
■ = Inform
● = Invoke

02.03.08 This iterative communication model works like a corkscrew. With each turn, people are drawn further in and ever closer to the moment when the potential of our message is fully released.

Think about the nature of a dialogue for a moment. Depending on the prior knowledge, personality, and disposition of both parties, a dialogue can be either long or short. If we're trying to inform one person, that person may need extra help understanding a certain aspect of the overall message—therefore our message must be protracted. To someone else, however, this emphasis might seem like a tangent—and it would be—for that person. They want a dialogue that is contracted.

For these reasons, we can see why it's *so* important that we understand the need to design our online resources to support messages that are *variable* and not fixed—to accommodate the needs of *various* people. We'll closely examine this issue in Chapters Three and Four.

02.04 Summary

As we've seen in this chapter, it's essential that we begin to view our role as experience designers as one of guiding people into comprehension of our online messages. When we effectively inform people regarding our ideas, they're well positioned to enter into response interactions with our Web enterprises. These response interactions are the natural by product of leading people through the three stages of our communication model. After initially exposing people to our online messages, these three stages involve *attracting* attention and interest, substantively *informing* them regarding our ideas, and then *invoking* them to respond by providing key insights as well as specific courses of action that can be taken. For these messages to be successful online, they must ultimately speak to people on an individual level. In this way the substance of the information we provide will likely be appropriate. The nature of these messages is that they're interactive, in that they closely parallel the process of real life interactions between people.

In Chapter One, we explored people's online motivations. We learned that, although we should always be attentive to people's need to easily interact with interfaces, the human mind and spirit need much more than mere simplicity to be inspired by information. In this chapter, we looked at the communication process that we must lead people through in order to convert these motivations into online results. In Chapters Three and Four, we'll take a closer look at the mechanics behind this process on a micro and a macro level.

GALLERY 02

02.00.06 – http://www.factordesign.com/drivedemo/
This functional tutorial for Driveway.com highlights how the online file storage service works. The training moves beyond simple next-and-last paging by animating a clear flow path of the process and by using animation to zoom closer on screen capture details. (Research found at http://www.commarts.com/CA/interactive/cai01/.)

02.00.10– http://www.andrethegiant.com/
This online resource showcases propaganda campaigns that were intended to "affect the reality perceived by [individuals]."

< 02.01.04 – http://www.swiftlab.com
SwiftLab, Eyeland Studio's latest project, allows visitors to create and purchase Flash games, animations, and interface online. SwiftLab also features free greeting cards which people can customize to include their own pictures and audio clips.

02.02.04 – http://www.ninjai.com

Ninjai, the Little Ninja is a Flash-driven, episode-based action/adventure series. The storyline follows Ninjai on his journeys as he travels throughout the Ancient World.

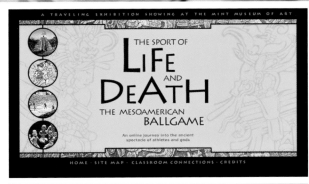

02.02.06 – www.ballgame.org

Ballgame.org is an educational resource that teaches about the first team sport in history—the Mesoamerican ballgame—while promoting the national exhibit tour. It takes people on a journey back in time to discover more about the land and culture and explore the game, then allows people to experience the game online.

CHAPTER 03

Composing Notions—
Making Online Information Meaningful

"Our educational institutions have a disappointing track record in educating our populace. One reason is that instructors are not able to listen attentively to their students. Teachers have too many students and too little time with each one. So their focus often turns pragmatically to the presentation of information, with quizzes interspersed and a concluding final test. It's what I call the 'tell and test' methodology, a traditional, convenient, and unfortunately very ineffective methodology.

"With today's technology, it's important that we not merely perpetuate failed models of the past, but use the new capabilities to truly overcome problems and make more effective models practical. We are no longer restricted to reciting our messages with the hopes that they are appreciated. We can once again listen and adapt our messages as needed. Through inexpensive ubiquitous technology, we can now communicate with the efficiency of the one-to-many model and have the effectiveness of the one-to-one model."

—Dr. Michael Allen

The best way to guide people into comprehension of our online messages is to lead them through a sequence of well-composed notions. I define a notion as a moment in the life of a message. I see a message as a series of notions just as a train is a series of cars. Just as the various types of cars on a train carry valuable cargo, the various notions in a message carry valuable thoughts. What's more, the whole of an idea can't be fully understood unless there's comprehension of the sum of its component thoughts.

Why is this such a big deal? From my perspective, online resources are too often designed to be diffused, branching networks of information, or tree structures, when in fact they should be designed to be series, or sequences, of information. The nature of a tree structure is such that, at every junction in the hierarchy, there are any number of branches that can be taken. This hierarchical approach can work on a limited basis when content is being sought, but when content is being encountered and ideas are being presented, I believe that branching must, in most cases, end, and a series—or sequence of notions—must begin.

03.00.01 Effective examples of notion sequences aren't encountered very often on the Web because the role of hierarchy in the organization of information has been widely misunderstood.

The purveyors of this misunderstanding—usability experts! Most usability experts are overly obsessed with empowering "users" to the degree that these "users" are given options to branch away from ideas they're endeavoring to understand, even when it's in their best interest to stay on the same track for a while[1]. If options to branch away simply must be provided, it would be better if people were given proper guidance regarding the benefits of branching into new directions. Effective guidance, however, is most often not provided. Even when branches are explained well, people can become discouraged when continually branching away from a central message because they feel as if they're not making progress in their understanding of core ideas.

Certainly there are times when parenthetical departures are appropriate, but allowances must be made to not let people lose a sense of context within the underlying message.

03.00.01
In the Web of the 1990s, Web enterprises forced people to go hunting for meaning.

[1] This issue of empowerment will be covered in Chapter Four.

03.00.02 The need to keep people on track is a familiar concept, but why is it so important?

It's important because fully understanding an idea, in most cases, requires *cumulative* comprehension of each supporting concept. Learning a subject like math provides some examples. We must understand the concept of *number* before we can understand the concept of *equation*. We must understand addition and subtraction before we can comprehend multiplication and division.

Cumulative, conceptual comprehension also comes into play in other non-educational communications, such as in marketing messages. We must understand, for example, that we as prospective consumers of a product or service *have* a need before we'll understand *how* a particular product successfully addresses that need. In any type of communication, our understanding of an assimilated concept is utilized and taken further in the transmission of succeeding concepts. We can't skip any steps, or we'll have gaps in our understanding. This again underlines the view of transmission of an idea as being a series, or sequence, of thoughts that must be taken in succession to one another.

In the remainder of this chapter, we'll explore the issues related to formulating an online resources microcosm—composing notions to express thoughts. In the next chapter, we'll explore the issues related to producing the macrocosm— the interactive sequencing of notions into effective trains of thoughts which express ideas that are appropriate and on target for individuals and a given situations.

03.00.01B
In the Web of the twenty-first century, Web enterprises will help people build meaning.

Attract   Inform   Invoke

03.00.03 To understand an information flow, it's helpful to first look at it from the microlevel and then from the macrolevel.

In my vernacular, a thought is a moment in the life of an idea. To be transmitted to others, ideas and their constituent thoughts must be put into messages and their constituent notions. A thought/notion represents the microlevel and an idea/message is the macrolevel.

I like the train metaphor because of its inherent flexibility and inter-changeability in terms of its constitution and sequencing. Just as a storyteller will alter the ways and means that a story is conveyed depending on who he or she is interacting with, an online resource must vary its transmission of an idea based on who it's communicating with. This requires an inherent flexibility in transmission. It's not that everyone doesn't need to understand the same concepts to understand the overall idea. They do need to. It's just that some people require a more protracted series of thoughts to understand the core concepts while others require a more contracted series of thoughts to understand the same concepts.

Figure 03.00.03 presents my view of the relationship between thoughts, concepts, and ideas.

THOUGHTS
CONCEPTS
IDEAS

Online Resource

THE HUMAN MIND

Note:
An important role of an online resource is to draw from the universe of thoughts, concepts, and ideas, and funnel them into the human mind as a sequence of well-conceived notions.

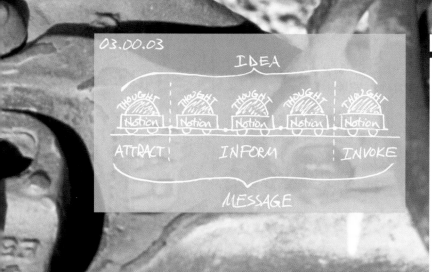

03.00.03

IDEA

THOUGHT · Notion
THOUGHT · Notion
THOUGHT · Notion
THOUGHT · Notion
THOUGHT · Notion

ATTRACT · INFORM · INVOKE

MESSAGE

Figure 03.00.03

1. As a car is to a train, a notion is to a message, and a thought is to an idea.
2. A notion is a component of an overall message and, like a car on a train, provides a container that holds an individual thought.
3. A concept could consist of only one thought, and be expressed in one notion, but may need to leverage any number of thoughts and require any number of notions to get its meaning across. This depends on how complicated the concept is as well as on how prepared a person's mind is to receive the transmission..
4. There are at least three concepts presented in a message, each corresponding to the beginning, middle, and end.
5. A message is an entire sequence of notions, or train of thoughts, which are linked together in order to present an overall idea in a way that's uniquely targeted toward an individual's comprehension needs. In other words, not all notions are meant to be accessed by everyone, but only those that are necessary for comprehension of a given concept.

FOR MARY TO UNDERSTAND AN IDEA

| Thought 01 | Thought 02 | Thought 03 | Thought 03.5 | Thought 04 | Thought 05 |

| Concept A | | Concept B | | | Concept C |

IDEA

FOR MIKE TO UNDERSTAND THE SAME IDEA

| Thought 01 | Thought 01.5 | Thought 02 | Thought 03 | Thought 05 | Thought 06 |

| Concept A | | | Concept B | Concept C | |

IDEA

03.00.04 Note that trains are of variable lengths.

A train is a train whether it consists of three cars or a hundred cars. In the same way, the beginning, middle, and end concepts of an idea could be expressed in a few simple notions, or they could extend far beyond that. At a minimum, the three primary concepts in a message should be as follows:

> Beginning concepts which *attract*—"There's something important that you need to understand, so please pay attention."
> Middle concepts which *inform*—"Here's what you need to understand. Does that make sense?"
> End concepts which *invoke*—"Based on what you've understood, here are the implications and the recommended course of action."

The beginning and end concepts often are simple introductory and summary thoughts that rarely need to be expressed in more than one or two notions. The middle concepts (or concept) are where the primary body of thoughts is presented. This is the substance of the message sandwich, and within it, any number of notions could be introduced depending on the situation and need.

03.00.05 To illustrate the variable nature of message length, let's examine a simple message that expresses the idea 'I love you.'

> Attract—Dear Mary,
> Inform—I love you.
> Invoke—Love, Mike

Apart from the introductory and concluding thoughts, which serve to attract and invoke (*Love,* Mike is an imperative, or command statement), the middle stage of the message presents three separate concepts in and of itself. These are the concept of *I,* the concept of *love,* and the concept of *you.*

Although the expression of these concepts and their relationships to one another could remain simply, "I love you," it could also consist of many stanzas that elaborate on these concepts, as in, "How do I love thee, let me count the ways...." Each of these words is, in fact, a mere label for extremely complex meaning. In response to this reality, the exposition of these concepts can become very elaborate, intriguing, and dramatic in their expressions of meaning. These are the concerns not only of the lover but also of the artist, the poet, the musician, the storyteller, the educator, and the marketer.

The key to effectively defining the constitution and sequencing of a train of thoughts is *appropriateness.* What follows in this chapter is an exploration of what constitutes appropriate communication on the microlevel of notions, themselves.

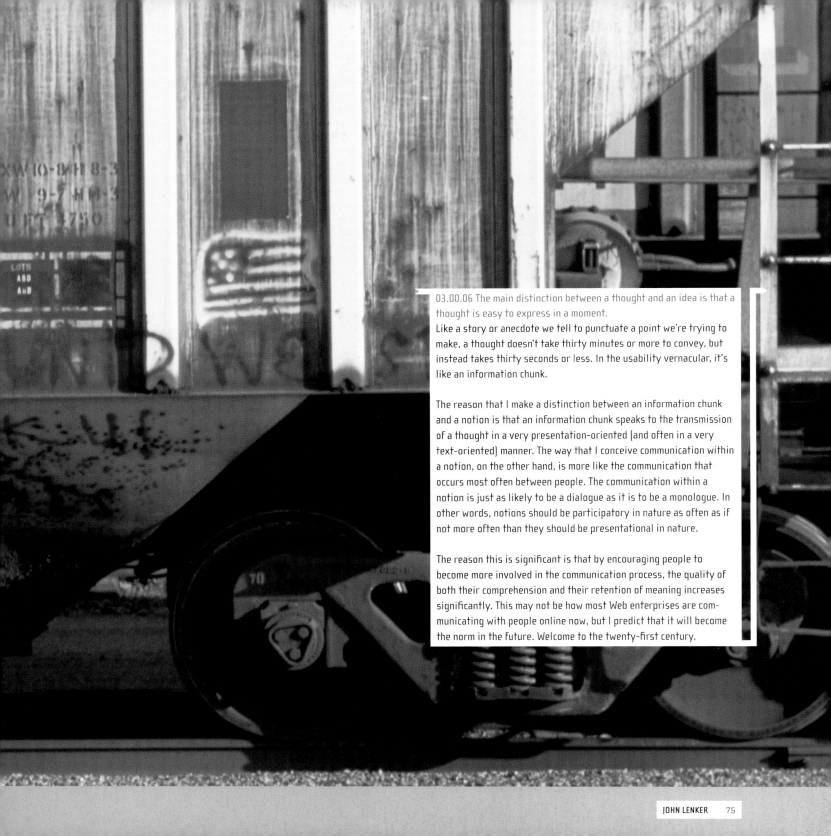

03.00.06 The main distinction between a thought and an idea is that a thought is easy to express in a moment.

Like a story or anecdote we tell to punctuate a point we're trying to make, a thought doesn't take thirty minutes or more to convey, but instead takes thirty seconds or less. In the usability vernacular, it's like an information chunk.

The reason that I make a distinction between an information chunk and a notion is that an information chunk speaks to the transmission of a thought in a very presentation-oriented (and often in a very text-oriented) manner. The way that I conceive communication within a notion, on the other hand, is more like the communication that occurs most often between people. The communication within a notion is just as likely to be a dialogue as it is to be a monologue. In other words, notions should be participatory in nature as often as if not more often than they should be presentational in nature.

The reason this is significant is that by encouraging people to become more involved in the communication process, the quality of both their comprehension and their retention of meaning increases significantly. This may not be how most Web enterprises are communicating with people online now, but I predict that it will become the norm in the future. Welcome to the twenty-first century.

03.00.07 Notions are the pearls that we string together to make our online messages valuable.

When making a pearl necklace, if the quality of any given pearl is of low value, it diminishes the value of the entire necklace. In the same way, if the ideas in our online messages are composed of vague or confusing notions, our ideas are going to seem mediocre and our online messages will basically stink. Moreover, the proper method of designing ANYTHING is to work back and forth between considering the parts of a thing and considering the vision for, and desired impact of, the completed whole.

When designing online resources, however, most organizations work only from the outside in—from the whole toward the parts. The result is that many projects get painted into corners. While the whole may *seem* intriguing, when push comes to shove, the component parts don't do a very good job of living up to people's expectations or effectively meeting their comprehension needs.

03.00.08 Experiential needs must be considered at the microlevel as much as they need to be considered at the macrolevel.

For example, the car manufacturer that wants to design and build a car with a certain external aesthetic appeal can conceptualize from the outside in to begin with, but the needs of the vehicle's occupants must be carefully considered as well. While the external vision will work its way into internal design considerations, the internal components will often mandate a reexamination of the external vision and, in some cases, even impose restrictions on it.

These impositions should be *driven* as much as anything by the needs of the people who will be occupying and utilizing the vehicle. Granted, some of these needs will be practical, but other needs will relate to aesthetics as well as to comprehension. So the overall design is the concern of the manufacturer as well as of the occupant, and must work well at all levels of granularity for the design of the vehicular experience to be a success.

Not only do many usability consultants work almost exclusively from the outside in, but what's worse is that by the time most organizations ever get around to formulating the components of information whose value determines the success of a Web enterprise, budgets have usually been expended. That means that the content must be thrown together without much information design actually going into it. No wonder that most commercial Web enterprises either have failed or are in the process of failing!

That being said, how do we determine the essence of an effective notion?

03.00.09 An effective notion provides the next rung in a person's ascent into understanding.

A notion helps a person to form meaning in the moment by providing the perfect piece in the puzzle of comprehension that fits nicely with what has already been understood as well as with what needs to be understood next for comprehension to continue.

Because it's impossible to teach people *much* more than they already understand in any given moment, it's important to really be on target with a notion. Being on target means that a thought that's being presented is within easy reach of a thought that's already been understood. If a new notion cantilevers out too far from a person's current conceptual framework, it will stretch a person's conceptual capabilities to the point that concentration will break. When this happens, a person tends to become overwhelmed and discouraged, and the likelihood of losing that person's motivation to continue with a message is greatly increased.

One way to look at the gravity of situations like this is that we're never more than one notion away from losing a person's attention.

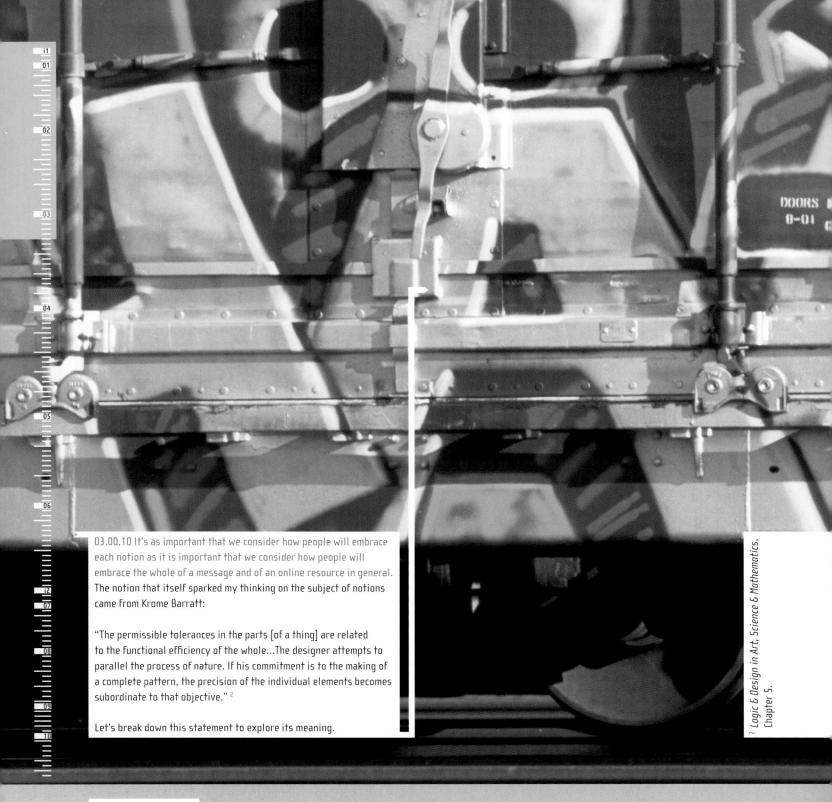

03.00.10 It's as important that we consider how people will embrace each notion as it is important that we consider how people will embrace the whole of a message and of an online resource in general. The notion that itself sparked my thinking on the subject of notions came from Krome Barratt:

"The permissible tolerances in the parts [of a thing] are related to the functional efficiency of the whole...The designer attempts to parallel the process of nature. If his commitment is to the making of a complete pattern, the precision of the individual elements becomes subordinate to that objective." [2]

Let's break down this statement to explore its meaning.

[2] *Logic & Design in Art, Science & Mathematics,* Chapter 5.

03.00.12 What is functional efficiency?

Components of a thing that are functionally efficient have a defined and precise role in the overall fulfillment of a specific need.

The worst communication mistake that a Web enterprise can make is to formulate its messages based on what it feels it needs to *convey* to people without first trying to assess what people *need* to understand and then formulate messages based on that assessment. This often leads to excessive, generalized, and wasteful transmissions of information that are anything but efficient and that are often not even functional. It's like trying to blindly develop understanding in a person from the outside in, instead of from the inside out. This almost never supports an optimum flow experience.

The better approach is to first find out what a person has to work with in terms of his or her current interests and understanding and then build upon those interests and that understanding. This leads to appropriate communications in that they precisely meet a person's need. The question is "How is this done?"

The answer is that we need to formulate a variety of notions to convey the same basic meaning from a variety of angles in order to address a variety of cognitive situations and needs. We must then interactively determine from which angle to approach the expression of that meaning. This can be done with or without soliciting the input of the person interacting with the notion.³

Based on this determination, an appropriate notion is activated from a possibilities pool and is introduced into the train of thoughts. Content and audience analysis can help determine the nature, variety, and scope of this possibilities pool and will provide great insight into what it will take to communicate an idea to different types of people within an online population.

03.00.11 What are permissible tolerances?

How do we determine the best way to compose our notions? Should we use words, pictures, audio, video, or a combination of them all? Should we provide a list of facts, or should we weave the facts into a story? What types of stories would be appropriate? Should we use charts or graphs? Should the presentation of a notion be fixed, or should it interact with an individual in some way?

The answer to all these questions is that the cognitive, emotional, and perceptual tolerances of the person we're communicating with online should determine the nature, character, and composition of the notions that we present to that person.

The idea is to attune our notions to the interests and understanding of the people in our audience sets and subsets in order to gain a strong foothold in their consciousness. From there, we lead them up into understanding. Although this can be quite challenging because everyone's needs are different, this is nonetheless the challenge of effective Web experience design.

The way this plays out is that if we know a subset of an audience is new to a product or service, for example, we must prepare notions for that subset in anticipation of its constituent's unique needs. It's not that everyone in that subset will receive the same sequence of notions. Sequencing depends on how each person interacts with the notions from moment to moment. In light of this, adequate preparation mandates that a pool of candidate notions be composed for a known subset so that these notions can be interactively sequenced as needed. If we don't prepare for our patrons' needs in this way, we're in no way practicing effective experience design methods.

CASE STUDY 3A

Becoming Human

Address: http://www.becominghuman.org
Client: Institute of Human Origins, Arizona State University
Experience Designers: Terra Incognita, Neon Sky Creative Media

Interactively retracing human evolution.

Becominghuman.org is an interactive webumentary that allows visitors to embark on a journey through the story of human evolution. Michael de Nie of The Scout Reports calls Becominghuman.org "... the best online documentary."

Instead of presenting text alone to tell their story, the project team created a rich, immersive, interactive multimedia experience that's a balanced synthesis of words, pictures, audio, illustration, and animation. The premise is to allow visitors to follow along and feel a sense of involvement with scientists in the field who are working on a paleontological dig.

In order to effectively educate various types of visitors, the Terra Incognita team conducted an extensive needs analysis and found that visitors would be divided into two groups: a goal-oriented group and an undetermined-focus group. The content was shaped to accommodate both audiences' learning tolerances by communicating ideas on various interrelated levels. Bart Marable, Creative Director and Principal, states:

"In Becoming Human, we had to accommodate different learning methods through a variety of navigation options. We also had to design the site to appeal to multiple interest levels. While some visitors would have a good working knowledge of paleontology, we knew that others would need a compelling introduction to the subject."

Read our interview with Terra Incognita online at:
http://www.trainofthoughts.com

03.00.13 What makes a pattern complete?

What makes beautiful patterns beautiful? Well, for starters, the essence of a pattern is that it presents a certain order. This order is the epitome of what Barratt defines as *elegance*. He defines elegance as something that functions well on multiple levels of awareness. This is definitely true of patterns.

When examining a pattern up close, we can see the precision with which a series of elements fit together to form one expression of the entire system. The characteristics that define a pattern can be appreciated at this level.

From a distance, the beauty and interplay of various relationships can, when taken together, reveal a broader vision for the individual series of elements that was examined on the microlevel. It reveals the pattern's potential complete with the subtlety of variation that confirms the uniqueness, completeness, and overall value that justifies the existence of a design as a whole.

The notions that make up an idea can also be likened to the elements that make up a pattern. There should also be an introduction, realization, and confirmation of the vision that an overall idea presents as a person moves deeper and deeper into each message. As in good storytelling, by letting the vision of a online message communicate on various, interrelated levels like this, we make an online experience not only elegant and beautiful but also comprehensible and compelling.

03.00.14 How do we subordinate design to an objective?

Organizations generally try to have reasons for the things that they do. The same can be said for the people who interact with Web enterprises online. Unfortunately, the rationale for the design and development directions that online resources take often has more to do with an organization's desire to play it safe and conform to the status quo than it does with being innovative in its efforts to genuinely support people's online objectives. To be effective, a Web enterprise must instead subordinate the design of its online resources to the needs of the members in its various audiences.

The key insight here is this: Although ultimately the formulation of a pool of notions is subordinate to the overall objective of a Web enterprise, if the notions aren't composed with the cognitive, emotional, and perceptual tolerances of the audience in mind, the development of the online resource may be an exercise in futility. If the objectives of the individual can't be reconciled with the objectives of the Web enterprise, the endeavor to create a successful online resource is doomed to failure and should not be attempted. In Chapter Seven we'll examine the process that will help ensure that this type of disconnect with the needs of a Web enterprise's patrons has very little chance of occurring.

03.00.15 We find meaning in a notion by associating the thought it expresses with what we already know and then by reflecting upon it until we gain either deeper or broader insight.

To close this section regarding the role of notions in our online messages, I think it's appropriate to take a quick look at how our minds comprehend and remember concepts. After all, the world of the mind is very mysterious, and most people aren't very familiar with how it works. Although no one really understands exactly how the mind works, we do have some excellent theories that seem to get at least the basic concepts mostly right. Examining one group of these theories more closely can help us better understand the objective of notion composition.

03.00.16 As mentioned in 02.00.04, the *Cognitive Constructionist Theories* address how we form and maintain our conceptual frameworks—sometimes referred to as knowledge structures, schema, or mental-models.

These frameworks are the tools our minds use to learn, assign meaning to, and remember the people, places, things, ideas, sensations, and so on that we're confronted with daily.

When the prior knowledge in our conceptual frameworks provides us with springboards for what we're learning—understanding comes easily. If, however, we don't have the conceptual springboards that associations with prior learning offer, "accretion," according to Dr. Donald Norman (see 02.00.05), "... requires repeating the material over and over again (rehearsing), using mnemonic strategies, or writing down the information."

When we first receive new information, we begin to search our conceptual frameworks for patterns, or networks of conceptual connections, that are similar in nature to the stimulus that we're currently encountering. When we find a network of meaning within a conceptual framework that's similar, we use that network as a starting point to relate the new information to what we already know.

03.00.17 Interestingly, we don't actually remember everything about a stimulus that we perceive.

Instead, we effectively store only what the new stimulus and existing framework *don't* have in common. When Web enterprises formulate notions to tap into and play into this innate associative learning strategy that we're all wired to thrive on, they'll have the best chance of helping people to both comprehend and retain the meaning that their notions are formulated to convey. In order to accomplish this, I believe that we must deliver notions that

> Match people's expectations
> Provide the appropriate balance of quality, quantity, relevance, and clarity
> Contain a balanced syntheses of media elements that are appropriate for a person's perceptual and conceptual needs

03.01 Expectation Influences the Efficiency of Comprehension

For people to ease their minds into an online message, it's essential that the notions that they're confronted with match or exceed their expectations. When expecting to access a certain type of message online, it's very difficult to interpret notions that don't seem to be consistent with that expectation. When we go to France, we expect the Eiffel Tower and baguettes. When we go to Italy, we expect the Leaning Tower of Pisa and spaghetti, and so on.

The problem is that more often than not, people are disappointed with the value of online messages. Rather than fulfilling expectations, our online messages tend to violate people's expectations. As a result, people lose their incentive to follow through with our presentations to the end. This happens when they realize that it's becoming less and less likely that their expectations will be fulfilled, and they lose confidence in our message's ability to deliver satisfaction, and they finally abandon it.

03.01.01 Expectations vary depending on the primary nature of a person's consumptive motivation.

In Chapter One, we outlined various types of consumptive motivations that people have when going online. The natures of these types of consumption have a lot to do with how people set their expectations for an online experience. Let's take a look at some examples that illustrate how the type of consumption a person is seeking online will dictate the nature of the experience that people are expecting. Types of consumption include

> Knowledge
> Products
> Services
> Diversion
> Propaganda

03.01.02 Knowledge—People generally expect that *finding* an online resource with appropriate information for their interests will take some effort.

After they find an appropriate resource, however, they'll not be as patient if it's difficult to make sense out of the content. An online resource will be judged very negatively if the value of its content is not readily seen. It goes without saying that people have ultra-high expectations for Web enterprises that sell information as a service. Expectations are still fairly high, however, for free online resources such as online news organizations that sell advertising. People recognize these examples to be commercial resources even though the content is free.

Expectations are lower for nongovernmental Web enterprises that exist as pure gestures of community service because people realize that these enterprises have fewer resources. Interestingly, although expectations are lower in terms of the presentation of the content, expectations for the relevance and accuracy of this type of free content are often very high. The reason is that only those who are extremely knowledgeable about a given topic are usually motivated to invest the time necessary to produce and maintain a noncommercial, free online resource of this nature.

03.01.03 Products—People's expectations vary when seeking products on the Web depending on the product's category.

It's important that Web enterprises promoting and selling products treat content related to their products in an appropriate manner. On the one hand, information about a toothbrush on a department store's dot-com isn't expected to go very deep. If it did, people would most likely find the unexpected depth of information cumbersome. People also expect it to be very easy to actually buy the thing. On the other hand, information about a Lear Jet is expected to be not only in-depth, but also of a substantially higher level of quality than the information about the toothbrush—unless it's highly innovative. Likewise, the actual acquisition of the Lear Jet is expected to be somewhat involved.

This comparison is obvious, yet online resources continue to violate these expectations by providing inappropriate information.

Figure 03.01.03

TYPE OF PRODUCT	EASE OF LOCATING	DEPTH OF CONTENT	QUALITY OF CONTENT	EASE OF TRANSACTION
Catalogue Item	High	Medium	Medium to High	High
Specialty Item	Medium	Medium to High	Medium to High	High
Major Purchase	Medium to High	High	High	Medium to Low
Collectable Object	Low	Medium to High	Low to Medium	Medium to Low
Capital Purchase	Medium	Medium to High	Medium to High	High

03.01.04 Services—Expectations for services-related resources also vary depending on the type of service being sought.

Commercial Web enterprises promoting services must often work harder to represent their services because services are less tangible and harder to evaluate than products. Qualities and characteristics of either the people or information involved must be evident in the content. If the content itself is the service, then it must be of a markedly higher level of value than similar resources offering free, noncommercial alternatives.

Figure 03.01.04

TYPE OF SERVICE	EASE OF LOCATING	DEPTH OF CONTENT	QUALITY OF CONTENT	EASE OF TRANSACTION
Web Entertainment	Medium	Low	Medium to High	High
Information	Low to Medium	Medium to High	High	High
Personal	Medium to High	Medium to High	Medium to High	Medium
Professional	Medium to High	High	High	Medium

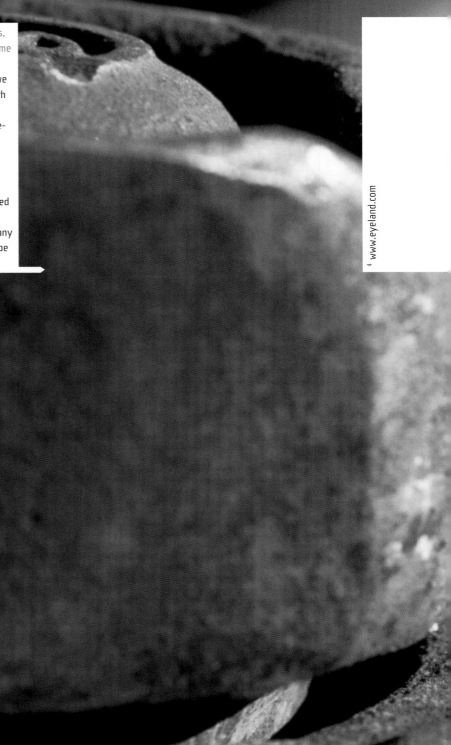

03.01.05 Diversion—Resources that offer diversions such as games, chats, and imagery on a free basis are not expected to be of the same caliber as resources that offer these same services for sale. Although we tend to be more forgiving of these online resources, we don't necessarily lower our standards, and we may not interact with these resources very long if they're not engaging. Often, however, free online resources offering diversion serve as promotional material for other online resources. In these cases, the quality of the content is expected to be high.

As an example, there may be a free online resource that offers arcade-style games as part of a promotion for a cereal manufactured by Big Dog Foods. My colleague Scott Hamlin[4], author of several books including *Flash 5 Magic* (which I contributed to), develops many such resources. In cases like these, the resources are expected to be of the same quality as the brand itself.

[4] www.eyeland.com

SPOTLIGHT ON:

DR. RICHARD HARRIS

Dr. Harris received his Ph.D. in psychology at the University of Illinois at Urbana-Champaign, with a specialty in psycholinguistics, in 1974. Since then he's been on the faculty in the Department of Psychology at Kansas State University. He's conducted research on a variety of topics in language and communication, including deceptive advertising, drawing inferences from text, figurative language, bilingualism, and memory for media, social cognition, and cultural knowledge.

His books include *A Cognitive Psychology of Mass Communication* (3rd ed., Erlbaum, 1999), *Cognitive Processing in Bilinguals* (Elsevier, 1992), and *Learning and Cognition* (with T.H. Leahey, 5th ed., Prentice Hall, 2001). He has been the recipient of two Fulbright grants for teaching in Belo Horizonte, Brazil (1982) and Montevideo, Uruguay (1994). Dr. Harris currently teaches courses in the areas of cognitive psychology, psycholinguistics, psychology of mass communication, and general psychology. He also gives community speeches on media literacy. My interview with Dr. Harris follows.

Lenker: Beyond issues pertaining to the learning theories covered in the text of this book, what other psychological differences exist in people (strengths and weaknesses) that require us to approach the communication of an idea in different ways to be effective for different people?

Harris: Different people have different knowledge and experiences, which causes them to interpret material differently and prefer different types of communication. Also, some people are by nature more visual learners and others more verbal. To some, a cogent diagram or picture crystallizes everything, while for others it obscures everything. Some people have disabilities which could limit their ability to use a Web site (e.g., color blindness and vision problems requiring large print).

Finally, communication differs as a function of the "Uses" someone makes of the medium (why using it—for entertainment? information?) and the "Gratifications" one gets from it (feel more connected, learn something, feel smarter). This approach is called "Uses and Gratifications Theory."

Lenker: Why are notions that are formulated to be a well rounded synthesis of appropriate media elements more effective than the presentation of text alone?

Harris: Text alone may be less effective than a multimedia synthesis in (a) maintaining interest, (b) avoiding memory overload, (c) dealing with diversity of learning styles, and (d) being scannable.

Lenker: Do you think that Web media can be emotionally engaging if it's stripped void of creative media elements (i.e. media would largely consist of HTML text and links)?

Harris: No, this is a bad use of the medium, which allows so much richer presentation of information. This reminds me of our early educational video technology which presented videotapes of a professor lecturing ("talking heads") with no other material shown. They might as well have used radio.

Lenker: What do you feel are the most important keys to guiding people into comprehension of our online messages?

Harris: Clarity is perhaps most important. There is no excuse for bad writing just because it's a web site. Construction of the site should be based on principles of the way people really think. A table of contents is helpful, as are aids like toolbars, back buttons, and ...

Read the entire interview online at:
http://www.trainofthoughts.com

Learn more about Dr. Richard Harris at:
http://www.ksu.edu

Buy *A Cognitive Psychology of Mass Communication* today at:
http://www.trainofthoughts.com

03.01.06 Propaganda—When people decide to invest some of their valuable time consuming information about a cause, they realize that an organization is attempting to persuade them, sway their thinking in some way, or solicit a contribution.

As a result, the expectation is that the organization will present compelling notions to support its arguments. If this isn't the case, the online resource will in no way be effective for anyone other than those who already subscribe to the ideology that the cause is purveying. It would seem that organizations that develop online resources for political, religious, or some other special-interest cause would be the most receptive to the principles presented in this book, and especially those presented in Chapter Two. The reason is that if they don't have messages that can persuade people to subscribe to their points of view, they don't have anything.

03.01.07 People's expectations regarding how technology should function vary widely.

One thing that varies regarding people's expectations of the presentation of our thoughts, concepts, and ideas is that of technical performance. This is relevant to the discussion of composing notions because technical performance issues must be factored into the design of the media elements that will be combined to transmit notions to our audiences.

To debunk a common myth, it's not necessarily wrong to design presentations that take considerable time to download. What's wrong, in most cases, is putting people in a situation where they must wait for large downloads that they're not expecting.

To debunk another myth, the use of multimedia elements doesn't necessitate long downloads. Well-designed multimedia elements with a high degree of artfulness in execution can meet any reasonable performance standard. It's not a question of usage; it's simply a matter of design and degree.

Beyond this, an overall difference between the expectation of people in consumer versus business audiences exists. Business audiences most often access the Web via a broadband connection. Organizations designing business-to-person[5] resources (B-to-P) will generally make allowances for slower connections than publishers of business-to-business resources (B-to-B) will. The trend is toward the average citizen moving to broadband, but projections vary regarding the timing of critical mass in terms of broadband market penetration.

[5] I don't like defining people as consumers either. People consume things, but defining them as such clouds our vision regarding the overall makeup of a person.

03.01.08

2 1 4 2 8 4 1

This illustrates a pattern of anticipation and a violation of expectation. Sixteen was expected, but one was given. This could be good or bad depending on the intent.

Note:
For the best example of the artful establishment of a dramatic pattern of anticipation and a positive violation of expectation, watch the Christopher Walken "watch" scene in "Pulp Fiction."

03.01.08 When expectation is met with realization, a person's mind becomes engaged in the flow of information.

Because the landscape of the Web is so cluttered with resources that violate people's expectations, resources that do otherwise are almost certain to attract and keep mass audiences. People not only have expectations for a Web enterprise but also aspirations (hopes, dreams, and goals). When the aspirations that a person has are realized, it's likely that a person will become engrossed in the experience. This leads to online sessions that are longer, more productive, more enjoyable, and more likely to lead to response interactions. Composing notions that are designed to be effective for individuals is the key to producing this level of success with our audiences.

03.02 The Constitution of Appropriate Notions

Although there are many characteristics of a great notion, the factor that determines a notion's success is the degree to which it engages the human mind. If a notion is thought of as being engaging, interacting with the notion is considered to have been meaningful. If a notion isn't thought of as having been engaging, it's not considered to have been very meaningful.

According to Byron Reeves and Clifford Nass, the meaning that a person derives from interacting with a notion should be similar to the meaning that a person derives from an interaction with another person. In their book *The Media Equation,* Reeves and Nass summarize research by H. Paul Grice, a philosopher and psychologist. Grice argued that conversations are basically an "exercise in which people try to be helpful." The question then becomes, what characterizes conversations that are helpful? Grice's answer is that people judge the value of a conversation based on four factors:

> Quality
> Quantity
> Relevance
> Clarity

Reeves and Nass feel that, just as in real life conversations, if the messages that our online resources transmit fail regarding any of these Q-Q-R-C factors, people will be naturally inclined to feel negatively about the experience. The remainder of this section will address these four factors in great detail.

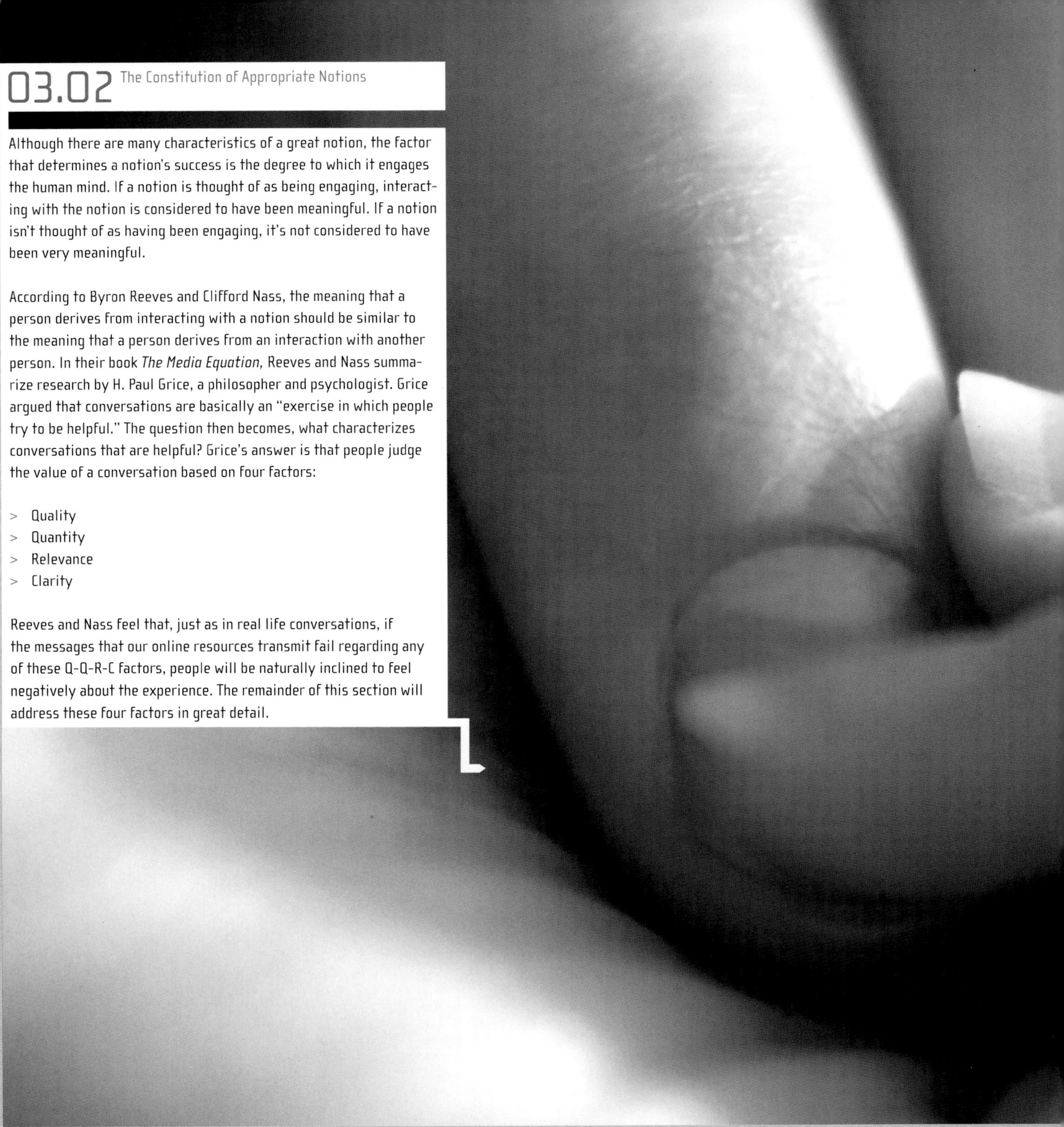

[6] *Things That Make Us Smart*, Chapter 1
[7] Ibid.

03.02.02 Allure factors into a notion's quality.

A notion must either attract or continue to hold the attention of the people who are interacting with a Web enterprise. This can't be accomplished through bland, monotonous presentations of information. Even when people are highly motivated to interact with the message, they can't help but tune out boring content after a while. It's cognitively involuntary. They're always struggling to refocus. Dr. Donald Norman paints a great picture of this[6]:

"Humans [...] cannot maintain attention on a task for extended periods. Basically, we are sensitive to changes in the environment: We attend to changes in events, not continual, ongoing ones. The same is true for memory: We tend to remember novel and unexpected events better than regular, recurring ones."

The role of creativity, which is the subject of Chapter Five, is of the utmost importance in developing novel and unexpected events. Allure also relates to the ability of a stimulus to involve an audience emotionally in the message. If we strip out all that is alluring in a task, it can have devastating results. As Dr. Norman states[7]:

"A worn-out mind leads to a demoralized [person], to someone who no longer cares about the [task] and who is apt to leave. [...] Worse [yet], the machine-centered approach to the design of a [task] leads to an uninspired society, where mental creativity is much reduced."

03.02.01 Everyone aims to have high-quality online communications.
The trouble is that most Web enterprises don't have a framework for evaluating their content's quality. As stated in the 03.00 series, while not the only consideration, the quality of a Web experience hinges on the quality of the notions it presents in its online messages. I find that there are four aspects to the quality of a notion:

> Allure
> Breadth
> Accuracy
> Memorability

CASE STUDY 3B

New Beetle

Address: http://www.vw.com/newbeetle/
Client: Volkswagen of America, Inc.
Experience Designers: Arnold Worldwide

Round for a Reason.

The Round for a Reason experience was originally created as a continuing marketing piece for Volkswagen to counter the misconceptions regarding the shape of the new Beetle. The design team at Arnold Worldwide used this online resource as a vehicle to further substantiate the design and safety of the automobile. Their goal was to create a fun experience while educating people about the car's safety points. Round for a Reason offers an engaging experience where all of the features and benefits of the car's design can be thoroughly covered.

Round for a Reason is the first in a series of three simple ideas that VW wants to communicate regarding the new Beetle. It's targeted to a specific audience: people who are interested in the car yet are apprehensive about its shape.

To convince buyers to accept their ideas, they present an explanation in a fun, lighthearted manner that people familiar with VW branding have come to expect. With these expectations in place, viewers are guided along a very specific, sequential path of explanation with their best interests in mind to influence comprehension.

Notions provide support for the message that the Beetle is "round for a reason," by engaging people in interactive activities such as "Crash a New Beetle," where they can watch the VW in a variety of crash scenarios, and "Fit Yourself," where they can play with height sliders to visualize headroom in the car based on personalized height specifications. To substantiate dimensional volume while relating to the audience, the experience uses photos and a QuickTime movie of the new Beetle containing large quantities of everyday items such as dashboard hula dancers and Ping-Pong balls. Relating to users in such a creative yet realistic manner creates allure while maintaining the audience's attention and piquing interest.

Read our interview with Arnold Worldwide at:
http://www.trainofthoughts.com

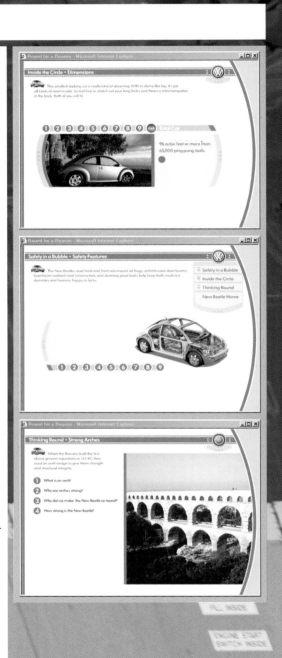

03.02.03 A notion's breadth factors into its quality.

For the quality of a notion to be high, it must cover the important bases. This doesn't mean that all aspects of an idea need to be crammed into one notion. It does, however, mean that our notions must be comprehensive enough to give those interacting with our messages confidence that the notion is a solid stepping stone on the journey toward comprehension of our ideas.

For example, if the subject of an online resource is *chickens,* the topic is *birth,* and the idea is that *chickens hatch from eggs,* a concept that supports this idea might be that *eggs must be incubated to maintain proper body temperature.* To flesh out that concept in the minds of various individuals, notions can be composed that communicate thoughts such as these:

> What the important considerations are when incubating eggs
> Why an incubator is needed instead of the mother hen
> The affordances of an incubator and descriptions of the function of its parts
> Statistics that make comparisons regarding the superiority of incubators over natural methods

A notion shouldn't necessarily be burdened with the task of expressing a complete concept, but it should provide enough information to make a solid impression in a person's mind.

03.02.04 A notion's accuracy factors into its quality.

From Grice's perspective, the quality of an interaction hinges on the accuracy of the information exchanged in a dialogue. The same is true of our notions. Although the presentation of concepts leaves much room for interpretation, it's important to strive for accuracy in the presentation of facts. Although we live in an age when there's so much information to keep track of that sometimes inaccuracies will occur in spite of our best efforts, it's important that we use due diligence to try and avoid them. Usually it's apparent when Web enterprises have attempted to follow through on accuracy, and it goes a long way toward establishing credibility with an audience.

If organizations are befuddled with inaccuracies, on the other hand, they can quickly lose their constituencies. Misinformation is seriously frowned upon in the online community. Ask the dot-coms who represented that orders of holiday gifts would be delivered by the critical dates. In the late 1990s, many misrepresented their ability to deliver, and they let down a significant portion of their customer base. Many of those dot-coms were never given a second chance.

03.02.05 A notion's memorability factors into its quality.

Here's a great quote from Reeves and Nass regarding memorability:

"If information in a message is presented in an order that mimics the established links between information in memory, then processing is relatively effortless."

For example, it's easier to remember this series of twelve words "My-Mother-Is-A-Wonder-Woman-And-I-Love-Her-Very-Much" than it is to remember this sequence of twelve words "Much-Woman-My-A-Love-Is-Mother-And-Wonder-I-Very-Her." The reason for this is that the first sequence of words followes rules of grammar that are well established in our minds. The second sequence doesn't readily relate to any conceptual framework at all.

In the same way, and as discussed in 03.00.15, it's easier for people to process, comprehend, and remember information that follows sequences that are already established in our minds. That's why we use tools such as stories, analogies, similes, and metaphors. We call up the memory in a person's mind of a certain script, and we liken our notion to that script. As a result, we give that person a conceptual handle with which to take hold of our notion. This can work when an analogy follows expectations because it fits neatly into a current conceptual framework.

Interestingly, new information doesn't always have to exactly follow an existing script to be memorable. Sometimes violating people's expectations through the use of story, analogy, or metaphor can be good because, being unique as well as unexpected, it burns an impression in their minds. This relates to the art of comedy and dramatization and can be effective if used appropriately.

03.02.06 We should strive to have an appropriate quantity of information in our notions.

As I've stated, a notion is a moment in the life of an message. As other's have stated, it's a "node" or "chunk" of information. A notion—boiled down to its most efficient state—is the minimum amount of information required to communicate a thought. It's the least common denominator for an online message. All these statements deal with how *extensive* a notion is. Extent, however, isn't merely a matter of word count. It's a matter of what the words and other media elements have been combined to communicate.

Whereas in discussing *quality*, we examined the issue of *breadth*, which dealt with covering important bases, *quantity* relates not only to the *volume* of communication that we employ to cover each base but also to the depth to which we delve into each base. We can be voluminous in communication yet not go very deep into a subject. We need to ensure against this. Similarly we can go very deep into a concept without expending needless communication. We want to ensure that we achieve this economy in communication on the Web.

03.02.07 It's not polite to ramble.

Rambling is rude and reveals a deficiency in social skills. It's awkward, irritating, and distracting when people do this to us in real life. It's equally disturbing on the Web because it becomes our task as people interacting with a Web enterprise's notions to sift through the sand in search of the elusive nuggets of gold.

Therefore, it's very important that we're courteous to those who are interacting with our notions and take the trouble to refine our communication. After all, why should someone bother to think through our notions if we haven't bothered to think through them ourselves? Sloppy communication dilutes the power of our ideas, devalues them, and is to be avoided.

We don't need to be in a rush to get to the point. It's just that every aspect of our communication must clearly be seen to play an important role in the presentation of our ideas—even if, as in storytelling, it's simply to make an expression of meaning more fun, vivid, textured, and interesting. Otherwise our ideas are viewed as excess baggage and aren't appreciated.

03.02.08 Effective series of notions are relevant to a person's comprehension needs.

"Interfaces that provide a *single* way of presenting information, without taking into account multiple goals of [people], risk violating the rule of relevance. Anger and frustration could be the result."

Reeves and Nass point out in *The Media Equation* that what we communicate through a notion should clearly relate to the purpose of the information flow. If extraneous information is included, it will detract from a person's understanding of the ideas contained in the underlying message. This rule is probably violated more than any other rule on the Web. It's almost impossible to engage with a piece of information without half a dozen irrelevant stimuli vying for our attention in the periphery. The fact that Web enterprises so often facilitate these distractions proves that the need for continuity in a presentation has been either completely misunderstood or else has been unwisely disregarded.

One implication for Web enterprises that have an advertising-based revenue model is that the distractions that the constant presence of ads impose is counterproductive to experience designers' efforts of keep people focused on a content stream. There are no easy solutions to the paradox that these enterprises must satisfy both sponsors and patrons to survive. It's a paradox because the goal of a sponsor is to use an ad to pull people's attention *away* from content. The goal of a patron, on the other hand, is to maintain focus on the flow of the message that they're pursuing.

03.02.09 A notion should represent a thought as clearly as possible for a given individual.

This can be accomplished through the synthesis of well-composed, appropriate media elements. Richard Harris states, "The meaning of something in the media, at either a cognitive or an emotional level, depends on how that information is processed during our experience of interacting with the medium."

Dr. Norman states that "the form of representation makes a dramatic difference in the ease of a task [...] Bad representations turn problems into reflective challenges. Good representations can often transform the same problem into an experiential task."

He goes on to state:

"The ability to find [representational] structures is at the heart of reasoning, and critical to serious literature, art, mathematics, and science. The ideal, of course, is to develop representations that:

> Capture the important, critical features of the represented world while ignoring the irrelevant.
> Are appropriate for the person, enhancing the process of interpretation.
> Are appropriate for the task, enhancing the ability to make judgments, to discover relevant regularities and structures."

What Dr. Norman seems to be saying is that media elements, which include textual representations, are the tools that we combine and use to express meaning to people in the way that most easily makes sense to them. The art of notion formulation lies in understanding the roles of these tools as well as understanding how to masterfully use them in combinations that maximize the effectiveness of our online communications.

03.03 Properly Representing Our Thoughts Within Notions

The way that we compose notions can determine the quality of a person's overall understanding. The proper synthesis of a set of media elements occurs when each is chosen for its ability to make a unique contribution to a person's understanding of a thought, a concept—and taken together, an overall idea.

The way information is represented to us is often not in an optimal form. Words are used to explain things that should be expressed through pictures. Pictures are used to express things that should be presented in diagrams. Tables are used to present things that should be bar charts. Language is used that includes unfamiliar vocabulary such as technical terms or colloquialisms.

The work of Web experience design is to find combinations of media elements that, when synthesized in the moment that a notion presents, are appropriate and effective for communicating thoughts and concepts to individuals.

03.03.01 Guiding comprehension distinguishes a Web enterprise. Although guiding people into comprehension of our online messages is the most crucial aspect of successful experience design, it's the aspect that Web enterprises seem to know the least about and give the least amount of attention to. As the Web moves forward, however, this will no longer be an acceptable practice. There's too much competition, and, as stated in Chapter One, the laws of natural selection do apply.

To illustrate this point, you've noticed when paging through a selection of books at the bookstore that you're attracted to some books more than to others. Why is this? Books pertaining to the same subject most likely present the same facts. What's the difference between them? A purchasing decision should be a matter of choosing the most inexpensive option and that should be the end of it. That is what's most practical, right?

The reality is that some books present their content in a manner that's more approachable and easy to follow than other options. The balance between text, figure, and page design—as well as the pacing of the information flow—is such that our minds quickly grasp the direction that an author is going with an idea. We simply find it easier to follow along.

It's the same with the notions that we present within our online messages. The manner in which we compose our notions and orchestrate them with various media elements will either make them seem approachable and easy to follow or will make them seem daunting, confusing, or worse—monotonous.

03.03.02 People have tremendous difficulty maintaining focus on things that are monotonous.

Everyone struggles with content that's *monotonous* in its presentation, but why is this? The answer lies in understanding the meaning of the word *monotonous*.

The word *monotonous* comes from the word *monotone*, meaning single tone. When people are presented with a single tone that has no variation, they let it slip from their consciousness, and it becomes part of the background noise that's made up of other competing stimuli. When this happens, their minds tend to wander.

That's why when presented with a range of options within a specific category, people tend to be drawn to the option that is the *least* monotonous. Just as we're more drawn to tones that are polyphonic or many-toned in composition, we're drawn to messages that show variation in their presentation because they're more engaging and therefore are more meaningful to us. This subject will be covered in more detail in Chapter Five.

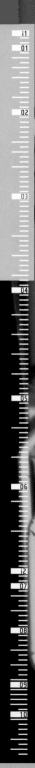

03.03.04 The Web is the most prolific medium within which interactive systems can function.

Before the Web, communication via mass media was *uni*lateral, meaning that it flowed only in one direction—from the publisher or broadcaster to the audience. Now that the Web has arrived, communication with a mass audience can be *bi*lateral, meaning that information can flow both to and from a person within an audience. What's more, these communications can be used to customize a Web experience to suit the interests and needs of an individual!

The essence of the distinction is that the presentations of our messages are no longer fixed but now can be variable. Our audience members can now have a sense of participation and dialogue with our Web enterprises. Their motivation can be escalated by the realization of the simple fact that what they think and do while interacting with an online message actually matters! It makes a difference in shaping the composition and therefore the value of the train of thoughts that they're engaged in.

THIS is the *real* power of the Web. This is the essence of true interactivity. This is what organizations must understand before they can design truly effective online resources.

03.03.03 Designing content for the Web is most often approached as an exercise in designing content for print.

Given the example of selecting a book from a range of choices in 03.03.01, it would seem that the task of designing information to be effective on the Web is the same as designing information to be effective in print. If one were to examine a sample of typical Web enterprises, this would seem to be the case. After all, aren't online resources most often referred to as collections of Web "pages?"

The fact is, however—and this is the good news—that this is NOT the case. It's good news because it turns out that, while having some similarities, the Web is truly an innovation after all—a new medium that affords new possibilities rather than one that merely duplicates the affordances of the print medium and simply adds a modern distribution channel.

What's more, the potential of the Web doesn't reside, as those with a more media-centric bent sometimes suppose, in styling it as a duplication of the mediums of radio or television. Much more than putting "TV on our computers" or even blending the print and broadcast mediums, as the word *multimedia* indicates, the greatest potential of the Web lies in its profound ability to improve the way that we *interact* with ideas.

03.03.05 The importance of interactivity in guiding comprehension can't be overemphasized.

Beyond how we employ various media elements to represent our thoughts within notions, it's often the case that true comprehension and long-term retention can only occur by creating situations where people are forced to *participate in* versus being merely *spectators in* the process of grafting meaning into their minds. What I'm talking about is the introduction of interactivity of various types that require a person to make some kind of decision based on the information they've received as input.

As an example, let's say that a mechanic is preparing to fix the transmission in an unfamiliar vehicle. As mentioned above, let's say that to succeed, the mechanic must understand how figure A evolves into figure B. Rather than merely demonstrating the procedure, interactivity can be used to require the individual to attempt the procedure by manipulating a dynamic model. The gestures and selections that are made can be tracked as feedback by the system and can be evaluated. Based on the person's performance in the task, the system can decide which notion from the pool of possibilities would provide the most appropriate response to the person's performance. If he or she got most of the steps right, maybe one particular notion would be called for next. If the steps were mostly wrong, however, maybe another would be required.

The mechanic scenario is an example of how guiding comprehension through a series of well-formulated notions truly works.[8]

The point is that if we continue to blindly stream information at people regardless of whether they're cognitively tracking with our messages, we're going to lose our audiences most of the time. Even if they actually "go through" all the information, they won't have gained anything of lasting value from the experience. The good news is that better solutions are looming on the horizon. What the online world needs is an epiphany. In Chapter Four, we'll move closer to understanding what the nature of that epiphany needs to be.

[8] For more on this type of interactivity, keep watch for Dr. Michael Allen's upcoming book on http://www.alleni.com.

03.04 Summary

How we communicate with the people who interact with our Web enterprises matters a lot. If we don't invest in composing notions that effectively communicate thoughts and concepts, our ideas won't come across meaningfully in our online messages. Since this hasn't been an emphasis in the past, Web enterprises have their work cut out for them if they're ever going to transform the Web into a medium that lives up to its potential.

We've examined what's been largely ignored—the microlevel of information design—and have been introduced to the concepts governing proper notion formulation. Now it's time to turn our attention toward the macrolevel of the presentation of our ideas as a whole to see how our well-composed notions will work together to form the overall meaning of the ideas contained in our online messages.

I think you'll find that designing effective flowpaths for our notions to flow along is simply an outgrowth of design-effective notions. This is true because the track that people's minds are on usually transcends the boundaries that we create for them. Let's turn now to see how the initial notions people encounter in online messages create what Krome Barratt terms *patterns of anticipation*.

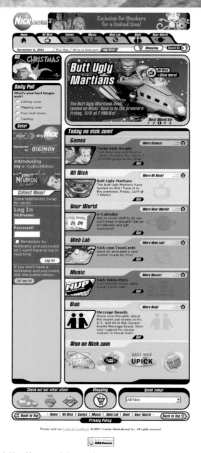

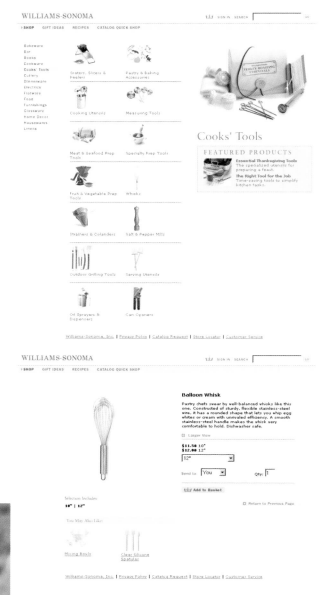

03.00.05 – http://www.nick.com/

Nickelodeon's Nick.com uses silly sound effects, bright colors, and animations appropriately geared toward a youthful audience to create a fun and playful experience.

03.01.04 – http://www.williams-sonoma.com

Williams-sonoma.com, a high-end online retail cooking store, provides their sophisticated customers with clear, logical organization and descriptions of the products just as customers would expect from the retail store.

03.01.06 – http://www.electrotank.com

Electrotank provides high quality interactive games for free while utilizing ad banners and corporate sponsors to supplement costs.

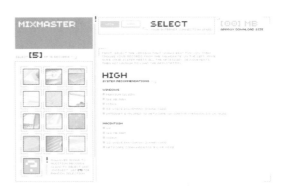

03.03 - http://www.focus247.com/killerapps/

To convey the spirit of "Detroit Techno," this online resource creates excitement for the Ford Focus by extending the techno theme with a virtual Mixmaster table that lets people mix their own custom-configured techno tracks.

< 03.03.03 - http://www.bumbleandbumble.com/

Bumble and Bumble, a high-end hair salon and beauty product enterprise, takes a creative Flash approach to string together notions in a successive flow.

CHAPTER 04

Patterns of Anticipation—
The Art of Flowstem Development

Get ready for what will perhaps be the most radical challenge to the status quo presented in this book. This chapter offers an alternative vision and paradigm for what has come to be known as *information architecture (I.A.)*. "Architecture" is a metaphor for the activities that are involved in "structuring" the information on a Web "site." Notice that these terms—*architecture, structuring,* and *site*—are all building terms that represent a very *fixed* system. Once buildings have been constructed, they don't generally change much without what is at best time-consuming and costly renovation, and what is at worst time-consuming and costly demolition and reconstruction. Because people and their information needs are not only varied but also dynamic, the paradigm of architecture seems less than optimal because people evolve and their needs change faster than information architecture can keep up with them.

Because Web enterprises seem to struggle so much to provide information in a "structure" that's effective for people, my assertion is that "architecture," both as a metaphor and as a process, has outlived its usefulness. The time has come to enlist a more powerful vision that reaches farther. Instead of information architecture, I believe we need to begin developing *Intelligent Flowpath Management Systems* that procedurally analyze the needs of individuals and then release appropriate sequences of notions[1]. These sequences must be programmed to guide people's minds naturally and in a manner that helps them to build anticipation of that which will ultimately succeed in fulfilling their expectations.

[1] See Chapter Three for an explanation of the role of notions in an online resource.

04.00.01 Information architecture (I.A.) generally fails to guide people into comprehension of our online messages.

An online resource isn't a destination but a territory that a person journeys through. It doesn't exist as a sole point in space but as a series of points—a line. People travel across these lines, or flowpaths, in pursuit of their goals. It's essential that we begin to develop systems that understand and then guide the people traveling these flowpaths in the pursuit of their goals.

Although people come to online resources to be guided, they're generally left on their own to fend for themselves. On most traditional "web sites," people feel like lab rats dropped into a maze. They scurry to and fro in search of the elusive cheese and generally hit several dead ends before they even taste a morsel. For most of us, finding messages that are relevant to our wants, needs, and interests is hit-or-miss. This is most unfortunate and has contributed to the failures of many

Web enterprises in recent years. By its very nature, the trial-and-error process of sorting through information diminishes the success of our experiences. There are too many false starts and stops. We never get into the groove of things—never get with the flow. It's difficult to maintain focus on the continuity of a message because that continuity is constantly broken. As a result, we rarely reach full comprehension of the ideas being presented. We even less frequently act upon them.

In response to this problem, database-driven personalization technologies have begun to be employed. This is definitely a step in the right direction, and I think that a very important key to an effective online future is hidden in these technologies. At this juncture, however, personalization systems are still widely subject to an overriding fixed information architecture that largely diminishes their value. There's not a unifying vision that guides the development of these systems. Consequently, they're generally not as effective as they might be.

04.00.02 Information architecture is complex and confusing.
Louis Rosenfeld and Peter Morville have written a popular book on information architecture titled *Information Architecture for the World Wide Web*. In it they describe what the work of designing information architecture is supposed to entail:

"Information architecture is about understanding and conveying the big picture of a website [... and is] composed of *organization schemes* and *organization structures*. An organization scheme defines the shared characteristics of content items and influences the logical grouping of those items. An organizational structure defines the types of relationships between content items and groups. [...] The hierarchical organization structures of websites often play the part of primary navigation system. The labels of categories play a significant role in defining the contents of those categories."

The work of an information architect from Rosenfeld's and Morville's perspective involves deciding how to formulate, arrange, group, and label information in a fixed way that makes the most sense to the most people. The trouble is that the only way to do this is to generalize information. The more generalized information is, the more of it there needs to be to cover as many bases as possible. Ironically, the more information contained in one architecture, the less valuable it is to individuals. Even Rosenfeld and Morville point that out:

"Far too many architectures are crushed under the weight of their own content. Large [institutions], rife with complex goals and messy politics, often have sites designed by ten individuals with their own vision of the site, their own deadlines and goals to meet, and their own politics to play. Is it any wonder that these sites often work so poorly, even when huge investments of time and money are made in them?"

Our Web enterprises become so complex and confusing because the goals of the committees that design information architecture are complex and confused.

04.00.02

Interest
Need
Problem
}

Information
Architecture

→ Solution

04.00.03 The result of I.A. is fixed information that can't possibly be optimal for everyone who interacts with an online resource.

If you've ever participated in a meeting in which a project team was developing the information architecture of an online resource, no doubt you noticed that it's often difficult for them to come to a consensus regarding what the final form of an information architecture should be. The reason that those designing information architecture often don't see eye to eye is that, while being professionals, they're still human.[2]

As noted in Chapter Three, each human being has a unique conceptual framework for any given topic. As a result, the final categorization, labeling, and arrangement of information will always be subject to personal perspective. If this is a struggle for the people designing the online resource—people who are extremely familiar with the material—how much more of a struggle will it be for the audiences that will be interacting with the information architecture[2]?

In light of this, the only way progress can be made on a fixed architecture is to compromise. When we compromise, we generalize. This waters down the solution to the degree that no one person trying to interact with the online resource feels that the architecture is optimal. When a person interacts with an online resource, that person doesn't want to be forced to bend his or her brain around a generalized architecture. Instead, the individual wants the information to bend itself around his or her own conceptual framework (with the aim of facilitating progress toward personal objectives) whether the framework is known to that person or it is yet undiscovered.

04.00.03
Categorization and labeling exercises are not very helpful because everyone categorizes and labels information differently.

Milk ?

Dairy Products

Ingredients

Perishable Foods

[2] I'm not suggesting that information architects are any more or less biased than any other type of design professional; rather I'm suggesting that the usual outcome of their work—a fixed, static architecture—is the wrong solution as it fails to accommodate people's different needs.

04.00.04 The opinion that matters in the arrangement of information is not the homogenized opinion of the project team.

Sometimes it's the opinion of the person interacting with that information. Just as often, however, the opinion that matters the most is that of an expert guide who can effectively steer a person in the right direction.

While seeking a very specific piece of information online is a valid activity, people often aren't even sure what they're looking for when they go online. In these cases they wander through an online resource in search of consultation and guidance. Instead of facilitating the identification and fulfillment of their needs, information architecture presents people with the stumbling blocks that accompany environments that are littered with inappropriate information. These barriers between people and their goals must be removed so that optimum flow experiences can be established.

Although some will agree that Intelligent Flowpath Management Systems can constitute these guides and might *supplement* a good information architecture, few are currently prepared to abandon information architecture altogether. I, however, contend that the branching nature of information architecture, combined with information design that speaks to everyone in the same, generalized voice, is unsalvageable and is, in fact, unnecessary.

04.00.05 Although information clearly must be organized in terms of its existence on the systems that serve information, as far as the people interacting with these systems are concerned, there's no need for them to be confronted with a fixed organization scheme or structure at all.

Because all individuals think differently about how information should be categorized, it's my contention that it's impossible to design organization schemes or structures that work effectively for everyone. What's more, the way we interact with Web enterprises by navigating through levels of a hierarchy is not natural. It's an activity that doesn't support the idea of an optimum flow experience. The effort to create these organization schemes and hierarchical structures, therefore, futile and should be abandoned.

This may all sound like new and extreme thinking, but it's really not. I'm just taking a stand on thinking that has existed for some time. Dr. Donald Norman:

"Searching through a spatially organized [information] structure only works for those who know the structure well … Will this scheme really work for all the knowledge of the world? No way. Through the years, people have tried various means of forming hierarchical organizational schemes that would put each item in its place, once and for all. Then, so the hope went, you could simply navigate through the various organizational structures until the item of interest was discovered, just in the proper location. The problems with these schemes are numerous … What are the alternatives? Simple: Why have organization? Why have a space? Want an example of this? Human memory—yours and mine.

"There is no need to organize material by alphabetical order. There is no need to put it together according to any organizational scheme. […] Instead, there can be multiple routes, multiple descriptions, and multiple methods that all get to the same ending point. What matters is that [people] be permitted whatever descriptions are most relevant to themselves and that the system accommodate itself to [them]."

My technical editor for this book, the outstanding Julie Dirksen, hastens to add:

"I think the point is that systems are frequently designed for the convenience of the folks who need to build or maintain them—and the systems themselves *should* be designed that way. The problem arises when once the particulars of a system are determined by the project-team, they assume that this same arrangement will work as an effective framework for the people that interact with it, as well."

04.00.06 Fixed architectures don't 'speak' to anyone in particular.
It's not that those who design information architecture aren't aware of the problems associated with over-generalized information. Rosenfeld and Morville outline one of the more recent tacks that information architects take to deal with this problem:

"In cases where there are two or more clearly defined audiences for a website or intranet, an audience-specific organization scheme may make sense. Audience-oriented schemes break a site into smaller, audience-specific mini-sites, thereby allowing for clutter-free pages that present only the options of interest to that particular audience."

I agree, but even when the primary organizational scheme of an information architecture is based on audience, there's still variation within an audience. Notwithstanding, fixed information architectures still inappropriately generalize to the subsets within an audience.

Say, for example, that a person accesses a specialty clothing store online that serves both men and women. Is it enough to categorize that person into a "male" audience and a "female" audience? Not at all. If no attempt is made to speak in a different way to a first-time visitor, to a fairly new customer, or to an established, loyal customer within the respective male and female audiences, the Web enterprise is very likely failing to provide effective Web experiences. When we misguidedly and annoyingly deal with all people within an audience *category* in the same way, we send an unspoken message that goes something like this:

"Hi! Even though we've seen you here before, we've taken absolutely no interest in you! We've therefore neither bothered to take note of any of your interests in order to make your experience here more valuable and more enjoyable, nor have we even bothered to remember your name. It doesn't really matter anyway, because we have all sorts of things to tell you about that you're bound to be interested in."

This seems really incompetent and presumptuous and gets back to the quality, quantity, relevance, and clarity (Q-Q-R-C) rules that guide helpful and polite communication which were examined on the microlevel of notions in Chapter Three. It also ties in to the Dr. Michael Allen quote in Chapter Two: "The prime objective of our work with interactive multimedia is to get people to do the right things at the right times." If we're going to be successful in doing what Dr. Allen is talking about, then we're going to have to figure out a way to deliver the right messages to the right people in the right way at the right times. For this to happen, we must learn about people's interests, needs, and their working knowledge of whatever it is that our online resources are offering them for consumption.

04.00.07 I.A. presents extraneous information that distracts people from concentrating on the flow of a message.
Most information architecture ends up being what amounts to nested layers of choices. To help people interpret these choices, I.A. tries to use appropriate labels, organizational schemes, and sometimes brief introductions to its messages. The problem is that since most I.A. is generalized to suit the needs of all audiences, everyone receives the same array of choices and introductions.

Because of this generalization, people are often forced to engage in a search for the proverbial needle in a haystack. People must systematically work their way through a screen of information linearly, attending to each and every option. This process is very distracting—with many starts and stops like in the rats-in-the-maze analogy. To add a third dimension to it, if what's being sought isn't found in the initial screen, a systematic "digging" process must begin into the nested clusters of information. What a time-waster.

What's more, when there are more than five to nine choices at any given moment, people are forced to think reflectively about information that should be experiential (see 02.00.05). None of us like it when several people are talking to us at once—even if they're trying to be helpful. We can only interact with one message at a time—one notion-flow with one goal. As mentioned earlier, most people look to an online resource to be guided. If they expect a solution and we instead hand them a puzzle,[3] we have not served them well.

Not only does I.A. present irrelevant information but even the information that *is* relevant doesn't usually follow the rules of proper communication. When people choose options that lead to subsequent screen-spaces, there's rarely a sense of continuity to the messages. There's no attempt to guide their comprehension of an idea. Ideas are generally not broken down into understandable thoughts at all. It comes across more like raw data, and people feel more like they're doing the hard work of a researcher rather than benefiting from the wisdom of sage guides. When they do encounter a couple of valuable screens of information and then expect to encounter equally valuable information in subsequent screens, they're often disappointed.

[3] It's important to not misinterpret this statement. To attract and hold people's interest, we often must present them with a stimulus that is unique in some way. The rule of thumb is that once a person attends to a stimulus, the interpretation of that stimulus should be evident with very little effort. If *no* effort is required, however, the stimulus will seem boring.

04.00.08 To solve the problems associated with information overgeneralization, what we need to be designing for the Web aren't Web sites at all but procedural Web interactions—dialogues between intelligent systems and individuals for the sole purpose of serving their specific interests and needs.

My prediction is that information architecture—at least the way it's commonly thought of here at the beginning of the twenty-first century—is going to go away. The reason is that neither the process nor the paradigm works. The organizations that succeed eventually abandon things that don't work. As stated in the opening notion of this series, I predict that in place of information architecture will evolve something more like what I refer to as *Intelligent Flowpath Management Systems* (*flowstems* for short). I refer to the process of creating these systems as *Flowstem Development.*

In addition to the writings of Krome Barratt, who as far as I know coined the term "flowpath," my thinking regarding flowstem development has largely been influenced by *computer-managed instruction (CMI)*, a form of artificial intelligence used in what is known as *courseware* in the *computer-based training (CBT)* market.

I believe that flowstem development will represent the turning point in the information revolution wherein Web enterprises switch their focus in a monumental way. Their focus will shift from trying to anticipate the intuition of their *patrons* and then design fixed information architectures to accomodated predetermined directions, to one of designing intelligent systems that are *themselves* intuitive and that *dynamically* formulate sequences of notions that move toward people's minds as people's minds move toward them. In doing so, online resources will allow people's minds to journey along appropriate and interesting experiential pathways that will, as I've said, "accelerate their insight and release their potential."

UTLX 201396
UNION TANK CAR CO

04.00.09 The basic gist of Flowstem Development is that it assigns proper roles to the designers as well as to the technologies that work together to guide people into comprehension of online messages. The role of the experience design team is to formulate individual notions and then define rules and procedural criteria for their sequencing by the flowstems. This ensures that an idea is represented in the best possible manner for a given individual's situation. The project team needs to consider all of the applicable principles related to psychology, understandability, and creativity when both anticipating and creating parameters for these flowpaths.

The design team will function like a team of pharmaceutical researchers who design medicines to treat certain ailments. People are really good at inventing things that address specific ailments. The intelligence built into the flowstems, on the other hand, will function like doctors who *prescribe* the right combinations of medicines to cure the specific ailments of the people interacting with a Web enterprise. Computers are really good at sorting through complex criteria to determine proper prescriptions that will efficiently and effectively solve the needs of the multitudes of individuals who will interact with the online resource.

Note:
An online resource generally serves many different audiences.

When we limit the scope of possible options to suit an audience, we're off to a really good start.

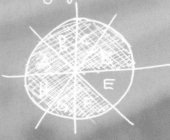

But when we further narrow content options to suit the needs of an audience sub-set, we've done much better.

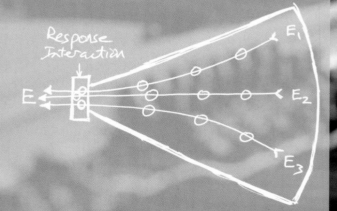

Response Interaction

D5 SPRING

WNED BY A BANK OR TRUST COMPANY UNDER
A SECURITY AGREEMENT FILED UNDER THE
INTERSTATE COMMERCE ACT, SECTION 20 F

04.00.10 Because people interpret messages by decoding them sequentially, the information we develop for online resources should therefore be viewed as *sequences* rather than as *structures*. Furthermore, these sequences are not fixed like the frames in a video or a movie but are variable like the frames in an interactive game. The decisions a person makes at any given moment affect what will be encountered in the next moment. The aim of this intelligence is to help a person maintain *focus* through the procedural analysis of individual needs and through the progressive formulation of variable sequences of notions that are appropriate to an individual and to a particular moment in time. If well executed, these sequences will produce what Mihaly Csikszentmihalyi envisioned when he stated:[4]

"If you want a sustained, optimal experience, the important thing is a continual flow of focused concentration: absolute absorption in an activity."

[4] *Flow: The Psychology of Optimal Experience*

A flowpath is the track that a person is traveling along when he or she begins an interactive journey through an online resource. A notion-flow is the online message that, like the cars on a train, is composed of notions that are linked together and sent traveling along a person's flowpath to meet that person "head" on. In a sense, a person's mind becomes the tunnel through which a notion flow enters his or her consciousness. One by one, a person's mind must engage the thoughts that these notions contain in order to progress from the *conception* of a thought through the *development* of a concept, and eventually the *delivery* of a fully formed idea.

As the *pregnancy* metaphor would suggest, the conception part—or the beginning part—should primarily provide sensory and emotional stimulation and satisfaction. It should also set an expectation that something of more substance will grow out of the initial interaction. The beginning part comes naturally and, in Dr. Norman's terms, should be "experiential," requiring little effort or concentration.

The middle part—or the development part—however should require us to, as Norman would say, "reflect" a bit more. Although elements of the experiential can be interspersed, we should be increasingly compelled to engage in a *legitimate thought process* that empowers us to work moderately toward comprehension of deeper meaning. The experiential aspects of our notions should at this stage be helping us to continually refocus our minds to more effectively comprehend the overall idea. As Dr. Allen always reminds us—if we're allowed to move through an experience without having to exercise our minds at all, we're unlikely to have truly learned anything from the effort. Being in line with this middle part is when we absorb the nutrients that will eventually cultivate our full understanding.

The last part—the delivery—is when the potential of our mind's endeavor is fully realized. It's when key insights are finally born in our consciousness. If our minds were satisfied in the conception, they're even more satisfied in the delivery. Now we have a sense that what our thinking has brought to bear is meaningful, lasting, and has been truly worth our every effort.

04.01.01 A notion-flow's unfolding is like the unfolding of a story. As we can see, the beginning, middle, and end components of a notion flow follow the story form. We learned in Chapter Three that the story form is one of the most ingrained cognitive scripts that we have. People recognize and can follow this type of pathway very easily. Once embarked upon, the story form is difficult to abandon until the end has been reached. Interestingly, we have already considered this same form in several different terms throughout the book:

Beginning	Middle	End
Ethos	Pathos	Logos
Exposition	Complication	Resolution
Conception	Development	Delivery
Introduction	Realization	Confirmation
Attract	Inform	Invoke

You may be wondering if this thinking can possibly apply to all Web experiences. Clearly it applies to what are normally thought of as typical educational situations and environments. Beyond these, however, and as we learned in Chapter Two, any person interacting with any online resource is engaged in a learning process. People enter our little stretch of road with a question mark, and it's our job to remove that question mark by the time they've exited.

CASE STUDY 4A
Lifescape Online Training Module

Address: http://sales.alleni.com/lifescape.htm
Client: Lifescape
Experience Designers: Allen Interactions Inc.

Learning through Practice

The Lifescape training experience was created for managers using Lifescape's Employee Assistance Program (EAP). The purpose of the training is to expand a manager's EAP knowledge through simulation of real-life employee management scenarios. Learners assume the role of a manager and are faced with a possible year's worth of employee situations. The training empowers managers to exercise discipline or take other actions and see the impact of their actions on such areas as productivity, morale, and management effectiveness.

The challenge for the design team at Allen Interactions was to engage learners in the training and motivate them to take appropriate action. Instead of simply presenting the facts in a series of next/last paging, the Allen team utilized principles of behavioral psychology and instructional design to create personalized training objectives specifically conducive to the real life environment. The training purpose and guidelines are immediately established while the content is chunked into meaningful segments that are presented as a sequential series of real life scenarios with a delayed judgment.

A wizard character is introduced, acting as a guide through the training while serving as a valuable resource if a student should need assistance in making a decision. The training further incorporates a game-like risk factor by challenging learners to make decisions and be accountable for them. Through this challenge, learners can immediately see the results of their actions and adjust future decisions accordingly.

Prior to the computer-based training, students formerly attended stand-up classes and read EAP training documentation. The benefit in shifting this training to a computer-based scenario allows an advantage of privacy where students can practice the training repeatedly until they achieve desirable results.

Read our interview with Allen Interactions online at:
http://www.trainofthoughts.com

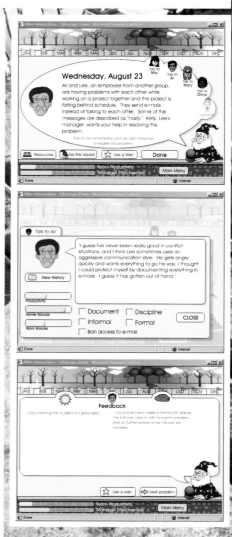

Or actually *speak* something, as is the case with some of the systems that Allen Interactions designs.

04.01.02 Some have trouble with this concept because they filter this new paradigm through past understanding.

They try to visualize a new paradigm as a variation of past experiences. To realize a more valuable online future, we must erase the old concepts of *architectures* with *structures* built on *sites* and replace it with a vision of *flowpaths* that channel *sequences* of *notions* towards people's minds.

To clarify, I'm not suggesting that we're *literally* telling a story in most online situations. What I am suggesting, however, is that every online situation should be a sequence of events that begins with determining a need and ends with satisfying that need. The *nature* of the middle part is determined by the cognitive and emotional circumstances of the individual. What's important is providing a continuity of appropriate compounding events that help people maintain focus and arrive at a satisfactory conclusion. This is the formula for Csikszentmihalyi's "optimal flow experience."

04.01.03 One of the most important tasks in providing a sense of continuity and progress in online messages is figuring out when and how to move people from the beginning to the middle and then from the middle to the end of a message.

The way that we transition—or modulate—between stages is important. Not only do people need to have a sense of having completed the stage that they're in, but they also need to have an accurate expectation of what will come next.

As an example, a good salesperson knows when it's time to ask for a sale versus when it's necessary to offer more evidence—or arguments—to support the idea that a given product or service will solve a given problem. If he or she tries to "close" too early or in a manner that is inappropriate for a given customer, that customer's expectations will be violated, and it's not likely that he or she will be persuaded to buy.

The craft of a salesperson is about becoming skilled at interpreting and then responding to a person's feedback as the sales process unfolds. The craft of those developing flowstems for an online resource is the same. The only difference is that online, feedback occurs when people click on a button, drag and drop something, or type something and hit the "enter" key.[5] Even though these usually aren't real-life interactions with other humans, the people interacting with our online resources still have definite expectations as to what should happen next. If expectations are violated, it becomes increasingly likely that a person will view a Web enterprise as being inept and, as a result, are much more likely to abandon the flowpath.

04.01.04 One of the most important principles that we need to understand is this: Although people may need to hear the same story, that story may need to be presented differently to different people depending on where they're 'coming from.'

We've looked at flowpaths in terms of communicating with people—telling them a story. What's more, we must break that story down into reasonably sized notions. In other words, and as mentioned in Chapter Three, if we want people to ascend to a higher plane of understanding, we need to give them reasonably sized steps to climb there. We want to meet people "where they're at" and then guide them up from there.

To get people there, we must tweak the Q-Q-R-C variables to match a message to the needs of a given individual so that we don't talk either over or under that person's head. Those who violate this rule are thought to be inconsiderate, or worse—rude. As Reeves and Nass have said, people expect us to be considerate and polite in real life conversations. They expect online resources to behave considerately and politely as well. Flowstem development is about making sure that this process happens. It's about presenting a person with the right notions that are presented in the right way, and that are presented at the right times—a valuable train of thoughts that effectively orchestrates meaning online for an individual.

[6] Information architects, who commonly have backgrounds in library sciences, are thinking that this is an ironic anecdote. In light of the fact that I've always found a knowledgeable librarian more helpful and enjoyable to deal with than a card catalogue, I think it's an appropriate anecdote.

04.01.05 More than merely cutting up information and filing the pieces away for people to access systematically as the practice of information architecture would have us do, we need to have multiple variations on each notion to present concepts in manners that accommodate the needs of various individuals.

As mentioned in Chapter Three, this doesn't need to be an infinite set of variations but maybe two, three, or more. The intelligence programmed into our flowstems needs to be smart enough to figure out how to string the right notions together like pearls on a thread. When you say, "I still don't get it," it's the built-in quality of a good guide that allows that guide to say, "I know just the thing that will help you understand."

As an example, put yourself in the shoes of not a *teacher*, who can plan for a homogeneous group like a third grade class, but of a *librarian* working in the history department of a library.[6] In your role, you must deal with a very heterogeneous group. You sit at your help desk waiting for a person to walk up seeking material on some historical person, place, thing, or event such as the Civil War. You need to be ready to help people find material not only appropriate to the *subject* but material that is also qualitatively appropriate for their *age* and for their *cognitive* capacity.

As it turns out, you're very passionate about history and enjoy getting others excited about it. You therefore not only point people to appropriate material, but also quiz them on their interests within the subject. Your aim is to somehow give them added insights as they pursue their learning objectives. To be successful, you've learned how to interact with a third grader as well as with a high school senior—with a more creatively minded individual as well as with someone who is more analytically minded. As a result, it's very easy for those you help to become engaged in the materials you recommend, because you direct them to resources that put a uniquely appropriate spin on a given subject.

Wouldn't it be great if we could guide people this way on the Web? The good news is that we can!

04.01.06 Carefully sequenced notion-flows are capable of setting into motion what Krome Barratt refered to as 'pattern[s] of anticipation.' As a person progresses through the thoughts in an idea that a sequence of notions presents, he or she is hopefully "catching on" to the rhythm and flow of that message. This helps the person to focus—to become absorbed in the ideas that an online message presents. This process is similar to the process that happens when listening to a song.

When you listen to a song, a sense of anticipation should build as the intertwined patterns of melody, harmony, and beat are recognized and understood. As a song progresses, a desire for it to develop and unfold in a manner that's faithful to the introduction builds both cognitively and emotionally. If the song doesn't systematically work its way to a climax and then to a satisfactory resolution, there's disappointment and expectations are negatively violated. It's the same with the notion flows of our online messages.

It's important to understand that patterns of anticipation *do* develop as people interact with our online messages. People unconsciously look for the patterns because familiar patterns provide a sense of context and direction—comfort and security. The recognition of patterns is fundamental to our comprehension, as patterns must correspond to the knowledge structures in our long-term memory.

When patterns of anticipation break down, violations of expectation occur. Krome Barratt explains:

"Violation of expectation can occur in both melodic and harmonic lines; if a pattern of anticipation is to be disrupted, it must first be established. The pattern must suggest a capacity to continue after the violation, if only as an echo. Changing the order of magnitude of just one term in a series is a violation of expectation. Any expectation is a projection into the future of past experiences or a combination of past experiences. [To] be anticipated, these should have a capability of fulfillment, if only in fantasy."

04.01.07 Different factors can cause things to go wrong in a notion, which will violate people's expectations:

> *Quality*—People are presented with a notion that's either of a lower caliber or of insufficient breadth compared to the ones they've been following.
> *Quantity*—People are presented with a notion that goes into either too much or too little depth than they're prepared to process at that moment.
> *Relevance*—People are presented with a notion that seems to be unrelated or unnecessarily tangential to the idea they're trying to follow.
> *Clarity*—As described in 04.01.03, people are presented with a notion that speaks to them in a manner in which they're not ready to easily process.

As mentioned in Chapter Three, there's a way to use violation of expectation in a positive way. Giving people *more* than they were bargaining for is one way. Another way is surprising people with something unexpectedly positive. This can add an intensity to the resolution and confirmation of a notion flow that might not otherwise have been achieved.

04.01.08 Flowstems successfully guide comprehension because they themselves are guided by a comprehension of an individual's needs. According to Reynolds and Iwinski[7], identifying a person's objectives is the most important part of the computer-managed information system that flowpath development largely hinges on. To understand how identifying and then responding to these objectives translates into an effective notions flow for an individual, we must understand the nature of the digital environments that our flowstems exist in. Dr. Ward Hanson points out Janet Murray's four fundamental aspects of digital environments in his book *Internet Marketing*:

1. *Procedural*—"A well-programmed computer can create wonderful illusions of intelligence, spontaneity, and attention to detail. Because digital environments are procedural (interactively respond to feedback), we can expect computers to perform well only if we understand and program the proper rules."
2. *Participatory*—"[People] become excited when [an online resource] responds to a choice. [...] Participation leads to both success in finding the proper information and satisfaction with the online experience. [...] The combination of procedural rules and participation leads to interactivity. [...] One of the most difficult challenges to Net marketing will be the creation of proper procedural rules."
3. *Spatial*—"A common complaint among [people who are new] to the Web is that they 'get lost.' [...] One of the best uses of spatial digital environments is to provide familiarity and comfort."
4. *Encyclopedic*—"Storage is cheap and compact, with hardly any need to delete content. This allows the volume, and value, of the digital environment to grow over time. Cheap bits allow a marketer to avoid the difficult choice between costly multiple [...] versions or ignoring smaller markets."

04.01.09 People who understand flowstem development will be extremely valuable to Web enterprise.

In *Things That Make Us Smart*, Donald Norman wrote:

"The power of the unaided mind is highly overrated. Without external aids, memory, thought, and reasoning are all constrained. The real powers come from devising external aids that enhance cognitive abilities. How have we increased memory, thought, and reasoning? By the invention of external aids: It is things that make us smart."

Are the online resources of this generation aiding us or making things harder for us? It's a matter of degree, I suppose, but it seems to me that the current practices of information architecture cause as many cognitive problems as they help us to solve. My entire aim in developing my *notion-flow* philosophy and in writing this book is to strive to reinvent or devise online resources to be tools that do a much better job of enhancing the same cognitive abilities that Dr. Norman writes about. According to Dr. Hanson, making sure that we craft information to be effective for people in enhancing cognitive abilities creates incredible value in the online marketplace:

"One of the most useful powers of the [Internet] is to take information as input, add value to it, and produce more valuable information as output. Rayport and Sviokla have referred to this as *virtual value activities*. [...] The five virtual value activities are *gathering, organizing, selecting, synthesizing,* and *distributing*. Each of these takes information as input and yields more valuable information as output. If they produce value, it is because they produce new kinds of information that help customers solve problems, make better decisions, or entertain themselves ... Proper selection and synthesis of information is closely tied to the market segmentation and personalization strategies of a Web site. Sophisticated sites try to build up a profile of usage so the most relevant material is the most obvious."

This is what Interactive Flowpath Management Systems (flowstems) are intended to accomplish.

[7] Multimedia Training

04.02 Artificial Intelligence and Interactive Notions

You're in a strange city and get into a cab. You ask the driver to take you to the airport. The driver looks at you and says, "Great! How do I get there?" You respond, "How should I know? If I knew my way around here, I'd have rented a car and driven myself!"

Giving people full control over their experiences is a misguided idea. Robert Mager once said, "If you don't know where you're going, you'll probably end up somewhere else." As we travel the highways and byways of the Web, this is often our experience. Many usability experts promote the notion that the chief aim of an experience designer is to put "users" in the driver's seat—to give them complete control over their experiential destiny. This is misguided. In most cases, the reason people go online is because they're looking for help with something. What we need are intelligent guides to get them to the right places, understand ideas, and to help them make the right choices—choices that will lead to their success. Dr. Hanson states:

"The huge array of consumer products and services can be dysfunctional ... There are too many products to sample and test. An explosion in the number of choices leads to consumer confusion ... The clutter of products leads to a clutter of messages."

04.02.01 Online resources should not be viewed as self-service tools. You call the phone company to talk with a customer service agent about a problem that you're having with your bill. Instead of a real agent, you're assaulted with a friendly, prerecorded voice that informs you that a comprehensive automated system will allow you to solve your problem yourself! The system ends up being more *exhaustive* than it is comprehensive. It's complex and slow because it puts too many layers of hierarchy between you and the interaction that you're seeking. You become frustrated as you try to quickly interpret the flurry of ambiguous options that whiz into your short-term memory. You wish that a live agent were available to respond directly to your question—or conversely, who could interview *you* like a doctor would to determine the best solution for your needs.

Why does it seem that so much of Web development is obsessed with devising systems that focus on enabling people to assist them-selves? Self-service is overrated. These systems almost never work very well. For people to assist themselves, they not only need to interpret the value of the content they seek, but they must also interpret and become proficient at navigating and utilizing the sys-tem itself. People don't want to focus on the tool; they want to focus on achieving the substance of their goals. People don't judge the value of a Web enterprise on how comprehensive it is in its attempt to provide self-service. They judge it based on how helpful it is and how much *choice assistance* it provides.

Note:
In a trainyard, the "hump" is where cars are joined together on a track. It's where appropriate cars are sorted and sequenced for a given situation and need.

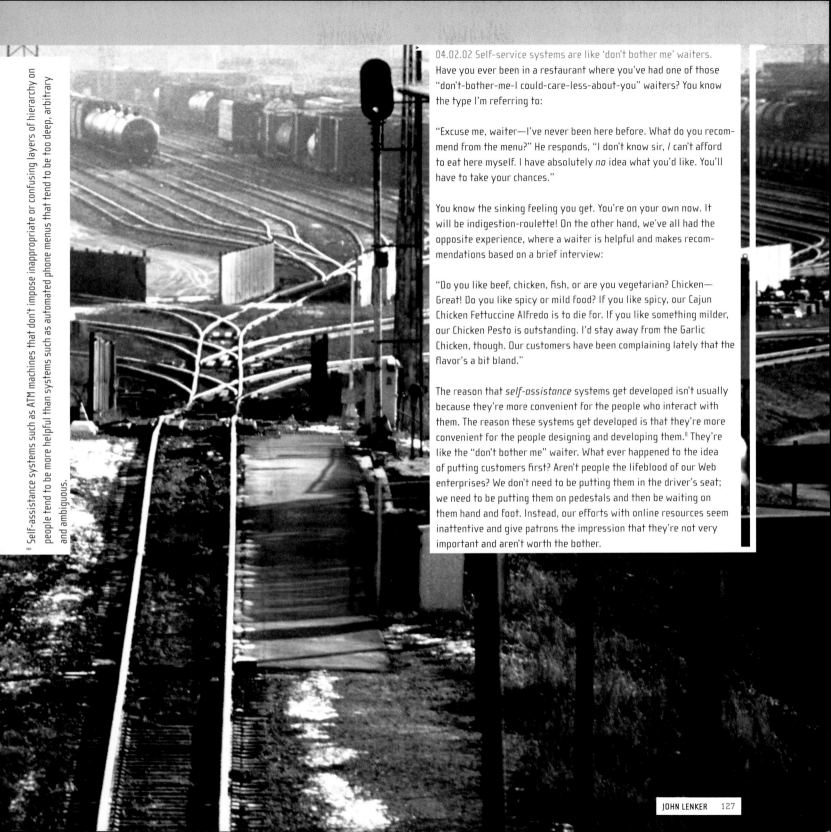

[8] Self-assistance systems such as ATM machines that don't impose inappropriate or confusing layers of hierarchy on people tend to be more helpful than systems such as automated phone menus that tend to be too deep, arbitrary and ambiguous.

04.02.02 Self-service systems are like 'don't bother me' waiters. Have you ever been in a restaurant where you've had one of those "don't-bother-me-I could-care-less-about-you" waiters? You know the type I'm referring to:

"Excuse me, waiter—I've never been here before. What do you recommend from the menu?" He responds, "I don't know sir, I can't afford to eat here myself. I have absolutely *no* idea what you'd like. You'll have to take your chances."

You know the sinking feeling you get. You're on your own now. It will be indigestion-roulette! On the other hand, we've all had the opposite experience, where a waiter is helpful and makes recommendations based on a brief interview:

"Do you like beef, chicken, fish, or are you vegetarian? Chicken— Great! Do you like spicy or mild food? If you like spicy, our Cajun Chicken Fettuccine Alfredo is to die for. If you like something milder, our Chicken Pesto is outstanding. I'd stay away from the Garlic Chicken, though. Our customers have been complaining lately that the flavor's a bit bland."

The reason that *self-assistance* systems get developed isn't usually because they're more convenient for the people who interact with them. The reason these systems get developed is that they're more convenient for the people designing and developing them.[8] They're like the "don't bother me" waiter. What ever happened to the idea of putting customers first? Aren't people the lifeblood of our Web enterprises? We don't need to be putting them in the driver's seat; we need to be putting them on pedestals and then be waiting on them hand and foot. Instead, our efforts with online resources seem inattentive and give patrons the impression that they're not very important and aren't worth the bother.

04.02.03 Personalization emancipates us from the bonds of boundless freedom.

Reeves and Nass said that "... rather than empowering through endless choices, media can empower through ease of use, and that often means freedom *from* choice."

What's the point? The point is that when we're faced with several unfamiliar choices, one of the first things we're inclined to do is relinquish some of our own control over the situation. In return, we attain some choice assistance from a guide that is more experienced, informed, and has our best interest at heart. This is what people need and what they really want when they interact with our Web enterprises. Wouldn't it be wonderful if online resources weren't Web *sites* at all, but interactive Web *guides* with specialized knowledge like the helpful waiter? Can you imagine how powerful people would find their Web experiences to be if these experiences were great at both communicating with people and at facilitating the achievement of their goals? Here's the good news—they can be! My hope is that reading this book will help best practices to get moving in the right direction in your little corner of the online universe.

SPOTLIGHT ON:

DR. PAUL BIEGANSKI

Paul Bieganski, Chief Technical Officer of Net Perceptions, has established himself to date as one of the leading thinkers regarding online personalization technology. In 1994, he began postdoctoral research in computer science and computational biology. His research included work on the GroupLens project, which eventually became the foundation of Net Perceptions' core recommendation technology. At the heart of this project was a technology known as *collaborative filtering*, a method of identifying communities of like-minded people, then tapping each community's collective experience to recommend information that would be relevant to the individuals within those communities. It quickly became the gold standard in this domain, fueling such online retail giants as Amazon.com.

Bieganski has a doctorate in computer science from the University of Minnesota and received a postdoctoral fellowship from the National Science Foundation. He has published numerous articles on algorithmic technology for computer analysis and manipulation of genetic sequences.

My interview with Dr. Bieganski follows:

Lenker: Why did so many Web enterprises fail toward the end of the 1990s?

Bieganski: Any time you have large infrastructure projects, initial investors often become casualties, but that doesn't diminish the value of what's been built. Examples such as the Panama Canal or the English Chunnel illustrate this. These were good ideas and have tremendous utility—it's just that there was an initial period of time in which people were still getting their bearings. Both businesses and individuals throw money into speculative ventures, and it's not until later that others can benefit from hindsight. It's periods such as the one we're in now—postboom periods—that provide excellent opportunities for new business ideas to emerge.

Lenker: What are the factors that most contribute to people really understanding what the value of a Web enterprise is?

Bieganski: The benefit of an online resource needs to be evident. Organizations often come up with sophisticated technologies and throw them at the general public thinking that people will approach them with a technical mindset. This is wrong. Most people are more of the mindset that they have a problem or need, and they want a Web enterprise to address it. They don't want to have to translate their needs into a technical language and then decode technical responses. They want to quickly see the benefit of an online resource as naturally and as socially as possible. We've built a lot of phenomenal technologies that can really benefit people, but if the experiential implementation is weak—let alone horrible—the whole enterprise is going to be irrelevant.

Lenker: How does personalization increase the value proposition of a Web enterprise?

Bieganski: Personalization technology makes online interactions with Web enterprises more convenient, intuitive, and less fractious. Personalization is actually all about what is referred to as "institutional memory." When an institution remembers vital facts and statistics about the people it serves and its interactions with them, and then leverages these data to ensure that future interactions are relevant and beneficial, the people that interact with that institution will perceive that they are served very well. If institutions make no effort to make interactions and transactions convenient in this way, their patrons will feel undervalued.

Lenker: What about the argument that capturing information about people is an invasion of privacy?

Bieganski: I don't necessarily agree with Scott McNeil who said, [...]

Read the entire interview online at:
http://www.trainofthoughts.com

Learn more about Dr. Bieganski at
http://www.bieganski.com/bio

04.02.04 The roots of personalization are in *Computer-Managed Instruction (CMI)*, which is a component of technology-based learning; Here's a summary of the history of CMI:

> IBM began working on technology-based learning in the early 1950s which centered on *Computer Assisted Instruction (CAI)*.
> The National Science Foundation funded several CAI projects starting in 1957.
> One of these projects took place at the University of Illinois. This led to a Control Data technology known as the PLATO system. Over several years, Control Data finally built a PLATO-based CMI system. It was called *PLM—PLATO Learning Management*. It was arguably the most widely used, most sophisticated, and most effective CMI system ever.
> By the late 1960s and early 1970s, most of the basic theoretical research was complete and emphasis moved to cheaper delivery.
> By the early 1980s, PLATO evolved into a desktop-based technology known as PCD3.
> In the mid 1980s, Dr. Michael Allen, who worked on PLATO and PCD3 for Control Data, bought the rights to the technology and created a CAI/CMI hybrid that's known today as Authorware. It was the first tool that provided an easy way to incorporate custome CMI development into a desktop-based CBT environment.
> Authorware became the top-selling CBT design and development tool and Authorware Inc. eventually merged with Macromind/Paracomp in the early 1990s. The company was renamed Macromedia after the merger.

According to Reynolds and Iwinski, "Computer Managed Instruction (CMI) [afforded a] way to let people focus on their deficiencies while ignoring topics they [had] already mastered." Speaking of the affordances of CMI, Chuck Buchanan popularized *Buchanan's Law,* which states: "No amount of time and resources can teach someone what they already know." CMI provided a method of ensuring that every person who engaged in the learning process was presented with a sequence of material that applied to each person's learning needs.

Robert Mager promoted the idea of breaking instructional materials down into content areas related to learning objectives. Within each learning objective, students would alternate between activities of testing, reviewing results, interacting with materials that the system prescribed in response to the test results, and then testing progress again. This process continued in this iterative fashion until each student met his or her learning objectives.[9]

[9] Reynolds, A. & Iwinski, P. (1996) *Multimedia Training,* NY: McGraw Hill, Chapter 2

04.02.05 The most important thing in education or training is an orientation to the learner.
CMI was the solution to the problem that people's learning styles vary, yet very few people have access to individualized education or tutoring. To help each person be successful with learning, these systems tailored instruction to each person's individual learning style. These differences in learning style include variations in

> Background knowledge
> Language comprehension
> Literacy
> Cultural background
> Biases and orientations
> Cognitive capacity

As Dr. Allen's opening quote in Chapter Three of this book states, "Through inexpensive ubiquitous technology, we can now communicate with the efficiency of the one-to-many model and have the effectiveness of the one-to-one model."

04.02.06 Notion-flows are managed by the artificial intelligence built into cybernetic systems.

Robert Weiner coined the term *Cybernetics* to, in Reynolds and Iwinski's words, "identify two significant branches of technology that developed independently in the first part of the century: communications, and control systems." They summarize:

"It is a process-oriented concept [...] in which information is transmitted, a feedback is elicited, and analysis of the feedback is made that governs the further transmission of information. Further, a prescription for instruction can be developed that will include each of these actions and be specific to an individual sequence of instruction, such as integration of learning theory, specific application requirements, available technology, learner profiles, and terminal educational or training objectives."

As can clearly be seen, Cybernetics has tremendously influenced what I call Intelligent Flowpath Management Systems—flowstems. Just as a person learning in a CBT application has specific needs that should dictate the sequence of learning, a person engaging in *any* type of online experience has specific needs that should dictate the sequence of notions in a message.

This procedural, cybernetic model, however, is only one of the two factors whose product is an effective Web experience. It exposes people to appropriate notions. The other factor that must be multiplied by cybernetics, and which was covered in Chapter Three, is *interaction design*. The person who designs CBT applications is known as an *instructional designer*. Those who have traditionally designed online resources are known as *information architects*. In my philosophy, however, these people should evolve into what I refer to as *flowstem developers*.

04.02.07 Web enterprises have already begun to explore cybernetics. The way the online design and development community has defined it up to this point, there are at least four types of personalization systems. These systems are *Rule-Based Systems, Computer-Assisted Self-Explication (CASE), Endorsement Systems,* and *Collaborative Filtering Systems.* According to Ward Hanson—and I quote:

> "*Rule-based Systems* use the information that a company develops about its customer base to make educated guesses about specific offers, promotions, and information that it should provide to visitors."
> "*CASE Systems* [... ask] visitors questions about what they like. [...] The goal of the system is to help [people] narrow their choices from thousands of possibilities to a few highly ranked alternatives."
> "*Endorsement Systems* work best when the product needs of consumers do not differ greatly, but judging quality and explaining the value of available products are a challenge."
> "*Collaborative Filtering* is a leading approach when the product space is complicated and preferences are highly subjective, qualitative, and complex. The goal of these systems is educated word of mouth. The system matches different guests who seem to share similar tastes."

04.03 The Future of Personalization

I believe that in the future, great notion composition combined with great procedural models will begin to yield the most effective Web experiences the world has ever seen. As Dr. Michael Allen has pointed out, the quality of an online experience hinges on the quality of its online interactions. As Dr. Hanson points out, "Because digital environments are procedural, we can expect computers to perform well only if we understand and program the proper rules."

So there we have it. Devise great notions, and devise great rules and procedures to prescribe notion-flows. Simple. Well, it actually is, but there are a number of prerequisites to these becoming standard industry practices.

04.03.01 Attitudes about the value of crafting content must change. Crafting content can't be viewed merely as an exercise in simplicity on the one hand or as an exercise in creating eye candy on the other. We can't burn our budgets on committees designing pointless information architectures on the one hand, and what a colleague of mine, Keith Craig, has termed "flaming intros" on the other. Those who are experts in finding moderation and are well skilled in the appropriate application of principles of psychology, understandability, and creativity to Web content must transfer their knowledge to the rest of the world.

CASE STUDY 4B

Reflect.com

Address: http://www.reflect.com
Company: Reflect.com
Developers/Designers: Reflect.com

Beauty — Made to Order

Reflect.com is an interactive, personalized beauty experience for women. Its concept is to offer a specialized service where customers can create personalized skin, hair, makeup, and fragrance products. It uses an interactive narrowing process to present a product that is blended with ingredients specific to an individual's characteristics, such as skin type. Realizing that women feel just as strongly about the packaging as they do the product, the experiences allows customers to play with label colors, packaging, and product names as well.

To ensure customer satisfaction, Reflect.com offers such incentives as free shipping, discount offers, and an unconditional guarantee to re-create the product if it doesn't meet expectations. These incentives help to ease fears of online purchasing while encouraging purchases. What's more, the pattern of anticipation that the online experience creates is not in any way violated when the product arrives. We were stunned with the meticulous care that Reflect.com took to ensure that the final presentation of the physical product was as satisfying as the online resource made it out to be. They packaged the finished product carefully using colored tissue and ornate mailing tubes. With this outstanding follow-through, the basis for a strong relationship is established; customers feel important, view the experience as memorable, and are motivated to return to the site again. Dennis Maloney, an original founder of Reflect.com, states:

"From the start, Reflect.com has tried to empower women by giving them the ability to take a very active role in the creation of their product. [...] The entire process constantly feeds back visual cues and information about the creation process to help assure the customer that we are not only incorporating her feedback, but using it to help create a product unique to her."

Read our interview with Dennis Maloney online at:
http://www.trainofthoughts.com

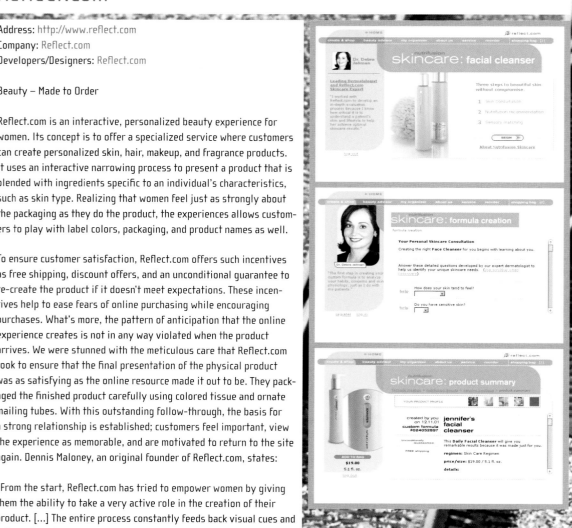

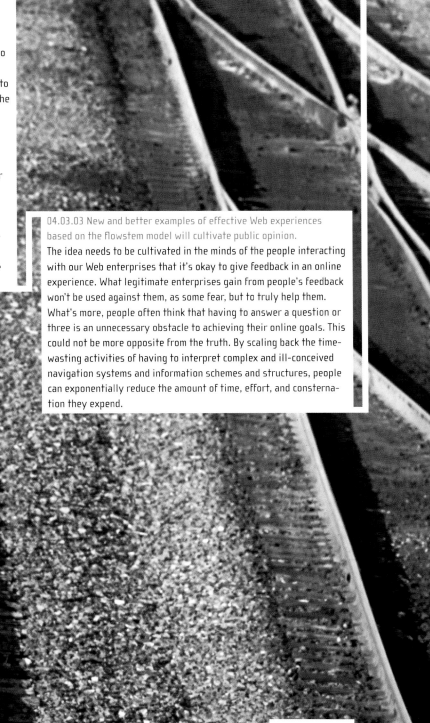

04.03.02 The teams that are responsible for online resources must become more well rounded in terms of the backgrounds of team members than teams commonly are today.

Those who understand flowpath development must get involved in helping devise better procedures so that our procedural systems approach true artificial intelligence (A.I.). Right now, the people who govern the development of personalization systems are engineers and marketing people. It's fine for engineers and marketing people to get involved—they should. They do, however, only present two of the necessary perspectives in designing these systems.

As I quoted Dr. Norman as alluding to in Chapter One, we need to make sure that we have psychologists, social scientists, aestheticians, interactivity specialists, computer scientists, subject-matter experts (SMEs), audience members, and sponsors involved in the development of systems that interactively generate notion-flows. This should not be intimidating. In some cases, and especially for projects of a smaller scale, the knowledge of as few as three multi-disciplined people can be combined to formulate these systems. If internal resources are limited, consulting firms such as my own are ever eager to pitch in and help.

04.03.03 New and better examples of effective Web experiences based on the flowstem model will cultivate public opinion.

The idea needs to be cultivated in the minds of the people interacting with our Web enterprises that it's okay to give feedback in an online experience. What legitimate enterprises gain from people's feedback won't be used against them, as some fear, but to truly help them. What's more, people often think that having to answer a question or three is an unnecessary obstacle to achieving their online goals. This could not be more opposite from the truth. By scaling back the time-wasting activities of having to interpret complex and ill-conceived navigation systems and information schemes and structures, people can exponentially reduce the amount of time, effort, and consternation they expend.

04.03.04 We need to supplement procedural systems that are based on rules and collaborative filtering with systems that are based on asking meaningful questions.

The industry calls these systems *Computer-Assisted Self-Explication (CASE)*. Before I even knew that there was such a thing as CASE, I used the term *Interactive Narrowing*, which I think is easier to say and remember. Ward Hanson speaks of the value of systems that utilize the *Interactive Narrowing Process:*

"A surprising result of recent marketing research is that a system that directly asks a [person's] preferences does a good job of predicting choice. One difficulty of rule-based systems is the need to guess preferences from behavior. A simpler way is just to ask visitors what they like."

If rule-based and/or collaborative filtering systems are making judgments based on people's online behavior, what happens when people's online behavior is really the result of misunderstanding the system? The result *might* be a snowballing effect of inappropriate information being presented to the poor, unsuspecting participant! That's why these systems must be informed by interactive narrowing systems. Hanson continues:

"The challenge is to ask [questions] in a way that encourages accurate, truthful, and useful answers. When this is achieved, complicated choices can be dramatically simplified. This is one of the most exciting areas of online personalization."

04.03.05 We must develop a much better understanding of people's patterns of behavior.

We need to understand people's fixations and fascinations—what inspires them and moves them to action. We need to understand their dreams and aspirations and then strive to help each person fulfill them. To accomplish this, we must understand that people fall into patterns of behavior to satisfy their fixations and fascinations—dreams and aspirations.

Just as the people interacting with our flowstems instinctively learn to recognize the experiential patterns that our systems present them with, our flowstems must learn to recognize the patterns of behavior that people exhibit when interacting with them. The hope is that a certain synergy will arise that will multiply the value of the notion-flows that the system generates for all stakeholders. Perhaps the most significant efforts that will yield the most profound results involve the experience design team recognizing, leveraging, and then influencing these patterns of behavior.

04.03.06 Our flowstems should demonstrate the qualities of good and reliable guides.

A good guide doesn't necessarily need to be all things to all people. A good guide must, however, be at least three things to be successful: an expert, a facilitator, and a friend.

An expert is someone who knows the subject at hand. The proverbial "answer man." An expert knows how to get deep inside a situation or subject and ferret out the critical issues. An expert has "been this way before"—has covered the ground over and over again. It's easy to identify experts. There's a certain sense of comfort and security that we get from being around them. It's easy to put confidence in them. If people get this same impression from our flowstems when they interact with them, they'll put confidence in the quality of our online messages.

A facilitator knows how to help others achieve their goals. It's one thing to know a subject well. It's another thing to know people. Good mentors and teachers know not only how to get inside a subject but also how to get inside the heads of the people they communicate with. The goal is always to transfer knowledge or skills to the student or apprentice. It's the same with our flowstems. People must feel that these systems make a connection both with their emotions and with *their* way of thinking. The difficult is made to be under-standable. That which is out of reach becomes attainable. The inaccessible becomes accessible.

A friend is concerned with the well-being of others. A friend doesn't have to be a close loved one to be a friend. Even a stranger can extend an act of friendship to someone in need. Although those who are cynical will say that people always have their own best interest at heart, according to John Nash, the most rewarding interactions in any medium occur when the person, business, or other interest bases its success on helping others to be successful.

Web enterprises need to go beyond solid subject matter expertise and strong communications skills. They need to try to put the needs of the people who interact with them before their own. It's so easy to see through phony marketing rhetoric. As much as I'm a proponent of the rhetorical process, I believe that our rhetoric will only be effective online when it's based on a sincere desire to protect the interests of those our flowstems are designed to benefit. This practice won't go unrewarded. By effectively serving others, we're sure to realize the greatest potential of our own businesses.

Chapter Seven discusses the importance of reconciling the needs of an organization with the needs of its sponsors and its constituents when formulating an online strategy.

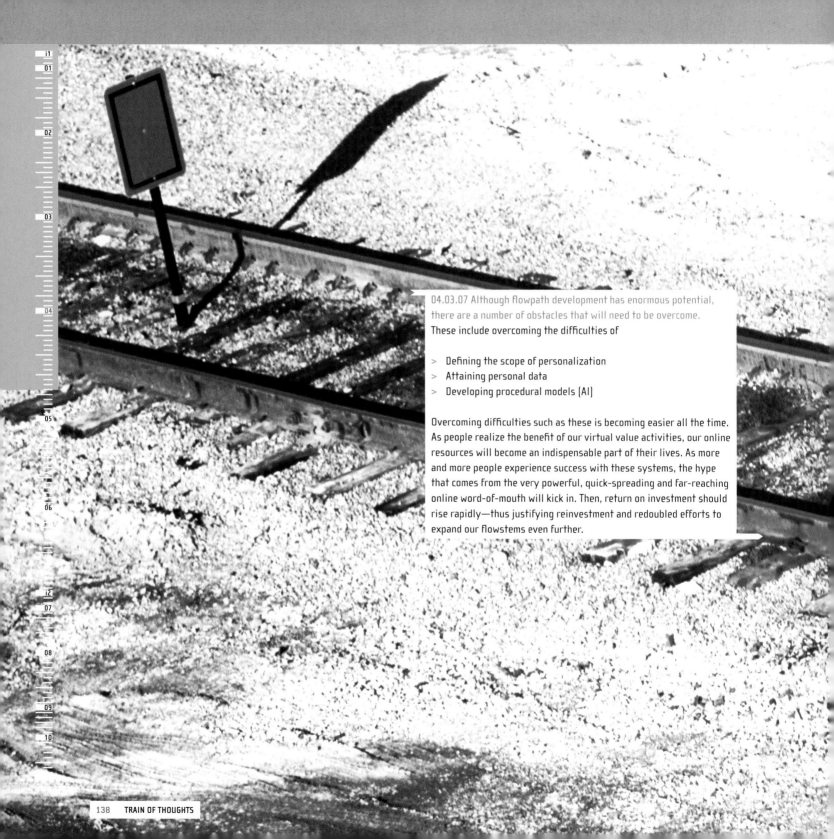

04.03.07 Although flowpath development has enormous potential, there are a number of obstacles that will need to be overcome. These include overcoming the difficulties of

> Defining the scope of personalization
> Attaining personal data
> Developing procedural models (AI)

Overcoming difficulties such as these is becoming easier all the time. As people realize the benefit of our virtual value activities, our online resources will become an indispensable part of their lives. As more and more people experience success with these systems, the hype that comes from the very powerful, quick-spreading and far-reaching online word-of-mouth will kick in. Then, return on investment should rise rapidly—thus justifying reinvestment and redoubled efforts to expand our flowstems even further.

04.03.08 Personalization cannot be developed properly in a vacuum. It needs to be based on the analysis of and reconciliation of all stakeholder needs. This analytical process must ensure that the key issues are drawn out and addressed. The capacity exists to do almost *anything* with personalization. The key is to *not* try and do *everything*. It's essential to determine the information that people will most value and desire to interact with. Beyond that, the procedures built into flowstems must be programmed in such a way as to provide an overall continuity between the notions that people will be exposed to in our online messages. Only then will people have a sense that their flowpaths are moving toward the achievement of their tangible goals.

04.03.09 It's a fact—people are reluctant to disclose personal information online.

Reasons for this range from inexperience with online systems to security concerns to conspiracy mythologies. There has been much written about these issues in other books, and I'm not going to cover it all here. I will say, however, that systems that make it easy for people to see the benefits of disclosing information will be more successful than systems that don't. The burden is on our online messages to guide people into comprehension of this idea.

Fortunately, our interaction with people online doesn't need to begin with asking for the disclosure of personal information. It's a myth that people must "log in" to a system to benefit from personalization. There are strategies through which systems can help a person on an anonymous basis. The hope is that in this way a person will see the benefit of the personalization before entering into a response interaction with the system by disclosing name, email address, and other basic information. Dr. Hanson's book *Principles of Internet Marketing* outlines three strategies for coaxing people into disclosing personal information:

> "Offer new information to consumers [which raises the system's overall benefits]
> Reduce the effort of using existing information [which lowers time investment]
> Remind consumers to use existing information [which helps them keep track of past benefits]"

04.03.10 Clearly, the burden is on our online messages to lead people to understanding the value that our systems have to offer.

The point of Part One of this book is to build a case for giving pains taking attention to the process of formulating these online messages. The reason is that these messages are the most powerful tool for leading people to a place of mental preparedness to enter into these response interactions.

"The procedural aspects of digital environments are some of the most complicated and important issues in online personalization," writes Ward Hanson. It's true that designing our online messages to be effective on the microlevel of notions is challenging. We do, however, have much more experience with that type of design than we do with the design of systems that possess artificial intelligence. Most cybernetic solutions in use, as of the writing of this book, are very limited in the breadth and depth of what they can really do for people. The result is that many of the options and messages that these systems generate are at best flimsy and tenuous, and at worst wholly inappropriate.

The fact that personalization systems come up short isn't a reflection on the ability of technology to handle greater solutions. It's a reflection on the inexperience of those who program these systems to think creatively about their programing and utility. Developers of these systems need to be possibility thinkers as much as they need to be computer scientists. Chapter Seven will address strategies for exploring these possibilities.

[10] Philip Kotler (1998). "A Generic Concept of Marketing," *Marketing Management*, Fall, pp. 48-54.

04.04 Building Relationships

Not only should interactive flowpath management systems benefit a person within the confines of one online session, but this information should also benefit the quality, quantity, relevance, and clarity of what it presents a person with in subsequent interactions with the online resource. As in any genuinely good relationship, the fruit of good communication should be a progressively better understanding of each party over time. Not only should a person become more familiar with a particular online resource, but also a Web enterprise should become more familiar with that person. As a result, the characteristics of the interactions between person and system should evolve over time.

Perhaps the best example of a system that attempts to do this, and, to a large degree succeeds, is Amazon.com. Not only does the intelligence of the system benefit the people interacting with it within the scope of one online session but also over the course of every interaction that these people have with the system in future sessions. The result is a *virtuous cycle* whereby all parties to the interaction maximize the benefit of the relationship. The customers benefit because the Q-Q-R-C of the messages that they're presented with is very high. Amazon benefits because the "time online," which is closely related to "time in store," is more efficient and effective and, therefore, far more fruitful. This leads to a greater customer lifetime value. The manufacturers of merchandise benefit because their products are being targeted to highly qualified audiences. This is not only the epitome of a virtuous cycle but also of what Kotler refers to as the *Individual Marketing Concept*.[10]

04.04.01 The Web has given life to the idea known as the *Individual Marketing Concept*.

According to Kotler, "The *Individual Marketing Concept* holds that the key to effective marketing is to treat the consumer as an individual and to use interactive dialogue to provide personalized products and services, improved quality, membership in communities, and to provide support."

Just as products are gaining access to global markets, the sizes of these markets are shrinking. People are increasingly coming to expect that the world that they interact with cater to them on an individual basis. This means that customization and differentiation not only of marketing messages but also of products themselves are becoming mainstream (see Case Study 4B). Department stores and specialty stores alike need to deal with this reality.

04.04.02 The *Individual Marketing Concept* is the latest in what Kotler outlines as a series of successive marketing concepts:

> *The Production Concept* held that consumers would favor products that were widely available. This was driven by the construction of the national roadways and railways, which enabled the mass distribution of products.
> *The Selling Concept* held that consumers would favor products that were most heavily promoted. This was driven by the radio and then the television broadcast technology that enabled mass promotion of products.
> *The Brand Management Concept* held that consumers would favor products that were targeted toward the segments of the market that they were a part of. This was driven by the development of computerized customer databases, which enabled direct marketing.

As can be seen, these concepts have always succeeded one another based on the available technology. Never before has there been a time when marketers could affordably engage in a one-to-one inter-action with every member of their customer base. Before the Web, the increase in interaction with the customer base made transactions more costly and *lowered* return on investment. People are expensive to employ. The more time they spend with a customer, the costlier the sale is to the business and the lower the gross profit margin on the sale. Now that the Web has arrived on the scene, the more time the business spends interacting with its customer base through its online resources, the *more* profitable the interactions become and the *greater* the return on investment. This is the essence of the *Individual Marketing Concept*.

04.04.03 Interactivity sets the stage for relationships to develop. When we individualize the messages that we present to the people interacting with our Web enterprises, we *create* value for each individual. The fact that we can actually *create* value—not by changing products, services, or facts but by making these products, services, and facts more meaningful for individuals—is a powerful notion. Bits are cheap, and for the first time we can talk to people without paying for printing, postage, long-distance phone charges, or broadcast time. Not only are interactions with the people we need to communicate with cheaper than it's ever, but also more effective than ever. Hanson has this to say:

"As sites tap into individual [needs] and become more interactive, customers dramatically increase their usage. [This is the result of increased system capabilities.] As interactivity rises, customers use a service more frequently, invest time to understand capabilities of the service, and increase the duration of their online activities. This creates opportunities for personalization, community building, and other avenues of real-time marketing."

04.04.04 Relationships build competitive advantage.

As a person gets to know an online resource and as its respective flowstem gets to know a person, the relationship becomes indispensable in the sense that the cost of switching to a competing Web enterprise becomes very high. The reason for this is that the person would have to, in a sense, "start over" with a new system.

A person who has been buying books on Amazon.com, for example, is not very likely to switch to Barnes & Noble.com (or vice versa) unless Amazon.com is perceived as having done something wrong. This *choice assistance* is extremely valuable because it keeps people focused on their interests, and they can avoid the painstaking work that's involved in sorting through the possibilities on their own. As people begin to rely on the convenience that choice assistance provides, people tend to become loyal to the organization that provides that system. This loyalty is based on the following factors:

> *History*—A person has a sense of being recognized and understood by the system. Sentiments such as "they really know me and understand me" are commonly held.
> *Track record*—The system has constantly performed favorably in past interactions.
> *Trust*—The system is perceived as being accurate and reliable.
> *Personable*—The system is perceived as being a helpful and reliable guide and friend.

As a result of succeeding in these areas, high rates of retention of these patrons can be expected. This can dramatically increase the projected lifetime value of the patron's relationship with the system. Hanson asserts

"Personalization has powerful *potential* competitive advantage. The first company to create an effective personalization approach in an industry can capture many of the most profitable customers. Personalization creates the opportunity to learn much more about current desires, future trends, and new opportunities for product features and extensions."

04.04.05 As with any relationship, it's important to not be too pushy up front.

When people perceive that a system isn't "in it for the quick kill," but for the "long haul," they're more relaxed and apt to believe that the desire of the system to build a relationship of mutual benefit is valid and not merely an empty marketing ploy. Organizations that develop these systems understand that if people enjoy their online experience, they're going to be back for more.

This relates to the prior discussion of attaining personal information. Just as it's rude to ask too many personal questions of a person we've just met, it's equally rude to ask too many personal questions of people interacting with our online resources. Gradual learning about a person's personality and interests over time can come from almost any interaction. A series of events that lead to a comprehensive understanding of an individual might go something like this:

> 1st visit: No personal information is gathered. Through the use of various technical strategies, preference information can be stored on a database without actually getting a name or email address. Maybe the system monitors choices and keeps track of them. Maybe it engages the person in an *Interactive Narrowing Process* and stores the answers.
> 2nd visit: The system recognizes that the person has interacted with the system before and formulates messages that are most appropriate to that individual based on monitoring selections during the first visit. This is likely to be refreshing to the individual because feelings of identification are being fostered. At this stage, it could be a welcome gesture to ask for a first name if it hasn't already been attained through a previous response interaction.
> 3rd visit: If a person hasn't already disclosed personal information via a past transaction or some other response interaction, it's definitely appropriate to do so now. The person has shown by a third visit that he or she has a serious interest in the offerings of the Web enterprise and is likely to be open to disclosing information. A person will likely be even more open if he or she perceives a tangible benefit from providing the disclosure of personal information.

04.04.06 The market value of a Web enterprise is directly proportional to the lifetime value of each of its relationships.

"Once the purchase and activity levels of customers are traced and recorded," writes Dr. Ward Hanson, "it becomes meaningful to talk about the lifetime profitability of a specific customer. This is the discounted net present value of the profits that are expected over the entire future dealings with a specific individual. The value of its customer base becomes the most important measure of how well the company is doing."

In his book *Principles of Internet Marketing,* Hanson outlines other benefits of these relationships:

> Lower acquisition, development, and retention costs
> Innovative messages and the possibility of a cycle of communication
> Customer support and online quality enhancements

It's important to understand that a person's lifetime value is directly proportional to the value that a person is receiving from the online resource. This value is based not merely on the practical value of the online resource but also on the overall benefit a person receives to his or her emotional, social, cognitive, and consumptive needs.

Because effective Web experiences largely hinge on our ability to successfully and consistently guide people into comprehension of our online messages, we must begin to interact with people in a more meaningful way. This requires an appropriateness, depth, substance, and continuity to our online messages that our Web enterprises have up until this point never been able to produce. As a result, the time for a new vision for information design and delivery has come. This vision relates to the way that we think about, design, and develop the messages that our Intelligent Flowpath Management Systems (flowstems) present. It also relates to the way we design our flowstems to interact with people.

What's more, our flowstems must accommodate the way that people naturally behave rather than force them to accommodate the way that technology naturally tends to behave. By doing this we'll continue to increase the level of satisfaction that people experience from our online resources. This will lead to a competitive advantage within a market space for Web enterprises that follow these principles. Furthermore, by designing our flowstems to guide people toward the fulfillment of their goals rather than requiring them to ferret out solutions on their own, we'll build goodwill and loyalty. This will lower costs and increase returns for all stakeholders of online enterprises' cybernetic interactions.

In the first chapter, we learned the importance of understanding people's online motivations holistically from not only a practical standpoint, but also from emotional, social, cognitive, and consumptive standpoints. In Chapters Two through Four, we learned the importance of formulating online messages that guide people into comprehension of our ideas on both the microlevel of notions and the macrolevel of flowpaths. We've seen clearly that in order to communicate effectively with people we must do several things. We must attract them, inform them, and invoke them to take action.

It's time now to look at the role that *creativity* has to play in each of these stages to make the experiential pathways that we develop as effective and meaningful as possible.

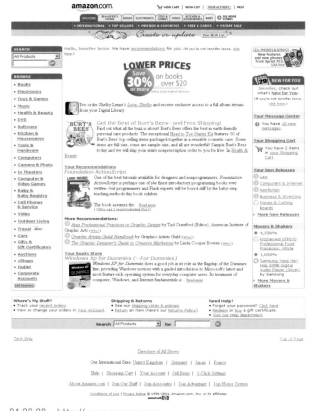

04.00.08 – http://www.amazon.com

Amazon.com recognizes their customers by presenting them with listings, ads, and promotions geared toward their interests.

04.00.08 – http://www.samgoody.com

SamGoody.com presents a generalized array of products but does not implement technology to present customers with customized product selections.

04.03.04 – http://www.nikeid.com

Nike ID allows customers to customize shoes based on a series of choices of color, style, and size while providing an online chat for further assistance.

04.04.02 – http://www.eyeglasses.com

Eyeglasses.com allows customers to upload their picture and try on various eyeglass frame styles.

04.04.04 – http://www.landsend.com

Lands' End builds customer relationships with "My Model"—a 3D virtual model that allows customers to "try on" clothes, configure outfits, and save their selections.

CHAPTER 05

Productive Originality—
Understanding the Role of Creativity Online

Save some of the more persnickety usability experts, most other experts acknowledge that creativity plays an extremely important role in getting people excited about information. The correct application of creativity in terms of meeting people's perceptual, cognitive, and emotional needs, however, is less well understood. In order to understand creativity's role in guiding people into comprehension, we must first understand what creativity is. What is creativity, and what role does it play in our online messages?

"The [conditioned] response to signals remains our most basic level of communication and is the most impelling tool available to the designer."

—Krome Barratt, *Logic & Design In Art, Science & Mathematics*

"Of all the accidental by-products of technology that help create the wasteland of the mind, the one I am becoming most concerned about arises through the technologies of entertainment, especially as they spill over to media of all forms, to education, and to the intellectual side of life. I am concerned that the new tools have moved us in unexpected ways to accept experience as a substitute for thought."

—Dr. Donald Norman, *Things That Make Us Smart*

05.00.01 As has been outlined in the first four chapters, professionals are at odds regarding what creativity is and how it should be employed online.

In one camp, we have those who subscribe to the usability point of view. Some of the more extreme Web usability writing amounts to a carte blanche condemnation of creativity. In the other camp, we have those who are "graphic-arts centric" and who generally defend the use of creativity even when they can't substantiate the reasoning behind their perspectives.

The aim of this chapter is to help those from both vantage points to understand that there is a moderate position that rises above the two extremes. This position is that not only *should* creativity be employed in the design of our online messages but also it *must* be employed if the successes of our online messages are to be maximized. But it's not the mere employment of creativity *itself* that will make the difference. It's the *appropriate* employment of creativity that will do more good than harm. This appropriate use of creativity strikes a balance between the perceptual, cognitive, and emotional parameters of people, and the ever-evolving parameters of the technology that we use to deliver our messages.

Note:
Although sometimes both the extremes of the abstract and of the blatantly clear can be beautiful, we need to make sure that we're _not_ designing to extremes that fail those who have more moderate intellectual needs.

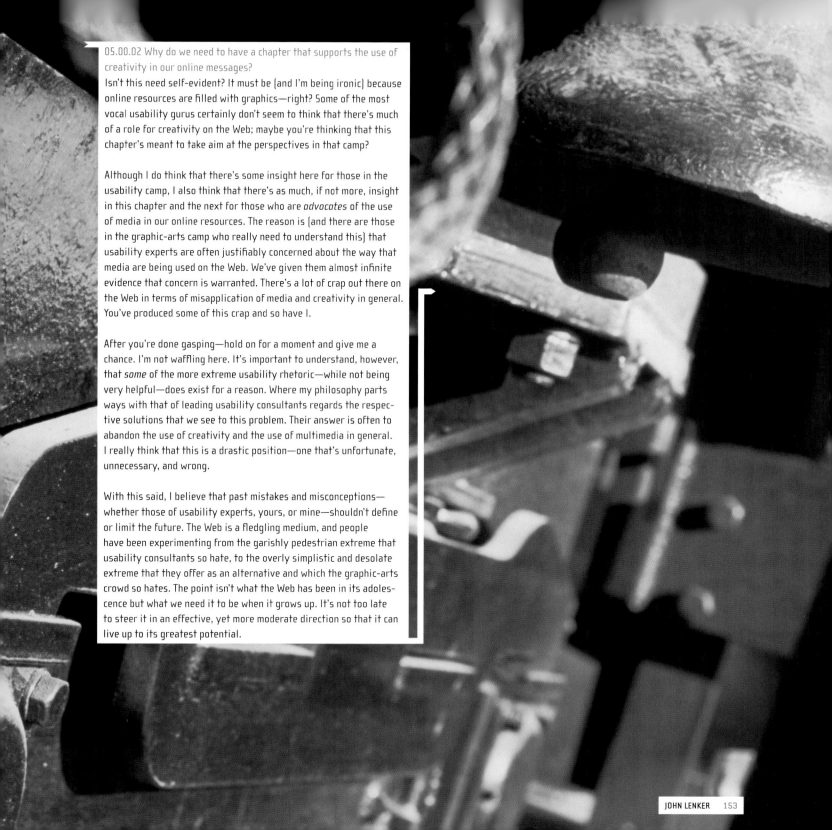

05.00.02 Why do we need to have a chapter that supports the use of creativity in our online messages?

Isn't this need self-evident? It must be (and I'm being ironic) because online resources are filled with graphics—right? Some of the most vocal usability gurus certainly don't seem to think that there's much of a role for creativity on the Web; maybe you're thinking that this chapter's meant to take aim at the perspectives in that camp?

Although I do think that there's some insight here for those in the usability camp, I also think that there's as much, if not more, insight in this chapter and the next for those who are *advocates* of the use of media in our online resources. The reason is (and there are those in the graphic-arts camp who really need to understand this) that usability experts are often justifiably concerned about the way that media are being used on the Web. We've given them almost infinite evidence that concern is warranted. There's a lot of crap out there on the Web in terms of misapplication of media and creativity in general. You've produced some of this crap and so have I.

After you're done gasping—hold on for a moment and give me a chance. I'm not waffling here. It's important to understand, however, that *some* of the more extreme usability rhetoric—while not being very helpful—does exist for a reason. Where my philosophy parts ways with that of leading usability consultants regards the respective solutions that we see to this problem. Their answer is often to abandon the use of creativity and the use of multimedia in general. I really think that this is a drastic position—one that's unfortunate, unnecessary, and wrong.

With this said, I believe that past mistakes and misconceptions— whether those of usability experts, yours, or mine—shouldn't define or limit the future. The Web is a fledgling medium, and people have been experimenting from the garishly pedestrian extreme that usability consultants so hate, to the overly simplistic and desolate extreme that they offer as an alternative and which the graphic-arts crowd so hates. The point isn't what the Web has been in its adolescence but what we need it to be when it grows up. It's not too late to steer it in an effective, yet more moderate direction so that it can live up to its greatest potential.

05.00.03 The role of creativity is often misunderstood.
Although many graphic designers confuse creativity with the modes within which it operates (e.g. they think being creative simply means using graphics, sound, or motion), an online resource can have elaborate media elements that are in no way, shape, or form creative. Usually people think that the role of creativity is to add *pizzazz* to an online resource. Although it's true that the initial role of creativity is to capture attention, many do not realize that it plays an equally important role in *managing* both attention and comprehension.

How, for example, do we use creativity to hold attention without distracting people from concentrating on the central focus of a message? How do we use it to inspire people's thinking throughout each of the attract, inform, and invoke stages of our online messages which were outlined in Chapters Two through Four? These are the issues that we'll be addressing in the remainder of this chapter.

05.00.04 Creativity often is erroneously used as diversion when what people really need are aids to comprehension.

Instead of inspiring thinking, many Web enterprises erroneously use what they view as creative media to add "entertaining" diversions to their online resources. Usually this is a cover-up for the fact that their messages aren't all that engaging. It's as if they were saying, "Look, we know that the substance of our message is really boring, so we'll make you a deal. If you'll agree to sift through our mangled, marginal messages, we'll provide some diversions to entertain you along the way." This is a really shallow and ineffective approach.

Don't misunderstand me. Adding ingredients that offer entertainment value can be productive if doing so serves the greater purpose of effectively informing people of the *ideas* contained in the online messages. Usually, however, Web enterprises don't work hard enough to find this better approach. Instead, gizmos and gee-whizbangs are stapled onto the side of the relevant content, and all that they tend to accomplish is to distract people from the information flow that they're *already* struggling to follow. I think that organizations that do this are doing it because they don't currently have a greater vision for their online messages. This is a situation that I hope this book will—to some degree—help to remedy.

The fact is that the interruptions to concentration that these diversions inherently create destroy the continuity of a message and make it much more difficult for people's minds to properly interpret and encode meaning. Although the people interacting with Web enterprises are often amendable to this practice, they often don't realize that the overall value of their interaction with an online resource's messages is dramatically diminished.

05.00.05 Creativity can address problems with concentration.

Before we look at how creativity must function in our online messages, we must first remember that the people who interact with our online messages aren't "users," they're people. In line with this, we must remember that people don't *effortlessly* absorb information like computers do. We as people think consciously, organically, and introspectively—ever striving to solve problems by making connections with existing conceptual reference points. Although this type of thinking is one of our greatest strengths, it also creates problems for us because it's somewhat unpredictable.

Our mission in designing effective Web experiences must be to identify and address these problems, and then figure out ways to help people overcome their limitations and frailties. Dr. Donald Norman views this as the chief aim of the tools that we create for people. We must supplement the cognition that people are inherently "bad at" so that they can spend more of their time engaged in cognition that they're really "good at."

This being the case, there's one impediment to people's ability to "think" that the application of creativity to our online messages can aid above any other. This problem concerns the inability of people to maintain focused concentration on a stimulus for extended periods of time—which generally amounts to anything longer than fifteen seconds. "Fifteen seconds" sounds a bit arbitrary, but in reality I'd guess it's pretty normative. Is there a way that we can more accurately assess how long people can maintain their concentration? The answer is that it depends on the product of two variables:

Sustainability of Focus = Mental Capabilities x Character of Stimulus

A person's ability to maintain quality focus is the product of his or her own mental capabilities multiplied by the character of a stimulus. And this, my friends, is where creativity comes into play.

Creativity is the strategy we use to shape the character of a stimulus in order to not only establish interest, but also achieve the desired comprehension when multiplied by the projected mental capabilities of a given audience set or subset.

05.00.06 Creativity can prevent experiences from becoming mundane and therefore cognitively blurred.

Since our aim, according to Mihaly Csikszentmihalyi (see 04.00.10), is to provide a "sustained, optimal experience" which is based on "a continual flow of focused concentration," we must *create* Web experiences that *allow* people to keep their minds activated and engaged in the flowpaths that our online messages are taking. The problem is that when the stimulus that we want people to focus on becomes monotonous, their minds increasingly try to set the stimulus aside as being familiar and therefore mundane and peripheral.

It's like listening to a boring lecture in school. As each minute goes by, we become increasingly restless and are almost in pain because of the persistence of the unbroken stimulus of the stoic lecturer's voice. Either our minds wander to other internal (distracting thoughts) or external stimuli, or we begin to fall asleep. The *quality of focus* is low because the *character of the stimulus* is flat—lacking dimension.

Remember the explanation in 03.03.02 regarding the nature of the *monotonous?* I stated that the word *monotonous* is derived from the word *monotone,* or single-tone, and that it's very difficult for people to maintain concentration on a single, sustained tone. There are numerous strategies that can be used to break this monotony, from introducing rests (or pauses) as well as other tones to achieve both rhythm and polyphony.

As a tone becomes familiar, it becomes mundane to us.[1] To our minds, the stimulus melts into the other familiar stimuli in our environment. Combined, these mundane stimuli begin to blur together into an unconscious background pattern that serves as a backdrop when some other stimulus comes and takes center stage. This same principle relates to stimuli that affect all other senses, including the senses of touch, smell, taste, and sight. When we try to maintain focus on any stimulus that's overly sustained and that, therefore melts into a perceptual background pattern, we have to *really* fight because our minds are extremely prone to wander to any stimulus that imposes itself in front of that pattern.

05.00.06

STIMULOUS →

TIME ↓

[1] This is not to say that all things "familiar" work against us. In fact, leveraging that which is already familiar to a person is one of the surest ways of making a new experience meaningful.

05.00.07 Creativity must help people distinguish 'figure' from 'ground' so that they can maintain content focus.

Because these mundane stimuli do form a pattern, our minds try to deal with them as they would with any pattern in general. In a visual pattern, for example, it's very difficult to zero in on any one instance of the figure that the interleaved elements, such as tiles, form. This is especially true from a distance, where a multitude of these uniform figures fill our fields of view. When each figure is equally weighted, it's very difficult for our minds to perceive a difference between the *figure* we're trying to focus on and the *ground* that the figure appears upon. As we fight to pull a specific figure to the forefront of our minds, our perception fights back and insists that it's not a figure at all, but a component of the background.

As an example, this is why it's so difficult to see a phone number on the two-page spread of the white pages. With four to eight columns of black text on white paper and with letters and spaces being almost equally weighted, we perceive what seems more like a gray background than what it really is—an array of separate black information chunks. Because our minds are not geared to cope with lists of more than about nine items (let alone several hundred), we *cognitively blur* the information into one of these mundane patterns.

Although we attempt to single out a unique figure, we struggle immensely. We can look right past the listing we're looking for and not even realize it because our brains aren't interpreting it as something unique enough to break the pattern of the mundane. After four or five passes up and down a column, the listing suddenly jumps off the page as if from "thin air." This effect is what Krome Barratt refers to as "the dazzling effect of plenty."

We need to do whatever it takes to prevent people from having to work so hard to maintain their focus on the ideas that we're trying to convey to them.

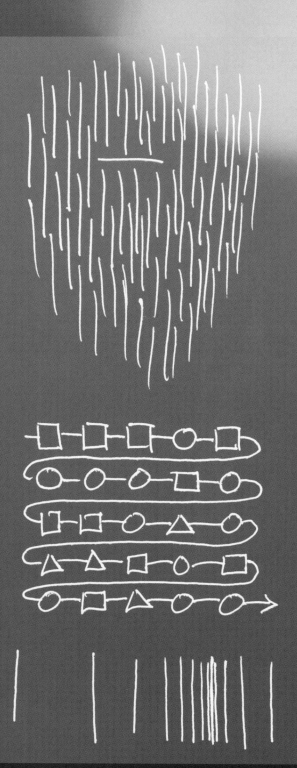

05.00.08 Our strategy in using creativity in our online messages is to break these patterns of the mundane that people subconsciously blur into the background of their conscious thought.

The essence of creativity's role in this process can be seen in this simple example:

_____
_____   _____
_____
_____
_____
_____
_____

Immediately we notice the break in the pattern.

Imagine the line representing a stream of information that's become monotonous to our minds. It all looks the same. It all sounds the same—even though it's not. Now compare this to the types of stimuli that people are exposed to in a typical Web experiences— HTML text on a flat-colored background—"page" after "page" after "page." Or maybe it's the latest trend in Web design with gratuitous eye candy—"page" after "page" after "page." Eventually we become numb to it all! We go into "scan mode," where we blur our minds and rush through information until a perceptual alarm goes off that tells us to stop and take notice.

In the end, we find that we have low comprehension of the messages we've experienced and an even lower level of motivation to respond to the message in some way.

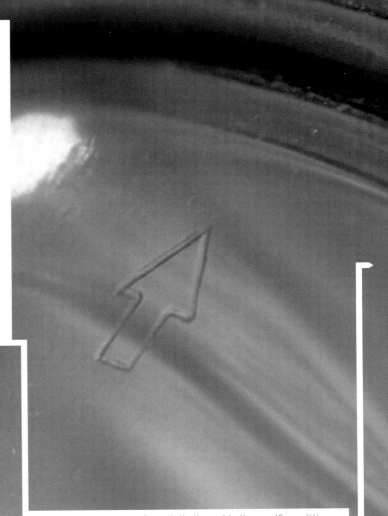

05.00.09 People don't choose to blur stimuli that are constant out of their minds; it's an involuntary phenomenon.

To the contrary, we often fight tooth and nail to stay engaged in a message. In the earlier example of the student listening to a boring lecture, the student understood that the professor had important facts buried within the drone of the lecture, yet he was unable to latch onto them because he couldn't stay "tuned in" to the message even though he tried.

Some of you may be thinking:

"Nice philosophy—so...how does creativity solve the problem if eventually any type of stimulus becomes mundane if it's sustained? What difference is there between a presentation that's based more on text than it is on graphics or other media?"

The beginning of the answer lies in the definition of the often misunderstood word *creativity* itself:

Creativity—productive originality, or producing and interposing something *unique* into a flow of stimuli that's constant.

05.00.10 The essence of creativity lies not in the specific qualities of a design, but in the fact that it introduces something unique and juxtaposes it to the other stimuli in the sea of that which has become perceptually, cognitively, and emotionally mundane (or blurred). In the example from 05.00.08, not only did I avoid the use of "graphics" to introduce creativity into the pattern of the mundane, but I also avoided using any stimulus at all! I demonstrated that the expression of creativity can be the *absence* of any stimulus whatsoever. Why? Because the absence of "line" in that *moment* introduced something unique to you that broke the pattern of the mundane within the flow of the column.

Did it work? Did you attend to my *anti*stimulus? Did you ponder the reason for its existence? Did your mind become engaged enough to comprehend, not so much the antistimulus, but the meaning that I've been trying to convey in these last few notions?

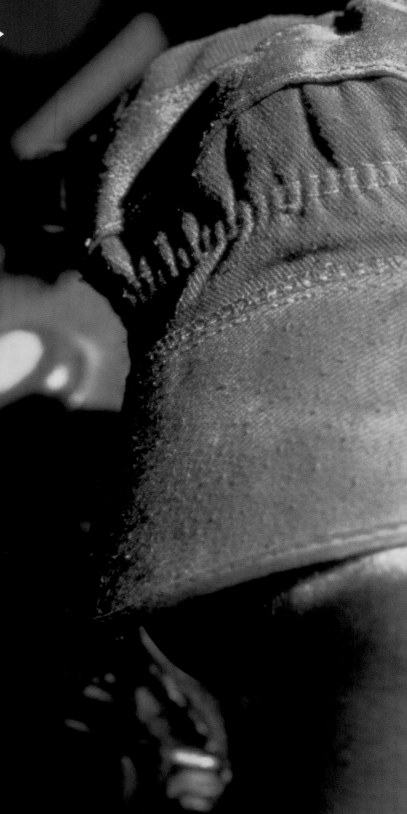

05.00.11 Creativity breaks the pattern of the mundane so that people are not only *willing* but also *able* to attend to our messages.

This is the primary role that I believe creativity plays in the way we communicate with people through our online messages. Their innate and conditioned responses to perceiving unique stimuli shocks them into awareness simply because a unique stimulus breaks the pattern of the mundane. This must take place not only at the onset of our messages—when we're attracting attention—but also throughout the development of our messages—when we're guiding people into comprehension. In the *inform* and *invoke* stages discussed in the previous three chapters, creativity becomes a powerful force to hold people's interest by making our messages more engaging and therefore more meaningful and compelling.

Well—there we have it! If only it ended there, it would be simple. Unfortunately, decorum and good taste would have us not resort to merely any tactic. For one thing, the unique stimulus that we present must *contribute to* and not detract from the message that we're trying to convey. For another, different people are equipped to maintain concentration in different ways. What might get the attention of one person would seem mundane to another. What might attract and hold the attention of a ten-year-old person is not likely to have the same effect on a thirty-year-old person (although it might). What might appropriately be used to attract people's attention at home might get them fired at work. Additionally, a stimulus might get negative attention versus positive attention.

The lesson? We must still strive to understand with whom it is we're interacting and then try to reach these people by shaping our creative ideas to be not only engaging to them but also appropriate for their situation and needs.

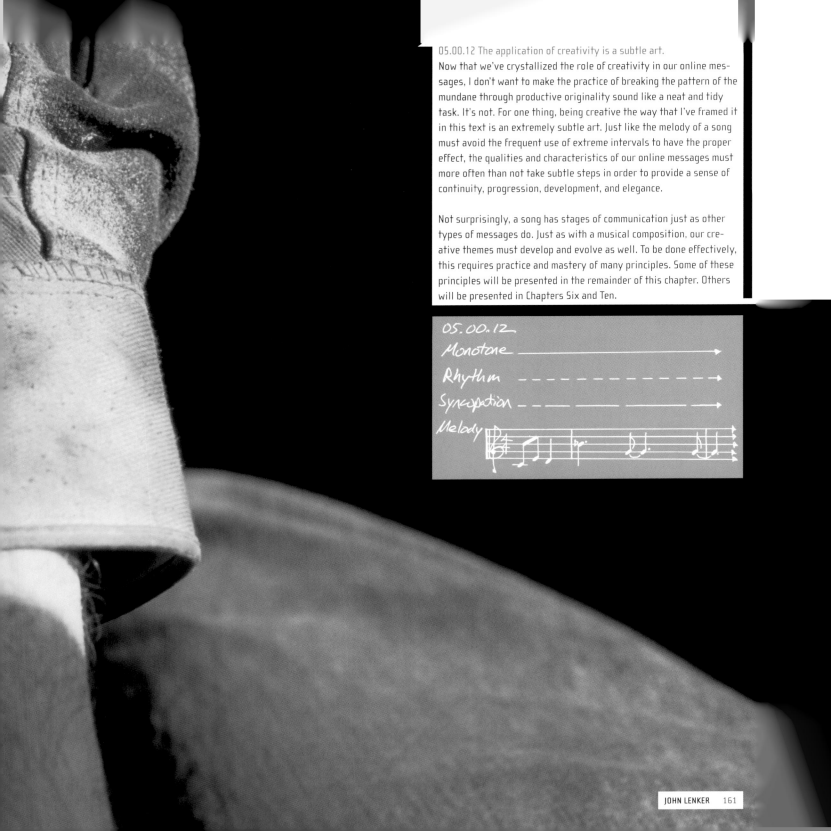

05.00.12 The application of creativity is a subtle art.

Now that we've crystallized the role of creativity in our online messages, I don't want to make the practice of breaking the pattern of the mundane through productive originality sound like a neat and tidy task. It's not. For one thing, being creative the way that I've framed it in this text is an extremely subtle art. Just like the melody of a song must avoid the frequent use of extreme intervals to have the proper effect, the qualities and characteristics of our online messages must more often than not take subtle steps in order to provide a sense of continuity, progression, development, and elegance.

Not surprisingly, a song has stages of communication just as other types of messages do. Just as with a musical composition, our creative themes must develop and evolve as well. To be done effectively, this requires practice and mastery of many principles. Some of these principles will be presented in the remainder of this chapter. Others will be presented in Chapters Six and Ten.

What makes music so engaging to the mind? Different people answer this question in different ways. There are, however, some foundational characteristics that are common to all[2] music, without which it could never be engaging.

> *Rhythm*—Breaking a sustained monotone into distinguishable units of hits and rests
> *Melody*—Substituting other tones from a modal scale in place of the monotone hits
> *Harmony*—Adding an array of complementary tones that add color to the melody and provide a context for it to move in
> *Orchestration*—Giving clarity, form, dynamics, emphasis, diction, character, voice, layer, and variation to a composition

By definition, a melody has both rhythm and temporal polyphony (tonal diversity over time). These are the minimum qualities required to make a melody distinguishable to people. A melody, or musical theme, is the idea that we're trying to communicate to people through a composition. Identifying a theme can be very tangible because it presents a finite statement like "Birds are heaven's flower blossoms." Its interpretation, however can be very subjective: "What's the composer thinking when making this statement? Where is this theme going? What is it leading to?"

[2] I'm primarily thinking about music that has a Western European Foundation.

05.01.01 In order for a composer to help an audience find meaning in a musical statement, he or she must often add harmony. Harmony frames a theme and provides the parameters within which an audience can seek interpretation of the theme.

Harmony adds dimension and elaborates on the color that a theme initially holds. Harmony can also be used to *recast* a theme in order to lead an audience into a deeper realization of a theme's potential.

Orchestration entails adding arrangement and instrumentation to a musical composition. Orchestration transforms a theme into a story. It writes the lines for the supporting characters and casts the players that will act out the parts. Orchestration is where the artfulness of subtlety can introduce the variations that are necessary to capture and hold an audience's attention while the story of the composer's theme unfolds.

Just as with music, the notions that flow into people's minds through our online messages should establish embraceable contexts for the ideas being presented. They should then present *variations* on those contexts and ideas until each person attains an ultimate overall comprehension of the underlying idea.

05.01.02 Interestingly—and I'm not trying to be religious here—the introduction of rhythm into a stimulus is reminiscent of the mythical prime creative act.

"In the beginning, God [*re*]created the *heaven* and the *earth* [...] and *darkness* was upon the face of the deep. [...] And God said, 'Let there be *light*' [...] and God divided the light from the darkness [...] and the *evening* and *morning* were the first *day*." —Genesis 01:01-05

When we give people limitless possibilities, we're in no way doing them any favors. When we present information as a constant, such as in endless singular columns of HTML text, for example, that information becomes perceptually intangible to people, and it subsequently overloads their minds.

Conversely, putting limits on a thing is really what gives that thing presence in people's minds. It defines it as being something that is *here* or *there*. Heaven without earth would be a constant and therefore would be nothing. Earth without heaven would be a constant and—while at the same time equaling infinity—would yet equal nothing. In other words, when we put limits on things (boundaries) these things becomes definable as quantifiable entities. The thing we call "earth" is only recognized as an entity because it has a space of emptiness around it. Likewise, the thing we call "day" is really only distinguishable by either the presence of light or its absence.

According to Abramic religions (Judaism, Christianity, and Islam), as well as many other world religions that purvey a creation story, when the God created heaven and earth, light and darkness, night and day—processions began that were fundamentally rhythmic.

CASE STUDY 5A

Adobe Studio

Address: http://studio.adobe.com/
Client: Adobe Systems
Experience Designers: Hillman Curtis Inc.

Communicating Community

Adobe Studio was established to exist as an online community resource for graphic design professionals and as an extension of Adobe.com, the online home to the graphics software company, Adobe. Adobe approached Hillman Curtis and his firm, to design this highly unique online resource. The goal was to organize and construct an environment that expressed characteristics of community and involvement while upholding high visual standards and expectations of the targeted audience.

Adobe Studio welcomes visitors to a clean, simplistic style with an underlying level of complexity beneath the visual surface. The visually inviting palette of warm hues draws people into the experience while a grid system is established with a series of hexagons acting as main navigation buttons. The purposeful choice of colors and shapes sets the stage for optimal content focus while implying structured guidance. The smooth, minimal animations extend content focus with interesting, yet subtle, sweeps of motion that invite people to watch them repeatedly without becoming bored. The lack of overuse allows these characteristics to break the pattern of the mundane and aid in comprehension of the design intent while invoking interest and curiosity. Hillman Curtis states:

"The goal was to create a design that could be used more organically. For example, the hexagons in the home page can be of any size and of any number, and filled with any content, [or] used as buttons to navigate anywhere. The idea was that the hexagons as an organic, changing group—the way they work together at different sizes and placement—become the identity. Again, in an attempt to reflect community."

Read our interview with Hillman Curtis online at:
http://www.trainofthoughts.com

05.01.03 The reason that boundaries are important is that stimuli that are all-encompassing are imperceptible—intangible.

If a bright light is turned on so that it floods out all shadow, that light becomes invisible—imperceptible. Likewise, if a sustained, audible tone is sounded, eventually it becomes inaudible. These fade into the pattern of the mundane.

What is needed to give both light and sound conscious presence are rests interspersed within each respective stimulus. For example, if light and sound are made to pulse in some way, they become perceptible. This injection of rests leads from the ambiguity of monotony to the clarity of diversity. Although very basic, the introduction of rhythm is the initial act of creativity. It interposes diversity among the invisible and inaudible constants. It's the most fundamental form of rhythm—an indefinite alteration between ons and offs, positives and negatives, ones and zeros.

DAY **night**　DAY **night**　DAY **night**　DAY **night** ...　　Rhythm
DAT_____ DAT_____ DAT_____ DAT_____ ...　　Rhythm

As a side note: I'm still waiting for the day when I hear the news that scientists have stopped trying to understand the universe as a reality that appeared out of nothingness and have begun to ponder it as a something-ness in which a nothingness suddenly appeared.

05.01.03

05.01.04 Measures of beats and rests establish the rhythm of a well-executed notion flow.

As indicated in 05.01.01, let's say that all of the information in an online resource was an enormous body of letters—a single, seemingly infinite word. Interestingly, this is how many ancient languages were rendered includeing Greek and Hebrew. Talk about a sustained monotone stimulus!

Here's the million dollar question. If it's considered a creative act to segment this stimulus into separate elements, why then isn't the presentation of segmented chunks of HTML text a sufficient expression of creativity? After all, this is common practice on the Web. It's known affectionately as *chunking*. Haven't I called the segmentation of a stimulus the prime creative act? I have! Furthermore, chunking is a practice usability experts espouse. This sounds very interesting—let's play out this scenario and see what happens:

> A seemingly endless stream of letters in an enormously long word is broken into a series of separate words. In music, these are known as *beats*.
> Each of these words is clustered into sentences. We'll equate these to what in music are known as *measures*.
> The sentences are combined to form paragraphs. In music, these are known as *phrases*.
> These paragraphs are grouped into chunks with headings In music, these are referred to as *sections*.
> The overall body of notions is broken into a series of pages so that each page only presents a moderate amount of information. In music, these are referred to as *movements*.

Great! We've definitely improved the situation. We *have* introduced a basic level of creativity. We've introduced an element of the unique into a constant stimulus . We've introduced visual segmentation to correspond with meaning. Now the mind has visual cues that help it make distinctions. The breaks between the words, sentences, paragraphs, chunks, and screens provide the *visual* rests that were desperately needed. It's easier to keep track of one's place while traversing the body of information. There's a sense of pacing to the stream of information, and this—as God alledgedly said—"is good."

05.01.05 By nature, rhythm forms repeating patterns.

Here's the bad news. You've got thirty screens full of this rhythmic textual presentation. After about a minute of reading through this material, the visual pattern that this rhythmic flow of information makes is beginning to become perceptually too familiar and is slipping into the backdrop of blurred stimuli that form the pattern of the mundane in a person's consciousness!

Unlike with printed text, when people try to engage in this information flow online, it quickly begins to wear on their minds. Their eyes become heavy. They begin to have trouble concentrating and keeping the information flow in the forefront of their minds. What's more, there are often a number of interspersed information chunks that either don't seem particularly relevant to some individual's comprehension of the overall idea, or just flat out don't seem to make any sense. Having to wrestle through these intermittent roadblocks to their optimal flow of concentration is wearisome in an already wearisome experience.

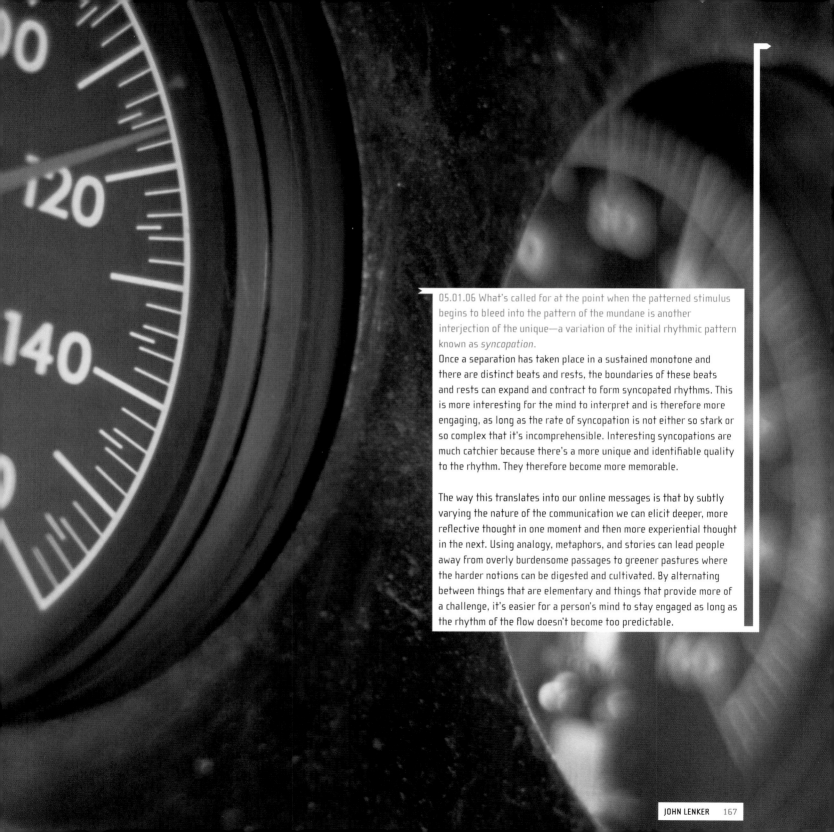

05.01.06 What's called for at the point when the patterned stimulus begins to bleed into the pattern of the mundane is another interjection of the unique—a variation of the initial rhythmic pattern known as *syncopation*.

Once a separation has taken place in a sustained monotone and there are distinct beats and rests, the boundaries of these beats and rests can expand and contract to form syncopated rhythms. This is more interesting for the mind to interpret and is therefore more engaging, as long as the rate of syncopation is not either so stark or so complex that it's incomprehensible. Interesting syncopations are much catchier because there's a more unique and identifiable quality to the rhythm. They therefore become more memorable.

The way this translates into our online messages is that by subtly varying the nature of the communication we can elicit deeper, more reflective thought in one moment and then more experiential thought in the next. Using analogy, metaphors, and stories can lead people away from overly burdensome passages to greener pastures where the harder notions can be digested and cultivated. By alternating between things that are elementary and things that provide more of a challenge, it's easier for a person's mind to stay engaged as long as the rhythm of the flow doesn't become too predictable.

05.01.07 No matter how much we try to syncopate opportunities for both experiential and reflective thought, if the writing is boring, it will inevitably begin to fade into the pattern of the mundane. Unfortunately, in the world of the Web, people will progressively struggle to pull it back into the forefront of their minds. Not unlike trying to listen to the boring lecture, trying to read page after page after page of sterile writing eventually gets wearisome. One very big reason for this is that every single sentence must be scanned and interpreted by the people in our audiences. This is the most labor-intensive form of accretion (gathering information) that we have. This is hard enough to do as it is. Do we really want to make everything that we present to the people that interact with our online messages feel like a lecture? Some of you may be thinking "No. Make it read more like a story. People have no trouble getting absorbed in stories." And you'd be right.

05.01.08 As melody combines patterned tonal variations to tell a musical story, our notions should provide tonal variations that combine to tell the story of an idea.

The distinction that I'm trying to make is between writing that comes across as being too technical and writing that comes across as being more creative. When we try to write creatively, we always write with an audience in mind. To make the writing engaging and interesting, we search for meaningful ways for our ideas to express themselves to people. The next degree of creativity, therefore, is to morph the syncopated monotone of a rough idea into meaningful tonal diversity. The result of this transformation is an idea that expresses itself in a diversity of ways through our notions. Like a good melody, we try to tell the story of our idea through our notions in ways that people are likely to find "catchy."

05.01.09

This is how we might syncopate the flow of information to aid attentiveness:

| = Easy, fun, experiential content

△ = Neatly packaged content that presents new information, but in a stimulating way.

□ = Reflective content that forces people to think.

⬠ = Summative challenge (test) to validate that comprehension and retention have occurred.

05.01.09 Just as harmony supports melody, the way we build around our ideas supports the central theme of our messages.

In music, although a lone melody can be very attractive, after a while—you guessed it—it becomes familiar, and it can easily fade into the pattern of the mundane as well. One way of trying to delay this eventuality is by introducing textual elements that harmonize with the central theme of the message. In music, a lone melody often lacks the color, depth, and nuances that are brought to it by adding the chords of harmony as an underlament. In the writing we do for our notions, we harmonize the central themes of our ideas with analogies, metaphors, and anecdotal stories that we interject to strengthen the presence that our ideas take in the minds of people.

Again, the aim of our messages is to guide people into comprehension of our ideas. As discussed in Chapter Three, these devices act as associative learning devices. They help people bridge the gap between what they currently understand and the understanding that we are trying to lead them to. For these types of interjections to be effective, however, it's essential that there's at the very least a basic understanding of the frame of mind that the people in a particular audiences set or subset have.

05.01.10 Expanding on a central idea with text online has some negative side effects.

While the harmonization of our ideas with textual representations of analogy, metaphor, and other literary techniques does introduce unique cognitive stimuli, there are no *perceptual* changes in the pattern that the visual stimulus has presented. Although using writing to provide cognitive aids solves the problem of helping people get a handle on our ideas, this practice unfortunately creates problems.

No matter how interesting what we've written is to people, they will still inevitably grow weary of the constant stimulus of our words flowing into their minds. As a result, people will either stop to ponder what they've taken in, or they'll become distracted by other competing stimuli as the impact of the words that they're reading fades into the pattern of the mundane.

Although we do indeed want people to intermittently rest from absorbing new information in order to productively reflect upon our ideas, this reflection is not very productive if it's a result of having overstimulated the visual senses.

By doing a good job supporting the central idea of our message by harmonizing it with several written examples, we have, in effect, made the presentation of our text much longer. The result is that we've created *more* of the stimulus that is causing the fatigue in the first place. This is the very fatigue that our interjections were intended to remedy, and is an example of what's referred to as a *vicious cycle*. By trying to make one thing better, we make other things worse. What we need is to somehow introduce what is known as a *virtuous* cycle. By making one thing better, it in effect makes other things better as well.

The problem is that we've only been able to take an idea so far through the melodic and harmonic voices that HTML text has to offer. We've done this to the degree that we wonder if there aren't more *efficient* alternatives to a strictly text-based presentation.

The answer is to develop our ideas in textual form in the most concise way possible, and then endeavor to harmonize it with supplementary expressions of meaning through other media elements in a way that creates the most synergistic and optimum effect on our audience's senses, minds, and emotions.

05.01.11 While composers orchestrate their music through arrangement and instrumentation, experience designers must orchestrate their online messages through the selection and layering of appropriate media elements.

When a musical composition—which is defined as having melody, harmony, and sequence—is orchestrated, two beautiful things happen. The first is that the composition is *formally* structured in such a way that the story that the melody has to tell can completely unfold with an introduction, realization, and confirmation—a beginning, middle, and end. In effect it's endowed with the power to attract, inform, and invoke an audience emotionally. This is yet another example of the threefold communication model that we've been talking about in previous chapters.

The second beautiful thing that happens is that the notes in each chord of the composition are divided into separate parts and are assigned to appropriate instruments. These instruments are selected on the basis of which one is the most appropriate vehicle to communicate specific aspects of the musical message. In fact, the entire art of those who orchestrate music is that of insightfully interpreting the meanings of musical ideas and then structuring fully developed musical messages by employing appropriate instrumentation.

One of the most fundamental ramifications of this process is that *layers of diversity* are added to the composition and bring the dynamics, emphasis, tone, tambour, and color which introduce the nuances which will cyclically break the pattern of the mundane.

In this very same manner, it's the art of those who craft the notion-flows that constitute our online messages to find the relationship between layered media elements that will most synergistically and effectively convey the meaning of an idea.

05.01.12 The synergistic orchestration of multimedia elements is the most powerful tool that we have to enable people to engage in optimum *cognitive* flow.

I do believe that it's fundamental to an effective Web experience to divide the expression of a central idea into boiled-down chunks of text. I also believe, however, that words should be used to do what words do best—help people gain specific conceptual insights that other forms of media might not necessarily make explicit.

To help support the central idea and to provide sufficiently unique stimuli to continually be breaking the pattern of the mundane, I believe that other forms of media should often be used. These elements should be orchestrated to be interposed between the textual elements that represent the central theme. Text that falls outside this central theme can often be replaced with media elements that have the power to manage the focus of people's attention.

As the cliché goes, if a picture paints a thousand words, why use words? There aren't many images that take as long to load into a Web browser as it takes for a person to read a thousand words.

Taken from another perspective, if musical underscoring can give a person instant recognition of the emotional tone a notion is trying to set or an overall message is trying to establish, why use words to try and set this tone? For anyone other than the most artful poets, the chance of successfully conveying meaning is greatly diminished when using words over music in order to establish emotional tone. If an animated model represents a process in such a way that it can be understood within seconds, why impose words when the interpretation can take minutes or longer?

05.01.13 Using HTML text alone will always fall short of providing optimum flow experiences.

As meticulous as we were in 05.01.04 through 05.01.09, and as hard as we tried, we were not able to fully utilize the metaphor of music for purely textual presentations. It's impossible because orchestration offers *so* many variations that allow a composition to live and function on multiple levels of awareness. Text alone numbs the senses and fades into the pattern of the mundane.

Remember that Krome Barratt wrote that an elegant design is one that functions well on many different levels of awareness. Remember also that Don Norman said "design should be like telling a story." These two statements alone should clue all of us in to the fact that creativity is the hallmark of not only successful online communication but successful communication, period! This being the case, it's time we all accepted a very important reality—one that encapsulates the key insight of my philosophy's message:

Neither humanity nor creativity can be separated, nor can they be contained. They're both explosive with variety. Their state of being can neither be predetermined nor legislated. Humanity is something that emerges from creativity; creativity is something that emerges from humanity. They both insist on reaching out passionately to one another. This is as fundamental and as essential to life as the relationship between heaven and earth, light and darkness, day and night, God and humanity.

Contrary to the views of some usability experts, I believe that people struggle perceptually, cognitively, and emotionally with experiences that are stripped void of creativity because they go against our diversely expressive nature. To attempt to do so is bad business.

Although I understand concerns related to bandwidth and other limitations as mentioned in Chapter Three, I believe that the issue of bandwidth limitations is largely misunderstood and often serves as the red herring that some usability folks use to maintain the status quo. I also believe that when bandwidth issues do come into play, necessity must become the mother of invention—or at least *innovation.* And for reasons outlined in this chapter, I say that creativity in our Web experiences is a necessity! Furthermore, I believe that for those who truly understand how creativity should be applied to Web experience design, our notions and flows can be designed to deliver the variety that the human mind and spirit cry out for while at the same time remain within the tolerances of existing technologies.

SPOTLIGHT ON:

LYNDA WEINMAN

It's hard to have a conversation related to online creativity without eventually having the name Lynda Weinman come up. Lynda is one of the pillars of the media design community. Long before others followed her lead, Lynda had a vision for making online content more enjoyable and more meaningful. She's been relentless in presenting her vision to the world through her interesting seminars and her thought-provoking books. Most notably, Lynda is a cofounder of the exceedingly popular Flash-Forward seminars that are held throughout the United States and the world. Lynda has stimulated a lot of thinking and has nourished many fledgling media designers. Through her encouragement, mentorship, and sponsorship, many of these people have become notable industry leaders in their own right. My interview with Lynda Weinman follows:

Lenker: What has motivated you to so deliberately nurture the online community toward appropriate creative expression?

Weinman: I love sharing information, especially about things that excite me. I believe that online communication is the single most significant advancement in publishing history, next to the invention of the printing press and movable type. Online communication has [changed] and will change our world. It's an honor to be able to teach people how to tap into it.

Lenker: In what ways do you see people being unproductive with their employment of creativity on the Web?

Weinman: There are those people who think that adding bells and whistles (Flash, Java, animated gif, sound, etc.) makes their site creative. The way to approach using creativity as a design element is to be conscious of your design hierarchy in terms of what you want to say or sell. Once you know that, the right solution will be based on a need, not on a preconception that something external will make it "cool."

Lenker: What are some general examples of ways that creativity has been employed to make online content much more valuable than would otherwise be the case?

Weinman: Sites like potterybarn.com, gap.com, and abercrombieandfitch.com use incredible photography to set the right mood for their products. They've invested in a creative approach to displaying their wares that makes their products more appealing. They didn't simply put their catalog online—they tai-

lored their site to fit their content. You can find zillions of mom-and-pop clothing sites that don't generate the same inviting feeling because they didn't preplan how to make their merchandise look good visually to their customers.

Lenker: What are some general examples of inappropriate ways that creativity is being applied within the context of online resources?

Weinman: I know that Flash gets dinged a lot because it can be over-the-top, too flashy, and actually detract from the purpose of the site. I'd like to compare tiffany.com's Flash work to that of barneys.com. Both are upscale sites and stores that chose to use Flash technology. Tiffany.com is much more conducive to viewing the catalog and getting the actual names and prices of items. Barneys.com is more of a fashion-show, mood-setting kind of site. Both are beautiful and visually engaging, but to me, the Tiffany site is much more practical. I think the days of creating a mood or style, instead of getting down to the business of making sales are probably gone in the current economic climate.

Lenker: What do you see as the solution to raising people's [...]

Read the entire interview online at:
http://www.trainofthoughts.com

Learn more about Lynda Weinman at:
http://www.lynda.com

Buy *designing web graphics.3* today at:
http://www.trainofthoughts.com

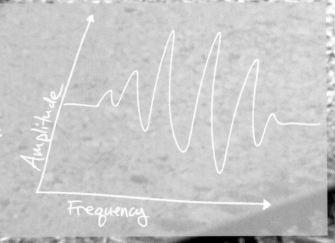

Note:
We must find the propper balance between _amplitude_ — which determines how intense (loud) that a stimulus is in a person's mind, and the _frequency_ — which regulates the pacing of the stimulous over time. The objective is to create a dynamic which builds from moments of serenity to moments of excitement and then back again.

05.02 The Roles of Creativity When Attracting, Informing, and Invoking

Just as a composer does with a musical composition, media designers should provide a *sensory* experience that unfolds with an introduction, realization, and confirmation of central themes and ideas. This unfolding parallels the attract, inform, and invoke stages of our online messages that we've been exploring in Chapters Two through Four. In Chapter One, we established that the goal of an experience design is to guide people into comprehension of our messages. In this chapter, we've seen that a big part of guiding comprehension is using creativity to keep people engaged in an information flow. What we turn to now is a discussion regarding how creativity expresses itself in the various stages of a message.

05.02.01 The most common way that people gain exposure to our online resources is through the investigation of the various options in the list that results from a search-engine query.

People essentially begin an *auditioning* process. According to Krome Barratt, when people are in these types of situations, they "compare new experiences with past ones to look for similarities that help [them] determine value." Based on this comparison, people make instantaneous judgments regarding what Reeves and Nass refer to as *valence* and *intensity*. These answer the questions: Is this good or bad for me? How good or bad is it?

Needless to say, to be a contender in this auditioning process where acceptance or rejection is instantaneous, the introductory notions must not only make a positive impression but also a *strong* positive impression. If the online resource makes only a positive impression, it's more likely that a person will set it aside in order to compare it to other possibilities. If the initial notion(s) makes a fairly *strong* positive impression, however, it's more likely that a person will become engaged in the flowpath and will forget about other options.

This strong first impression is important, but must be followed up with progressively more engaging and valuable notions. The reason is that the initial strong positive impression has set in motion a pattern of anticipation. When this occurs, a person isn't likely to abandon a flowpath unless there's a bad violation of expectation.

For this strong positive initial impression to occur, it's essential that a person perceives the introduction to a message as breaking the pattern of the mundane.

05.02.02 How do we break the pattern of the mundane when introducing people to our Web enterprises in the *attract* stage of our online messages?

Most people's solution to this question is to produce things that they view to be "exciting and cool!" They figure that the opposite of being mundane is being "exciting and cool."

Unfortunately this usually isn't the answer to the question. The reason it's not is that even the most "exciting and cool" stimuli become mundane after they become familiar. In a world where everything's exciting, we actually begin to notice the things that are *boring*. In a *Las Vegas* world, things that are dull stand out. When people's senses are overstimulated, they become overloaded, whether there are bells, whistles, and flashing lights everywhere or only text-based arrays everywhere.

No. The secret to breaking the pattern of the mundane isn't to present something exciting but to interject into the mundane, or familiar, something that's unique. It's the only way to raise a person's mind from "scan-mode" to "engage-mode."

There's only one method that I know of to come by the formula for constructing a notion to have the desired effect. This is to conduct an audience analysis and reconcile it with what competing Web enterprises are doing with *their* online resources. The information gleaned from this exercise can then serve as a basis for the formulation of the creative construction of the notion (see Chapters Seven and Ten).

05.02.03 Creating a strong first impression results from finding unique ways to address the criteria unearthed through analysis. More than merely touching on the quality, quantity, relevance, and clarity (Q-Q-R-C) issues outlined in Chapters Three and Four, an effective experience design will create a strong positive impression by virtue of its productive originality, or uniqueness. In other words, beyond being helpful and polite by making our transmissions of meaning of good quality, quantity, relevance, and clarity, we want to make the transmission of meaning both interesting and intriguing.

The goal is to formulate initial notions to give people the impression that the Web enterprises that they're interacting with stand head and shoulders above other competing systems in a given category. Again, the goal of introduction is to attract people into continuing with a sustained notion-flow. To summarize past discussions, this is done by providing:

> An aesthetically gratifying environment—When given a choice and all else being equal, people will choose to interact with the online resources that provide the *strongest* level of appropriate aesthetic variation. Reeves and Nass support this view when they say that "visually dynamic messages will create more favorable responses [...] than visually static messages."

> Motivational relevance—The way productive originality is used to help people find easy social, emotional, and consumptive identification is of prime concern. Online messages that strive to reach out to people on all of these levels stand the best chance of building an emotional bridge with these people. People seek long-term relationships with online resources with which they can closely identify. This identification can be established through the unique employment of media elements that reinforce a person's *own* unique sense of self.

> Cognitive congruence—People are most comfortable in communication when they feel like they're being "talked to" in a voice that's easy to identify with. I'm referring to the way that all media elements can be orchestrated to "speak" to a person in an appropriate social and emotional tone. This reinforces a person's identity and sense of self. This type of communication requires less reflective interpretation. Some people just feel better when they're greeted with, "Hey, man! How's it goin'?" than they do when they hear, "Well hello, sir. And how are you doing on this fine spring morning?"

05.02.04 When we strive to build a realization of an idea in the *inform* stage of our online messages, we're trying to find the best conceptual approach.

At this stage, we've already qualified people's interests and have worked with them to determine an appropriate flowpath for them to follow. The work at this stage is to provide resources for our interactive flowpath management systems (flowstem) to procedurally prescribe the most appropriate antidote for a given cognitive ailment.

Since the simple aim of our communication is to help people to "get it" (or REAL-ize it), we must try to identify and overcome any obstacle in each person's mind that prevents him or her from really attaining enlightenment. The *inform* stage is also referred to as *realization,* and aims to make ideas *real* in people's minds. In light of this, we must progressively add layer upon layer to the substantiation of our central message until people have a real sense of both cognitive and emotional fulfillment.

The work of creativity in this effort is to try to find new metaphorical and anecdotal antibiotics to attack incomprehension so that the substance of a train of thoughts isn't unnecessarily protracted. The goal is never to prolong a person's interaction with our notions but to move them to the closing stage of confirmation/invocation in an *appropriate* and reasonable timeframe. Although this doesn't necessarily mean that a message will consist of a contracted sequence of notions, it does mean that people won't feel like it's dragging on and on.

05.02.05 Creativity helps people *realize* what ideas mean by adding dimension to the central theme.
Rosenfled and Morville state

"Some sites are thought provoking. [...] Great writing and intelligent page layout aren't what's obvious about these sites; their ideas are. The intangible qualities of this type of site are its quality writing, copy editing, and overall ability to communicate ideas effectively."

There are so many approaches and angles to take when trying to help someone understand a concept or idea. Creativity comes in when we try to formulate the individual notions to do a good job of communicating a thought in that moment in the life of an idea. This formulation process is essentially the same as the orchestration process highlighted in the 05.01 series. The job is to take the portion of the central theme that extends through the notion, and then add the underlying harmonization that will put this particular part of the idea in the best light for a person.

Deciding what angle to take is an important part of the formulation process, but deciding how to use media elements to add the "instrumentation" to the chords is just as important. As outlined above, a notion can't consist of mere HTML text alone; that would cause the expression of the harmony to get too lengthy, and people would struggle to keep their minds from blurring the text into the background pattern of the mundane.

Instead, the task becomes that of examining competing online resources that endeavor to express similar meaning. The task then becomes that of trying to discover a more effective means of expressing that meaning.

05.02.05
We need to prepare to be able to "hit" a person's mind from a number of different (angles) directions to ensure that comprehension occurs. (see Figure 02.00.06).

Once there was a guy who went to a job interview...

It's like riding a bike.

HUMAN MIND

Remember when you aced your first math test?

Begin at step #1 and pro...

According to your profile, you would really enjoy...

It's like a hot knife in butter.

05.02.06 Creativity provides meaningful conceptual constructs that cause ideas to make strong impressions on people's memories.
"Shapes and textures, souls, words and phrases resonate in the mind. The process of trigger and response that forms and informs our awareness is based on resonance. Words like 'compassion' and 'empathy' record the human capacity for resonance [because they reveal that how another person feels can be identified with.]"

—Krome Barratt, *Logic & Design In Art, Science & Mathematics*

How will we lay hold of territory within a person's mind? Once we've touched a person's mind with one of our notions, we can't hang around to make sure our idea stays locked up in there. Instead, we spend our resources trying to make our transmissions of meaning so effective that people simply can't forget them.

While it's important to leverage prior conceptual structures to aid with comprehension, this is not enough to make a new idea memorable. For a person to remember a concept by grafting it into his or her existing conceptual framework, that something must present itself as being unique enough to justify being given its own somewhat permanent residence in a person's long-term memory.

The ways that this uniqueness can express itself in our formulation of notions is almost limitless. For one thing, almost any aspect of a notion can be singled out to be given special treatment. Beyond that, there are almost unlimited approaches to transforming any one of those aspects into a memorable stimulus.

CASE STUDY 5B

KobeTwo

Address: http://www.adidas.com/kobe/
Client: Adidas
Experience Designers: SBI and Company

Brilliance. Above and Below the Ankle.

KOBETWO is the Adidas clothing and shoe line designed for the famed NBA player, Kobe Bryant. Bryant, who plays for the Los Angeles Lakers, was approached by Adidas to assist in creating a signature shoe and clothing line. SBI and Company's goal was to establish a personal connection with the target audience, comprised of young athletic males seeking stylish performance footwear. To attract people and make this connection, they utilized Kobe as a narrator. He talks to his audiences about the ideas behind his line—specifically regarding the design, intention, and focus of the KOBETWO brand.

The story of the shoe's development is told through the use of voice and music audio, imagery, and animation. It's unfolding is syncopated in that it continually shifts accent in composition from Kobe to KOBETWO. This method, blended with the art of storytelling, allows for greater mental digestion of the brand message while maintaining interest through subtle variations. The central theme of the message is further supported by presenting a visual style that's congruent with the shoe design—simplistic, clean, and fluid. The minimalism and distinct grid suggest an air of elegance, while subtle animations of muted transparent boxes introduce a layer of dimension that exists in Kobe as an individual and as a player.

As the design story informatively unfolds, Kobe reveals the design sketches, concepts, and influences of the shoes and clothing while providing further explanation of the process. The sneak peak into the development and inspirations of the shoe creates an extended visual memory while leaving a lasting impression on the audience.

Read our interview with SBI and Company online at:
http://www.trainofthoughts.com

05.02.07 Creativity confirms the ideas contained in online messages and reinforces them in people's minds.

Creativity also helps people interpret, comprehend, and remember them. If we've been effective in our transmission of meaning in our flow of notions through the *attract* and *inform* stages of our communication model, it's been because we've found associative-learning approaches that both triggered existing knowledge structures and encoded new information into long-term memory. Now in the *invoke* stage of our message, an even more substantial expression of the unique must be used to drive home the key insight.

The goal of this last application of creativity to the online communication process is to elevate the status of our *new* transmission of meaning *above* the prior knowledge that a person had regarding the subject. The combined effect of the key insight and its creative expression should be that people are left with a very profound sense of enlightenment and enjoyment.

05.02.08 When the key insight comes, it must be profound to be powerful and compelling.

The purpose of our three-stage communication model is to tell the story of our idea complete with a beginning, middle, and end. The job of this *end* part is to

> Summarize the overall message in as neat and tidy a conceptual package as possible
> Recast the interpretation of a concept that people already have
> Compel people both cognitively and emotionally to respond to the call to action

People recognize the story form as being a cognitive script. When they encounter it, they can't help but set in motion a pattern of anticipation. Patrons of our online resources *expect* that the rules of what is essentially *drama* will be employed by our online messages—just as the story form mandates. As a result, a substantial dramatic peak needs to occur toward the end of the presentation of our messages where a person can attain a sense of *emotional* gratification. Otherwise those who follow along to this stage will experience disappointment, violation of expectation, and letdown. Their reaction may best be expressed in a statement such as:

"You're kidding me. That's IT!? I went through all that, and all I get from this darn resource is this!?!"

The fact is that we need to give people a sense that their time has been worth some effort. This is why we need to save our best creative, mundane-pattern-breaking act for last. We must drive people from the fringe to the very center of the realization that our communication with them has not only been valuable but also essential to their own personal lives. After all, the magician always saves the best act for the very last!

05.03 Summary

In this chapter we've learned that creativity doesn't have as much to do with the way media elements are treated as it does with the role that these elements play in our online messages.

Because sustained stimuli eventually become constants that slip below the threshold of people's abilities to make perceptual, cognitive, or emotional differentiations, people cognitively blur these stimuli. Web enterprises must therefore employ creativity to introduce stimuli that are unique in order to continually refocus people's concentration on the idea that's being presented through the various notions in an online message.

As with musical compositions, introducing subtle variations in the way we orchestrate the expression of meaning has a lot to do with helping people to maintain both interest and focus. What's more, the way we interpose various media elements in the midst of the textual components of our notions has much to do with conserving people's abilities to stay perceptually, cognitively, and emotionally engaged.

Finally, the synergistic strengths of properly combined media elements can contribute greatly toward attracting and holding people's focused concentration as we lead them through the attract, inform, and invoke stages of our online messages.

In the next chapter, we'll address specific design tactics that, can maximize the success of the refocusing process that productive originality is intended to facilitate.

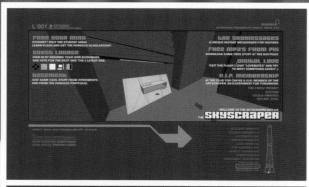

05.01 – http://www.themagicmountain.com/
Themagicmountain.com creates a sense of pacing and rhythm through the use of animation, variation in color schemes, various imagery, and photographs.

05.00.10 – http://skyscraper.paregos.com/
Skyscraper is the representational site of Paregos media design and uses metaphoric references of a building to structure the experience while dressing it in a fresh and fun style.

05.02.03 – http://www.sabrinawardharrison.com/
Sabrina Ward Harrison's Web experience infuses narrative with expressive art by using her colorful, dramatic artwork to tell her story and generate interest for her book, art, and teaching.

05.01.02 – http://www.absolut.com/
Absolut.com is an online experience marketing various flavors of Absolut vodka. The enterprise employs precise doses of creativity by blending pacing and rhythm in perfect harmony with engaging content and interactivity.

CHAPTER 06

"The presence of matter determines the structure of space."

—*Bernard Riemann, German mathematician*

The Time/Screen-Space Continuum:
Designing Perceptually Experiential Media

The universe in which we live is not at all fixed but is variable. It flexes. It ebbs. It flows. Moreover, no object in the universe exists in a vacuum, as previously supposed. Not only is everything connected, but in fact the very presence of one object bends the existence of everything else around it. The time/space continuum flexes *around* an object traveling through it. The degree to which it flexes is a function of the mass and velocity of the object itself.

What this concept means to our study of designing perceptually experiential[1] media is profound. As a person's mind travels through a message in the time/*screen-space* continuum in the universe of the Web, the *expression* of an idea must bend to accommodate that particular mind. The degree to which the message bends is a function of a person's cognitive mass and intellectual velocity.

As outlined in Chapter Five, we must find the best way to creatively *flex* online messages not only to attract people's interest but also to continually refocus their concentration on the information flow. This refocusing effort must persist until each person comprehends the message that's being conveyed. Actually formulating online messages to convey the *meaning* of ideas experientially through media elements can be quite challenging, however.

Challenging as it may be, it's the mission of an experience design team to determine the overall qualities of and relationships between a set of media elements that express an idea both spatially (within a singular screen-space) and temporally (across a progression of screen-spaces).

[1] See 02.00.05 and 02.01.06 for an understanding of the idea of *experiential*.

06.00.01 Because many experience designers view design for the Web as an extension of print design, much of the multimedia that's produced for the Web is perceptually ineffective.

The reason is that when we follow the print paradigm online, we create unconscious perceptual expectations that the Web medium has difficulty following through on. People *expect* physical documents to have a certain set of affordances, but documents online instead behave in ways that are incongruent with our perceptual conditioning regarding how they *should* behave. When we try to duplicate print media electronically, we strive to make them live up to the standards that are set in the *print medium.* This is almost impossible, however, because of limitations in the way that information must be transmitted and displayed online.

Although these limitations manifest themselves in many ways, one manifestation can be seen in the way people make visual comparisons between two or more "pages" of information. It's not as easy to flip back and forth, so to speak, in order to quickly make comparisons between Web "pages," because there's generally too much of a delay between views. Being able to quickly make comparisons between spatial arrangements of information, however, *is* a vital part of how people interpret and comprehend ideas. In light of this, providing people with ways of making these comparisons that work efficiently within the electronic medium of the Web is very important. When we come up with good ways of doing this online, however, they inevitably will involve departures from practices commonly employed in print media.

Another example of how electronic versions of print media violate people's perceptual expectations relates to the style and nature of typical print layouts. People have come to almost expect several large continuous-tone images (photographic quality images) on every "page." The trouble is that they *also* come to perceptually expect instant gratification when trying to access layouts containing these images. People want it to seem just as easy as turning the page in a book or magazine.

The problem is—and now I'm sounding like a usability consultant— that except for those who have broadband, latency issues on the Internet don't typically allow instant gratification when dealing with large continuous-tone images. It's not that we can't employ continuous-tone images online—we can. It's just that we must have a good rationale for using them within the context of a given online resource, we must employ good production technique, and we must make allowances for those who will inevitably have latency issues.

06.00.01

Making a visual comparison between items on two physical pages involves two distinct actions—sliding and focusing. We do these comparisons very quickly!

slide

focus

focus

The nature of the limited screen-space is such that we can't perform this instinctive slide/focus process very quickly online. Several other actions in addition to slide and focus must be performed when viewing print-style layouts online. This interrupts optimum cognitive flow.

Screen Space | Screen Space
Print | Space

06.00.02 People's frustration with latency problems isn't a matter of impatience, but a matter of conditioning.

Although it may seem as if people who use the Internet are really impatient, impatience isn't the problem. Our frustration is the result of experientially programmed neural subroutines in our brains.

These subroutines keep tabs on how long certain tasks are supposed to take and alert us if things take longer than they're supposed to. When the paradigm we're led to follow tells us that we're dealing with electronic *documents*, our unconscious expects them to *behave* like physical documents. This is a problem. Our brains are accustomed to being able to flip a physical page and get instant results, and when instant access isn't achieved our neural subroutines send out an alarm signal to our consciousness, warning us that something has gone wrong.

As a result, neural responders begin to send out stress signals, which trigger our adrenal glands. A fight-or-flight response then ensues. It's as if our subconscious was telling us, "Hey, this isn't going so well—maybe somebody's trying to kill us or something, my precious." Our rational mind quells these fears, but the energy that's built up to deal with the potential threat needs to vent somewhere, so it gets expressed as frustration.

06.00.03 The Web does have a role in helping people access information that's been designed for the print medium.

After all, the Web has made it much, much easier to gain access to documents designed for the print medium. Leveraging the Web as a distribution channel for documents such as Adobe® PDF files, which are primarily intended to be printed and then read, is a very smart idea. But by failing to move away from the safety and comfort of the print paradigm for resources that are intended to be interacted with online, we're inevitably left with poor substitutes for printed materials instead of powerful engines that can facilitate understanding.

What the online community is going to benefit from the most in the future isn't mere reference materials but smart *knowledge modules* that can be intelligently activated to grow people's understanding.

06.00.04 The ineffectiveness of the way rich media elements have been used in the past has caused usability experts to steer Web enterprises away from employing rich media elements in the future. As previously stated, I understand the latency concerns of those in the usability camp. But despite what these multimedia detractors might say, multimedia elements *can be* and *must be* interposed among textual expressions of meaning if for no other reason than that people need the emotional stimulation that perceptual diversity offers. The task becomes that of finding new, more effective methods of both formulating and leveraging these media elements.

To get things moving in the right direction, those who design Web experiences will need to have old ideas regarding how to design screen-spaces overwritten with new ideas that provide a theoretical foundation for the twenty-first century. This is of the utmost importance. After all, media elements are the avenues through which we gain access to people's minds to express our thoughts, concepts, and ideas. Media is where the rubber of our ideas, so to speak, meets the road of people's minds.

For those who still subscribe to the philosophy that rich media elements are anathema on the Web, here's what I hope is a thought-provoking question. Which is better—to frustrate people because information they've tried to access doesn't appear instantly, or to frustrate them because the information that they've accessed instantly isn't helping them build comprehension or enthusiasm for our ideas, even after minutes or hours of "page-turning"?

The obvious answer is that neither option is better—nor is anything that exists on the continuum between these two extremes. What's needed is a solution that exists on a higher plane than the dilemma itself. What's needed is a new paradigm for expressing our ideas to people through our online messages.

06.00.04
In the late 1990s, dynamic and stimulating online resources were viewed as being diametrically opposed to fast performance.

Dynamic / Slow ←——— OPPOSED ———→ Static / Fast

In the twenty-first century, static, boring online resources won't be associated with good performance, but with bad design.

06.00.05 We need new and innovative media-design paradigms to match a new medium.

As stated in Chapters Three and Four, the rigidness of fixed-form paradigms such as either a building's architecture or the printed page are inadequate for the Web. What's needed is a paradigm that more closely matches the variable and sequential comprehension needs of the individuals who interact with our online resources. There are many such paradigms from which to choose. The paradigm itself isn't important. What's important is that the conceptual model an experience designer chooses must have built-in flexibility.

For myself, and as Chapter Five foreshadowed, the best paradigm that illustrates the need for precise expressions of an idea in the moment, while at the same time illustrating the need to interactively blend these moments into a meaningfully fluid whole, is the paradigm of *improvisational music orchestration* and *performance.*

In the same way the chord that harmony and melody strike is a moment in the life of a song, the thought that meaning and expression strike is a moment in the life of an idea. Although a song's underlying melody and harmony are composed before a performance, during a performance much adaptation can happen, depending on the inspiration of the moment and the interactive feedback of a responsive audience. As a result, the musical idea can express itself in a variety of ways through the various instruments in an ensemble.

To prepare for a performance, a music composition can be orchestrated to lay a tonal foundation upon which each of the various instruments can improvise during the performance itself. Similarly, an online message can be orchestrated to set a cognitive and emotional tone upon which the expression of an idea can be improvised to accommodate the unique needs of each individual interacting with it.

Because our thoughts are cognitive constructions and because communication—musical or otherwise—is an act of expression, I believe that the nature of any good paradigm for online transmissions of meaning must be both *constructivist* and *expressionistic.*

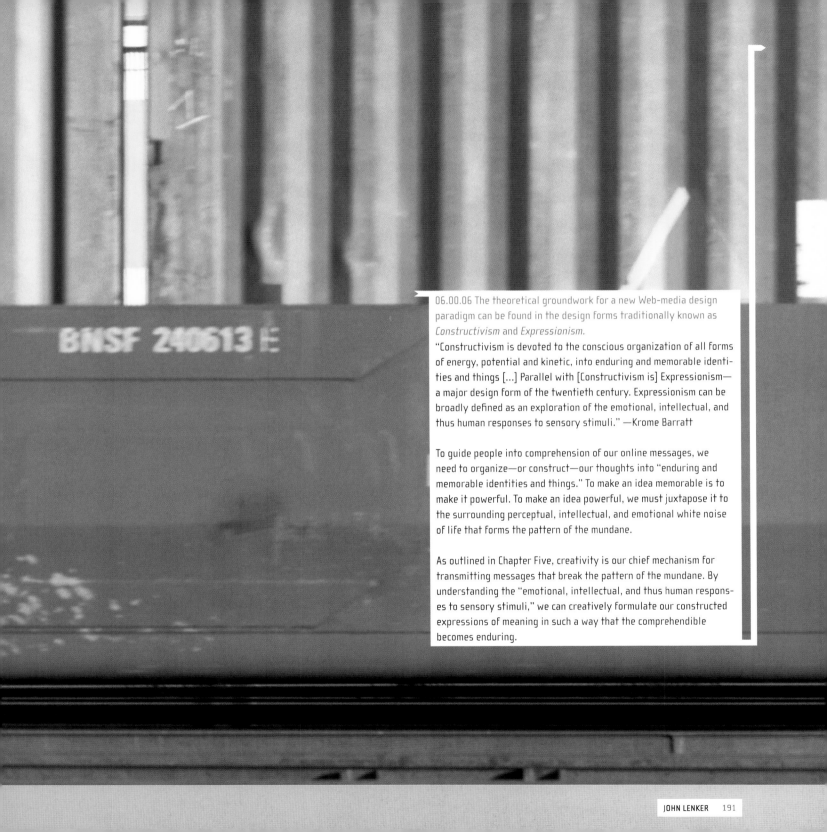

06.00.06 The theoretical groundwork for a new Web-media design paradigm can be found in the design forms traditionally known as *Constructivism* and *Expressionism.*

"Constructivism is devoted to the conscious organization of all forms of energy, potential and kinetic, into enduring and memorable identities and things [...] Parallel with [Constructivism is] Expressionism— a major design form of the twentieth century. Expressionism can be broadly defined as an exploration of the emotional, intellectual, and thus human responses to sensory stimuli." —Krome Barratt

To guide people into comprehension of our online messages, we need to organize—or construct—our thoughts into "enduring and memorable identities and things." To make an idea memorable is to make it powerful. To make an idea powerful, we must juxtapose it to the surrounding perceptual, intellectual, and emotional white noise of life that forms the pattern of the mundane.

As outlined in Chapter Five, creativity is our chief mechanism for transmitting messages that break the pattern of the mundane. By understanding the "emotional, intellectual, and thus human responses to sensory stimuli," we can creatively formulate our constructed expressions of meaning in such a way that the comprehendible becomes enduring.

06.01 Meeting People's Perceptual Needs

If we want to be successful at using creative multimedia to construct enduring and memorable messages, we must first understand how the media we use to express our ideas affect people. The first thing we need to know is that, although the purpose of communication is to be helpful, many Web enterprises prove to be anything but helpful because they don't follow the quality, quantity, relevance, and clarity (Q-Q-R-C) rules discussed in previous chapters.

As a reminder of these rules, we *show* people too much stuff (often the wrong stuff) at one time; people don't know where to look, and their continual flow of focused concentration is constantly interrupted as they try to sort it all out! There's so much of the stuff they *don't* need to look at cluttering things up that they can hardly find the things they *do* need to look at.

The second thing we need to know is that people want to understand our *ideas*, not our organizational schemes and structures! It's time we let our ideas come to the foreground where people can focus on them, and move the mechanics behind accessing our messages into the background where people don't have to worry about them. To be successful in this endeavor, experience designers must understand the effects that visual relationships have on perception. As Krome Barratt wrote:

"The transmissions of ideas as well as the ideas themselves are limited by the designer's sensitivity to visual relationships [...] Design is about the making of things that are memorable [and understandable]. Understanding is based on making sense out of certain relationships between elements amidst the expanse of other stimuli."

06.01

Noise Noise Noise Have Noise Noise
We Noise Noise Noise Noise Noise
Noise Noise Noise Noise Perceptual Noise
Noise Noise Noise Noise Noise Noise
Noise Want Noise Noise Noise Noise
Noise Noise Noise Noise Noise Ease
Noise Noise TO Noise Noise Noise

Noise Noise Noise Noise Noise To Noise Noise Noise Noise Noise Noise Noise Noise Noise Noise Noise Noise

We Want To Have Perceptual Ease. →

Noise Noise Noise Noise Noise Noise Noise Noise Noise Noise Noise Noise Noise Noise Noise Noise Noise

06.01.01 When people first look at a screen-space they begin a visual orientation process.

Just as our contemplation of an idea is a *cognitive* orientation process, our examination of a display is a *visual* orientation process. What we're orienting to is the center of energy within our field of view. When we say that we're "seeing" something tangible within a field of view, what we *really* mean is that we're *scanning* the stimuli within that field of view. Reeves and Nass explain:

"Visual experience is a progression of separate glances [that are] all tied together to serve some goal, but none capable of providing the big picture."

The way that we perceive visual stimuli is through light sensors in our eyes. These sensors capture and instantly transmit information through our optic nerves right into our brains. We don't interpret all light coming in through our corneas equally, however. There's a depression with about a two-millimeter diameter in the center of each retina called the *fovea centralis*.

The fovea is the only portion of our retina that has a high enough resolution to see detail. As a result, to identify a visual stimulus our eyes must dart around (scan over) various parts of an object, environment, or information array to put those parts that contain a specific stimulus within the bounds of our foveal focus. Once we identify a stimulus for interpretation, our minds take "snapshots" of these various parts and place them in short-term memory as our brains piece them all together. This continues until we've gathered enough information about the stimulus to interpret what it represents in our long-term memories.

The easier it is and the shorter the amount of time it takes for a person to interpret and evaluate the relative importance of any given snapshot, the more expediently he or she will zero in on its center of energy. The more ambiguous an information array is *perceptually*, the longer it will take to zero in on this locus.

06.01.02 When engaged in the visual orientation process, we're preconditioned to zero in on centers of energy.

As Descartes correctly observed, people prefer to focus on only one stimulus at a time. When we're engaged in the scanning process described above, we're attempting to zero in on the singular stimulus that has the greatest focus of energy and then use that as a basis for defining a relationship with secondary and tertiary centers of energy. Barratt states:

"All thriving, interactive conglomerates of forces develop centers of energy. Given a set of forces and an assurance that equilibrium prevails, the human sense of balance is so finely developed that it directs us to their focus. It is the responsibility of a designer to ensure that the [centers] of energy of an organization [are] where [they] should be. [...] These need to be clearly formed into a hierarchy so that an observer can move freely from one to another using both peripheral and foveal receptivity."

A number of attributes attract our attention when scanning an "expanse of stimuli," including relative size, shape, configuration, groupings, tonal value, and/or color. The point isn't what *specific* attributes a stimuli has, but that some attribute or combination thereof uniquely sets apart the stimulus from the expanse of the other stimuli around it.

This being the case, there are two very important things that we must design within any given screen-space. First, we must design the screen-space to have primary, secondary, and, if needed, tertiary centers of visual energy. Second, we must make sure that these centers of energy form a *substantial perceptual hierarchy* that highlights the components of a message necessary to maintain focused concentration on the comprehension of an overall idea.

The problem with most screen-space designs is that there's either no center of energy or the centers of energy are misplaced on elements that are tangential to the current flowpath.

06.01.03 When there's no center of energy, dazzle occurs.

The visual information we're accustomed to looking at on the Internet doesn't generally emphasis particular elements. Instead Web enterprises either seem schizophrenic in their numerous appeals that vie for our attention (several distinct centers of energy), or they appear as bland arrays with overwhelming numbers of options that barely distinguish themselves at all (no distinct center of energy). Because of perceptual ambiguity at either extreme, we struggle to concentrate on any one stimulus in particular. Rosenfeld and Morville touch on these issues when they state

"Pages crowded with text, links, graphics, and other components make it harder for [people] to find information on those pages. Many designers forget that white space[2] is an important a component of a page as anything else ... We've all yawned our way through long pages ... without a break for the eye."

Richard Harris further underscores this point when he states, "Before we can comprehend much from media, we must select some information to attend to and process and neglect other information." To do this with most online resources, requires scanning through the various groupings of information on the screen to find what we're interested in attending to. This is a slow and distracting process. What's more, we're not set up very well cognitively to deal with these types of information arrays.

When you think about it, there's nothing like it in nature. These types of arrays are completely man-made. The result is that most people become zombies as they try to deal with information overload. As mentioned in Chapter Five, the effect of this information overload is what Krome Barratt refers to as *dazzle:*

"To become rhythmic, stimuli need to avoid the dazzle of plenty by grouping within our small number threshold.[3] Larger numbers need the grouping of groups ... The need for focusing both senses and mind leads to recognition of figure and ground. Insecurity, ambiguity, dazzle arise when positive and negative stimuli compete without the ultimate supremacy of one or the other as figure. Normally, dazzle is avoided by emphasis of [particular] elements ."

To *avoid* the dazzling effect, we must establish positive and negative asymmetry. As outlined in Chapter Five, the alternation between beat and rest is what forms rhythmic patterns. To be effective, however, the beats and rests can't be a continual procession of symmetrical alternates. Otherwise the stimulus would become monotonous.

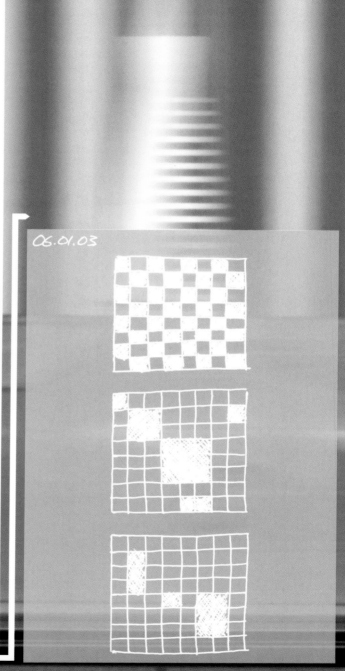

06.01.03

06.01.04

- Almost everyone instantly recognizes this as the concept "three."
- Almost everyone instantly recognizes this as the concept "five."
- Many people instantly recognize this as the concept "seven."
- Some people instantly recognize this as the concept "nine."
- Almost _no_ one instantly recognizes this as the concept "twelve" without first counting in order to decode meaning.

06.01.04 People need the security of visual boundaries.

When we begin a visual orientation process by scanning a screen-space with our eyes, it's just like piecing together a puzzle. We try to define the border first to give us the security of a sense of scope. It's easier to feel like we have a handle on the situation.

The obvious question in light of this is that if we find security in defined boundaries, what effect does the typical indefinite scrolling browser window have on us? The answer is that it makes us unconsciously insecure because we don't have a handle on the scope of the situation. We need to go exploring and try to find the edges of the situation to ensure that we're up for whatever might be hidden "below the fold." The problem is that while we're worrying about this, we're losing focus. What are the implications?

One implication is that we should move beyond the vertically oriented, indefinite scrolling browser windows, because our monitors have a horizontal orientation. Doesn't it make sense to design our presentations to be congruent with that orientation? For another thing, according to Reeves and Nass, it's a fact that people respond more favorably to horizontal orientations. Speaking here of television screens, they state the reasons why:

"Screens that are more horizontal approximate more closely the aspect ratio of human vision, as people can see farther to the sides than they can above or below the point of focus. Horizontal screens are likely more arousing because more action occurs in peripheral vision, that is, to the left and right of visual focus. This is the same in real life: most information arrives laterally."

[3] The small numbers threshold is the point at which the items in a group are too numerous to recognize without consciously counting. For most people, this is between five and nine items. It's helpful to keep items that people are considering within these cognitive tolerances. Otherwise items that fall outside of these boundaries will fall out of short-term memory.

[4] Please note that I'm not suggesting that horizontally oriented screen-spaces should scroll, although in some cases maybe they should. Cases when this might be appropriate relate to arrays of information, such as geographical maps, that are inherently spatial in nature.

CASE STUDY 6A

Creative Edge

Address: http://www.8edge.com/
Client: (Self Promotion)
Experience Designers: Creative Edge

Moving Toward Elegant Clarity

Creative Edge is a design firm located in Malibu, California. The design team wanted to establish an online presence that really moved people emotionally. They sought to create an experience that appeals to classic corporate palettes while remaining technically savvy and design wise. Their solution is a very unique and interesting environment that establishes clear visual relationships between figure and ground.

Within 8edge.com, content focus is shifted through animated grid flexure and modulation. This is driven by a person's own interaction with the environment. As a person moves his or her pointer to one region of the screen, that region becomes prominent as the other regions recede. This effectively aids a person's natural process of visually orientating to clearly established centers of energy.

The experience is well orchestrated with calculated precision as attention is funneled from key moment to key moment. From a comprehension standpoint, this helps prevent information overload (see 03.02.08). From a perception standpoint, this helps avoid what Krome Barratt calls the dazzling effect (see 06.01.03). By not showing too much to people at one time, it's much easier to convey intent and ensure that proper interpretation, comprehension, and encoding of the key messages will occur. The navigation paradigm matches people's expectations as its animations aren't arbitrary but instead are a direct and appropriate result of people's interaction.

Steve Marsh, creative director at Creative Edge comments:

"We were tired of the busy interfaces that look cool but didn't really do anything. To be dynamic and still have classic design was the challenge. [We wanted to communicate] that good design can cross all media whether it be Web or print."

It has received a "Best of the Web" awared and the "Flash Forward Best Navigation" People's Choice award.

Read our interview with Creative Edge online at:
http://www.trainofthoughts.com

06.01.05 Not only are there flowpaths over time, but there are flowpaths in a screen-space.

After we've found our boundaries, our eyes are drawn like magnets toward the primary and secondary centers of energy. It's important that we leverage this perceptual process to full advantage. By defining a clear visual hierarchy—not in the branching sense, but in the order-of-magnitude sense—our eyes can begin to follow the flowpaths that the centers of energies form. To be effective, every spatial layout must have these flowpaths—or master lines—that lead the eye through the various visual media elements.

When we're talking about flowpaths as lines, we're not necessarily talking about literal lines. What we're referring to is the invisible lines that connect the centers of each visual element in a flowpath. If there's an inherent order to this invisible flowpath, as in Figure 06.01.05a, our visual journey seems to flow rhythmically from one center of energy to another. If this visual journey is met with disorder, our eyes dart to and fro trying to define a flowpath. The result looks more like Figure 06.01.05b.

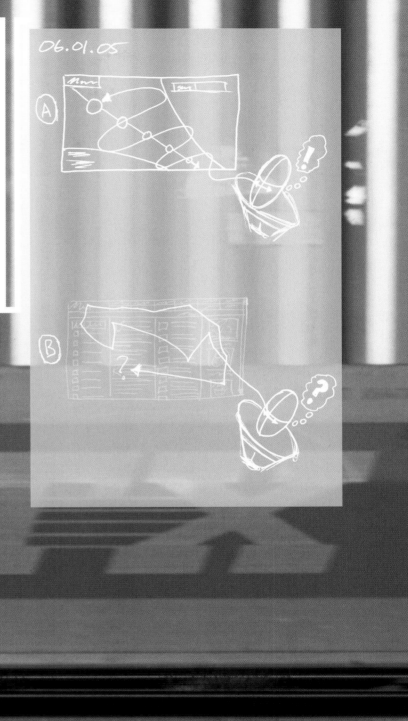

06.01.06 Flowpaths are the visual roadways that our eyes journey along within a screen-space.

If the shortest distance between two points is a straight line, what's up with all the curvy lines that are popping up on online resources these days? The fact that new technologies make these lines technically and practically feasible aside, what is their real value?

The answer is that they're of no value if they're not employed to fulfill some perceptual role. When used to help guide the eye toward meaningful centers of energy, however, these curved lines can become both powerful and practical perceptual aids. Curved lines are more interesting to us than straight lines because their innate compression creates drama. Barratt shares these insights:

"The senses need guidance across [a screen-space], and although cognition often seems to be instantaneous, its process is sequential, involving a scanning along a path that's rarely straight ... Difficulties usually arise from failure to define flow-paths, and thus the hierarchy and sequence of units to be read."

Barratt clearly defines the problem that exists with the vast majority of screen-spaces on the Web today. We have trouble grasping online messages because we don't read them. First, we can hardly find them, and when we do find them, we can't understand them. Most environments offer evenly weighted cluster after evenly weighted cluster of visual information. These information arrays aren't designed to let people unconsciously—or experientially—follow along so that they can search for meaning.

When information arrays are not designed to make thinking experiential for the people interacting with them, these can't be intentional decisions, can they?

06.01.06
According to Barratt:

— Horizontal lines represent the horizon which is stable and infinite.

| Vertical lines defy gravity and represent objects that stand up from the earth.

✕ Linear discord occurs when lines cross at right angles. The eye is held at the intersection.

⇗ Sloping lines are in transition from one state of being to another. This suggests movement and draws the eye to follow.

Ɛ When a line turns and curves, the center of energy, and the eye movement, is toward the tighter curves.

—–→ A break in a line draws the eye toward itself.

Two curved lines can funnel our focus and create more intensity. Daniel Bernoulli discovered that as fluid is constricted as it flows through a tube, pressure and rate-of-flow increase. It's the same when we funnel a person's visual orientation process. As the curving lines converge, the intensity of perceptual focus is elevated.

06.01.08
Our first job in aiding perception is to take the body of possible visual elements...

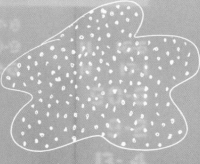

...and "slice" them like a pizza into audience-appropriate sections.

We must then assign these elements to screen-spaces that correspond with the notions that our flowstems prescribe (see chapter four).

06.01.07 The way that leading usability experts approach screen-space design plays right into the dazzle problem.

If it's our tendency as people to be overwhelmed by more than five to nine options at any given moment, why do leading usability experts suggest that people benefit more when they're exposed to screen-spaces that allow them to take in as much information as possible[5]?

It's not that this notion can never be true—it can be. The key, however, is that information must maintain its ability to be perceptually and experientially *meaningful*—especially when there's a lot of it.

Interestingly, the only way for there to be information arrays that are both voluminous and experientially meaningful is to avoid words by using symbol systems that have strong visual relationships. As I've quoted Richard Harris as pointing out, "Before we can comprehend much from media, we must select some information to attend to and process and neglect other information." This is especially difficult when there are numerous, equally weighted textual elements on a screen that we must sift through to interpret.

Web enterprises have been led to believe that creating these conglomerations or organizational schemes and textual content is what builds a sense of value in people's minds for a Web enterprise. This is ridiculous! People don't want to go on a treasure hunt that turns into a wild goose chase when they interact with a Web enterprise; they want to be helped in some way. They don't want a thinking process that should be experiential and effortless to end up being laborious and reflective. If we're ever going to be helpful in our communication with people online, by definition we're going to have to learn to be more helpful in our presentational style. This directly relates to how we design our screen-spaces to be congruent with people's perceptual needs.

To comply with the Q-Q-R-C principles, we must learn more about the people who interact with our online systems so we can give them more targeted information. As stated in Chapter Four, one major tool we use in clearing away irrelevant information—and thus reducing the quantity of perceptual screen garbage—is the *Interactive Narrowing Process* discussed in 04.03.04.

[5] In *Designing Web Usability*, Jakob Nielsen states: "It is *much* faster to perform most tasks when you can take in more information at a single glance."

06.01.08 The number of visual relationships affects the strength of centers of energy.

As Barratt states, "Number is an awareness of separation." If we want people to distinguish centers of energy within a screen-space, we need to keep the number of recognizable forms within perceptual tolerances, which is nine or less (see footnote 4 on page 194). For people to perceive the separations—or the visual rests between beats that media elements provide—we must make those rests large or long enough so the separations don't become ambiguous.

Anything that's uniform is ambiguous and therefore bleeds into the pattern of the mundane I talked about in Chapter Five. What this implies to the coordination of the centers of visual energy into flowpaths is clear. We must avoid straight, uniform, horizontal, or vertical information arrays that exceed nine items. The problem with these uniform arrays is that the eye can move in either direction without finding a greater concentration of energy to latch onto. To avoid this situation, we must create weighted flowpaths that help the eye zero in on the heavier end as a starting point from which it can proceed to other, secondary and tertiary centers of energy. Again, Barratt's comments are valuable:

"The sensory weight of a unit is affected by its proximity to other units, their centers and their boundaries .... Number is an awareness of separation, of an independence that is also interdependent. As two stimuli are moved apart, their two-ness is progressively overwhelmed by the interval [between them] and they become isolated entities. Apparent proximity affects our awareness of number."

Establishing primary and secondary centers of energy is very important, but what determines their strength?

06.01.09 Size and tonal variation must be used to create and balance centers of energy.

When talking strictly about monochromatic visual elements, the amount of power a stimulus has to draw the eye is actually defined as a mathematical formula called the *Law of Moments*, which we borrow from physics. The basic gist is that the power that a stimulus has to attract the eye to that stimulus is a function of its spatial volume multiplied by its perpendicular distance from a fixed invisible point—or *fulcrum*—on the screen. The quantitative value of this mathematical expression is known as a *moment*. To achieve balance of visual elements around this fulcrum, we need to achieve equilibrium in the equation that these elements form.

To try to grasp why this equation works, imagine a teeter-totter or an old fashoined scale. If your goal is to balance the scale, you have a few choices. To achieve balance you can

a. Place two equally weighted items equal distances from the fulcrum (the center point on which the lever rests on)
b. Place a heavier item closer to the fulcrum on one side and a lighter item at the extreme end of the other side. On a 10-inch lever, if the lighter items weighs 1 units and is sitting 5 inches from the fulcrum, its *moment* is 5. If the heavier items weighs 2 units and is resting 5 inches from the fulcrum, its moment would be 10. This is an imbalance. To achieve balance, the heavier item must be moved closer to the fulcrum so as not to exert excess leverage. In this case, equality is achieved when the heavier item is placed at a point 2.5 feet from the fulcrum.
c. Place two or more lighter items at various points on one side of the fulcrum to compensate for the weight of one or two heavier items on the other side. In this case, the same math applies; however, we must use addition to find the sum of each item's moment on any given side of the fulcrum.

When dealing with colored or otherwise toned visual elements, the equation changes slightly. We must not only multiply the spatial volume of the element by its perpendicular distance from a fulcrum on both sides of the equation; we must also multiply that product by the magnitude of tonal variation from the average value of the background tone.

Figure 06.01.09 illustrates how these equations work.

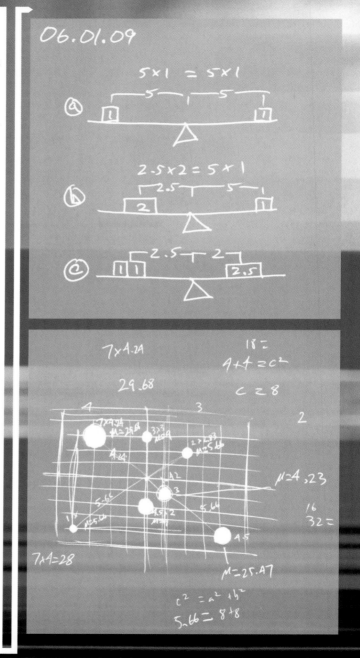

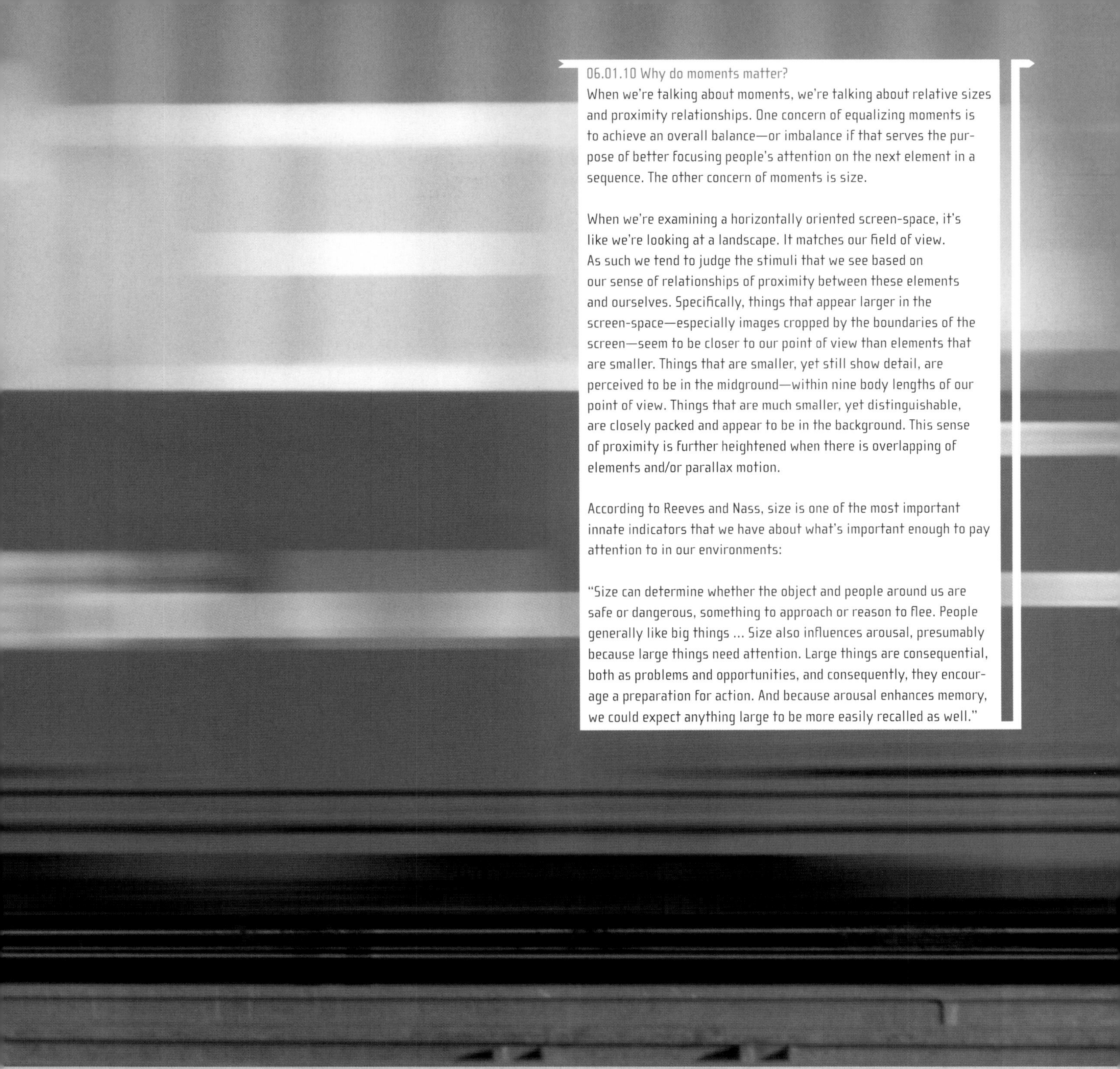

06.01.10 Why do moments matter?

When we're talking about moments, we're talking about relative sizes and proximity relationships. One concern of equalizing moments is to achieve an overall balance—or imbalance if that serves the purpose of better focusing people's attention on the next element in a sequence. The other concern of moments is size.

When we're examining a horizontally oriented screen-space, it's like we're looking at a landscape. It matches our field of view. As such we tend to judge the stimuli that we see based on our sense of relationships of proximity between these elements and ourselves. Specifically, things that appear larger in the screen-space—especially images cropped by the boundaries of the screen—seem to be closer to our point of view than elements that are smaller. Things that are smaller, yet still show detail, are perceived to be in the midground—within nine body lengths of our point of view. Things that are much smaller, yet distinguishable, are closely packed and appear to be in the background. This sense of proximity is further heightened when there is overlapping of elements and/or parallax motion.

According to Reeves and Nass, size is one of the most important innate indicators that we have about what's important enough to pay attention to in our environments:

"Size can determine whether the object and people around us are safe or dangerous, something to approach or reason to flee. People generally like big things ... Size also influences arousal, presumably because large things need attention. Large things are consequential, both as problems and opportunities, and consequently, they encourage a preparation for action. And because arousal enhances memory, we could expect anything large to be more easily recalled as well."

06.01.11 Screen-space grids should be designed to aid the visual orientation process.

We judge visual relationships based on not only proximity relationships between visual elements but also the proximity of these elements to our own vantage points. In light of this, we must design the grids of the screen-space environments to best leverage our abilities to visually focus both foveally and peripherally.

Things that appear closer to our point of view have either already been chosen by us or are in the process of violating our personal space. Things in the background are too far away to be current options, so they are cognitively blurred—perceptually ignored. These form the pattern of the mundane. Things that are valid candidates for turning our attention appear in the midground. After we make a choice, either we move toward it or it moves toward us, and it becomes bigger in our field of view as it moves to the foreground.

Because it's not my recommendation to design screen-spaces to perpetually house vast arrays of choices but rather a limited number of applicable choices, I don't believe that the fundamental question when designing a screen-space is where to put the navigation. Although I believe that some navigational elements are necessary, I believe that the proper, intelligent sequencing of appropriate notions can drastically reduce the burden that people are currently placing on navigational elements. In keeping with this, I believe that the first question at hand is determining the best design grid to express ideas through content and then making appropriate modifications to accommodate navigation.

Although it's not my intention to try to define a one-size-fits-all design grid, I think that there are certain parameters that we must stay within to avoid the dazzle effect. The reason is that the nature of a design grid greatly influences a person's ability to interpret the stimuli presented upon it. Barratt makes these recommendations:

> 3x3 cells are the minimum rhythmic subdivision of an area.
> 5x5 cells support optimum comprehension according to psychologists.
> For grids beyond 5x5 cells, the dazzle effect can be subdued by establishing a hierarchy of one set of parallels over another.

BNSF 2374

06.02 The Instrumentation and Sequencing of Rhythmic Notion-Flows

One of the issues that is very controversial today, but that will become less and less polarizing over the course of the twenty-first century, is that of communicating with anything but textual expressions of meaning on the Web.

In print, we use the written word as well as pictures to communicate within a space. In television, we use the spoken word as well as still or moving pictures to communicate over a period of time. As mentioned in the opening series of this chapter, the print paradigm has traditionally been followed on the Web. Although this has been changing over the past few years, our use of media hasn't necessarily been an evolution toward a higher calling. We've merely begun to saddle our textual expressions with pictures, animation, streaming video, and audio. Neither the initial adaptation of the print paradigm nor recent efforts to add broadcast-type features to online resources have fully leveraged the capabilities of the Web.

The paradigm of an improvisational music ensemble can shed light on what an improvement on this situation might look like.

06.02.01 Listening to an ensemble that doesn't have its act together is a troubling experience.

One of the worst things that can happen to a person's music is for it to be publicly performed by a group of instrumentalists who sound like they've never played together before. Their sound isn't "tight" or buttoned up. There's a lot of redundancy harmonically. People just play "whatever" and aren't necessarily considering how to develop synergies either rhythmically or harmonically with other players. In a musical ensemble, having a bunch of instruments of expression in the room doesn't necessarily mean that the sound that's produced will have any redeeming musical value.

In the same way, using a variety of media elements to express meaning within a notion doesn't necessarily mean that the message that's communicated will have any redeeming value. The problem is that this is exactly how most online resources come across when trying to use media elements. Words communicate meaning that is better captured in pictures. Pictures and words overlap in their expressions of meaning in a way that makes the redundant words extra baggage. Words are used to explain processes that would be much easier to follow if either diagrams or simulations were used instead. Meaning is expressed in words in a way that would be much more engaging and emotionally compelling if the spoken word was used as the instrument of expression. The list goes on and on.

As outlined in Chapter Three, the challenge of formulating effective notions becomes that of trying to figure out the best way to get all the instruments of mediated communication to work together— enhancing one another and complementing one another's strengths while compensating for one another's weaknesses. Skilled arrangers of music learn the strengths not only of each instrument but also of the people who will be playing the instruments. Arrangers then figure out the best way to convert the simple chords that harmony and melody combine to produce in the original music notation into parts that work together on a more expanded basis when played by several instrumentalists.

The key to success is understanding the role that the various instruments need to play and using them in ways that are appropriate to a situational expression of meaning within the context of a specific musical composition.

06.02.02 There's a key to the effective instrumentation of an expression of meaning.

The key to the effective instrumentation of an expression of meaning is...well, let me back up a second.

Most harmonic instrumentalists can play an entire music composition by themselves. Imagine a person singing and playing the guitar or singing and playing the piano—which can both be valid expressions of a musical composition. The sign of amateur instrumentalists, however, is that when they get together with *other* instrumentalists, they each play the same part as they would when playing alone. This is just plain wrong.

There's no surer way to muddy up the sound of a performance than by having everyone simultaneously covering all of the harmonic bases in a song. The work of orchestration is to assign *part* of the harmony and melody and rhythm to *each* of the instruments in the ensemble. Alone, these parts wouldn't produce the complete chord, but since they're playing together, they don't need to, and they'll ruin the subtlety of the performance if they try.

It's the same when we're coordinating the various media elements that will combine to express meaning within a notion. The *key* in using several media elements together isn't to saddle our textual expressions with extra "stuff," but to take "stuff" away from each element until they all piece together to form the entire unified expression. Remember this Krome Barratt quote from Chapter Three?

"The permissible tolerances in the parts [of a thing] are related to the functional efficiency of the whole ... The designer attempts to parallel the process of nature. If his commitment is to the making of a complete [expression], the precision of the individual elements becomes subordinate to that objective." [6]

Part of what Barratt is saying is that how much or how little we use a particular element is contingent on filling the needs of the whole. To be elegant, there must be no needless redundancy unless the redundancy is a part of the intended expression, such as in musical unison, wherein more than one instrument plays the same note.

[6] *Logic & Design In Art, Science & Mathematics*—Chapter 5

SPOTLIGHT ON:

HILLMAN CURTIS

Hillman Curtis is a name that engenders respect throughout the international Web design community. Not only is he a hard working, visionary designer and author, but he's also a really nice guy. From Adobe to Pavarotti, Hillman has created not only some of the most interesting online resources but also some of the most successful. His many awards are a small testimony to his numerous accomplishments.

Because Hillman has spent years trying to achieve the delicate balance between designs that are elegant and engaging, yet also simple and useful, I've asked him to offer some insights regarding the power of dynamic media to capture and hold people's attention.

Lenker: Someone types in a URL—then the screen goes blank, indicating that an online resource is about to take center stage. From a perceptual standpoint, what's the most important thing that needs to happen next?

Curtis: It has to load! Quickly. There are two ways to communicate on the Web: one is visual (colors, fonts, layout, copy, motion); the other is functional. How a site loads can say as much as what it loads and how it functions. How one navigates through it can say as much as the info/product one navigates toward. I am a strong believer of time being a real currency of the Web. Here at hillmancurtis inc we use terms like "cost" and "charge" to describe file size. "How much is that file going to cost me?" "What are you charging the user for that animation?" It helps us to stay focused and to keep the audience always in mind.

Lenker: Why is it so crucial that our designs help people visually orient to the content focus?

Curtis: That's why we design, I think. To draw attention to something. It might be a movie poster that visually tells a story...and a good movie poster tells you exactly what the movie is about. It draws attention to the theme. And you respond to that. Or it might be the iconography at international airports that makes you feel comfortable in a country where your native language fails you. There's a reason we have graphic design...and we have all grown up responding and relating to graphic design. I think it's important to acknowledge its power as a common visual language; then once you do that—or at least once I do that—I'm able to get into a mindset

to design for communication. The idea is to use this common visual language comprised of color, type, layout, motion, sound, and interactivity to try and reach people.

Lenker: What are some of the most important ways that you feel dynamic media can aid in this visual orienting process?

Curtis: Hmmm...well, Mark Rothko once said of his paintings, "They are not pictures, I have made a place." And that's a quote I keep always in mind when I design. I don't want just a pretty picture, I want to design a place. Often I'm able to do that; sometimes not...but I think that with dynamic media, with interactivity, audio, motion, and the ability to program behaviors that change according to how the user interacts, we have so many tools in which to create that place.

Lenker: How do you find a balance between giving people ready access to a range of valuable options and giving them clutter-free screen-spaces? [...]

Read the entire interview online at:
http://www.trainofthoughts.com

Learn more about Hillman Curtis at:
http://www.hillmancurtis.com

Buy *Flash Web Design* today at:
http://www.trainofthoughts.com

06.02.03 There are two categories of media in a screen-space. The first category is composed of the elements that a person needs to focus on to understand the notion currently under consideration. The second category is composed of the elements that are not of immediate concern but must represent choices that are readily available for whatever reason.

The treatment of the elements of focus must be such that they're set off in some way from the other elements. This can be done with size, shape, color, movement, value, grouping, or whatever it takes to form a primary center of energy. These elements must not compete with one another, but must come to one another's aid in their aim to express meaning. Any type of media, including sound, motion, illustrations, continuous-tone images, or even video is fair game as long as its use falls within the permissible tolerances of the technology supporting the delivery medium. Anyone who doesn't think this is possible hasn't properly understood the role of technology.

The treatment of the elements in the periphery must NOT in any way compete for the attention of the person interacting with the notion. This means no unnecessary bells and whistles. No animation. It especially means that the moments of these peripheral elements must not combine in some way to overshadow the elements of focus; otherwise, ambiguity will be the result, and the dazzle effect will be constantly gnawing at our audience.

While visual representations of other notions in a visual flowpath can have the force of secondary centers of energy, these should clearly fall in the midground of our three-dimensional proximity grid. Elements such as navigational options that don't directly relate to the flowpath should be relegated to tertiary centers of energy and should be extremely subdued. This doesn't mean that these elements can't be stylistic and elegant. They should be. But their treatment, especially their color and tonal value, must not draw the eye away from the flowpath.

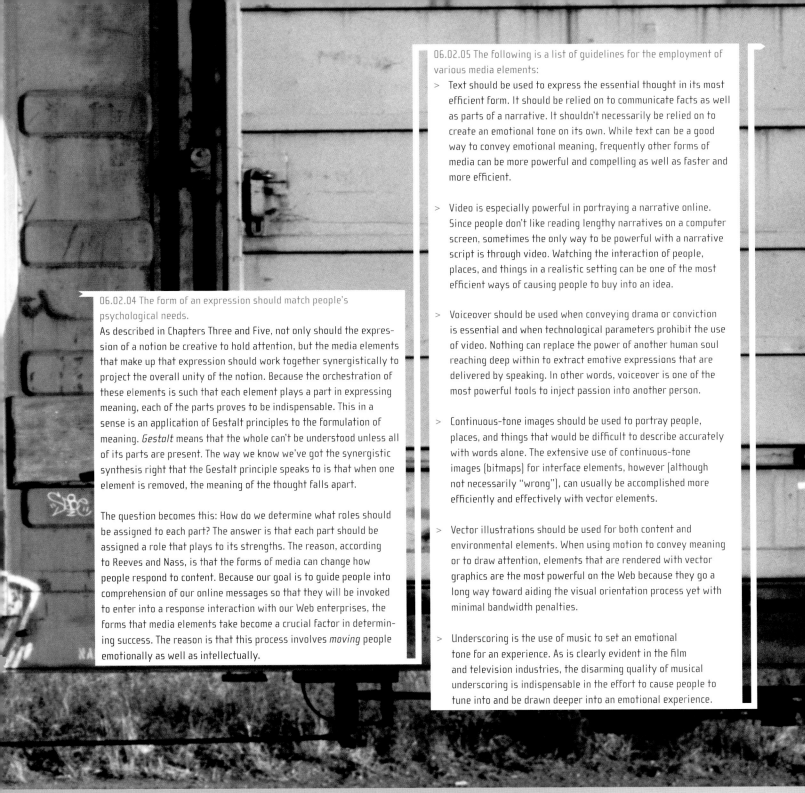

06.02.04 The form of an expression should match people's psychological needs.

As described in Chapters Three and Five, not only should the expression of a notion be creative to hold attention, but the media elements that make up that expression should work together synergistically to project the overall unity of the notion. Because the orchestration of these elements is such that each element plays a part in expressing meaning, each of the parts proves to be indispensable. This in a sense is an application of Gestalt principles to the formulation of meaning. *Gestalt* means that the whole can't be understood unless all of its parts are present. The way we know we've got the synergistic synthesis right that the Gestalt principle speaks to is that when one element is removed, the meaning of the thought falls apart.

The question becomes this: How do we determine what roles should be assigned to each part? The answer is that each part should be assigned a role that plays to its strengths. The reason, according to Reeves and Nass, is that the forms of media can change how people respond to content. Because our goal is to guide people into comprehension of our online messages so that they will be invoked to enter into a response interaction with our Web enterprises, the forms that media elements take become a crucial factor in determining success. The reason is that this process involves *moving* people emotionally as well as intellectually.

06.02.05 The following is a list of guidelines for the employment of various media elements:

> Text should be used to express the essential thought in its most efficient form. It should be relied on to communicate facts as well as parts of a narrative. It shouldn't necessarily be relied on to create an emotional tone on its own. While text can be a good way to convey emotional meaning, frequently other forms of media can be more powerful and compelling as well as faster and more efficient.

> Video is especially powerful in portraying a narrative online. Since people don't like reading lengthy narratives on a computer screen, sometimes the only way to be powerful with a narrative script is through video. Watching the interaction of people, places, and things in a realistic setting can be one of the most efficient ways of causing people to buy into an idea.

> Voiceover should be used when conveying drama or conviction is essential and when technological parameters prohibit the use of video. Nothing can replace the power of another human soul reaching deep within to extract emotive expressions that are delivered by speaking. In other words, voiceover is one of the most powerful tools to inject passion into another person.

> Continuous-tone images should be used to portray people, places, and things that would be difficult to describe accurately with words alone. The extensive use of continuous-tone images (bitmaps) for interface elements, however (although not necessarily "wrong"), can usually be accomplished more efficiently and effectively with vector elements.

> Vector illustrations should be used for both content and environmental elements. When using motion to convey meaning or to draw attention, elements that are rendered with vector graphics are the most powerful on the Web because they go a long way toward aiding the visual orientation process yet with minimal bandwidth penalties.

> Underscoring is the use of music to set an emotional tone for an experience. As is clearly evident in the film and television industries, the disarming quality of musical underscoring is indispensable in the effort to cause people to tune into and be drawn deeper into an emotional experience.

06.02.06 The fidelity of our media elements is an important yet surprising consideration.

Conventional wisdom dictates that we try to make our visual images as sharp and high resolution as possible. In reality, however, this isn't the chief predictor of the success of visual elements.

First, the content is of prime importance. What the image conveys must contribute meaningfully to overall understanding of the notion. Second, the image must be honed to contribute indispensably to the overall expression of meaning among the media elements as a whole.

The reason that resolution isn't so important compared to other considerations, according to Reeves and Nass, is that most of our field of view falls into the peripheral zone, where we don't have the capability to perceive detailed resolution anyway. Only visual stimuli that fall under our foveal focus appear to have any detail at all. As a result, detailed continuous-tone images that fall into the peripheral zone can in many cases be a waste of bandwidth (see Figure 06.02.06).

Audio fidelity is a different story. According to studies conducted by Reeves and Nass, " ... audio fidelity can also help visuals, quite apart from the technical quality of the pictures, because good audio can even make people think that the visuals look better." It turns out that we have a much lower tolerance for poor audio fidelity than we do for the fidelity of visual images. In fact, audio that is exceedingly poor can actually detract from a person's overall comprehension of an expression of meaning.

The moral of the story is that if audio and imagery are to be used together, spend your bandwidth tokens on better audio fidelity (less compression) rather than on image or fidelity (more compression).

06.02.07 The rhythmic sequencing of media layers is crucial to establishing unity.

Just as in a musical score, various media elements form layers of textures that evolve over time. In a musical performance, the various instruments alternate between times of being the central focus and times of providing more of a supporting role for another featured instrument. As mentioned in Chapter Five, the reason for this diversity is both to keep a composition interesting as it unfolds over time and also to tell a musical story—to lead an audience on an emotional journey through the introduction, realization, and confirmation of various related musical themes.

The key to succeeding with creating these layers is to make sure that the patterning of each layer syncs with the patterning of the others (see Figure 06.02.07). Barratt explains:

"Rhythmic patterns can be generated by superimposing two or more...but not too many...scales. [Superimposed scales] need to be wedded; either by keying to produce a consonant beat frequency or by a transition from one scale to another. In music this transition is known as modulation."

The reason that we need overlapping rhythmic textures, according to Barratt, is that repetition dulls the senses. He says, "Even the most exciting events require [periods] of rest in which their reverberations may be subsided before they are repeated." When the mind is given a chance to rest and recover, it can contemplate and anticipate the reintroduction and possible embellishments.

This idea of repetition dulling receptivity can be seen when we stare at a color swatch such as the color red for too long. The cones in the retina become overstimulated and require a time of rest. This is why if you close your eyes a negative impression of the swatch can still be perceived in the mind. The other colors can still be perceived, but the color red is temporarily turned off.

06.02.08 Unity must be maintained over time.

In addition to providing rest for the senses, the other primary reason for using a complementary set of media elements to express the meaning of an idea is that each layer can offer a unique vantage point from which to examine a thought.

It's like being at someone's house for dinner and having the family tell the story from their last vacation. The father tells his version of the story. While doing so, the mother adds minor embellishments here and there. They play off of each other and sometimes blurt out details in unison. After the story's been told, the son insists that the parents didn't have it quite right and repeats the story from his perspective—offering his unique voice and insight. If there are other siblings, maybe they chime in to embellish as the mother had when the father was telling the story. In the end, the father acknowledges some of what the children had to say but qualifies the input and wraps up the story. This is exactly how the instruments that express meaning in a song and the media elements that express meaning in a notion work together to tell the story of an idea.

In most cases, the various instrumentalists in an ensemble don't all begin playing at the same time. What happens instead is that they layer in over the course of the performance. Let's say for example that the percussion and base guitar kick a song off by laying a rhythmic and tonal bed. They set forth the "rules," so to speak, for the other instrumentalists to follow. The rhythm that the percussionist and bassist lay out forms a pattern that's interesting to listen to, but that would become monotonous if allowed to continue very long without the incorporation of other tonal colors and textures through the other parts that are eventually added. This is the essence of providing orchestration in a notion-flow.

According to Reeves and Nass, "If there is no rest afforded by the stimulus, it will be initiated by the viewer." What this means is that if we don't layer media diversity over our textual expressions, people will get overstimulated from the reading and will be tempted to interrupt their consumption of the message. This is the way that people give their mind time not only for rest but also for contemplation and reflection. According to studies conducted by Reeves and Nass, these rests help improve the recollection of the stimuli.

06.02.09 *Sensory* introduction, realization, and confirmation must follow our three-stage communication model.

Unity must exist between design elements as they follow a theme and as the expression of an idea's meaning unfolds. These elements must come across "like they've played together before." Their collaboration must be tight. Like musicians in an ensemble, each must assume a role that supports the song's storyline.

Alternating periods of experiential thought and periods of reflective thought must be triggered by our communication. In the beginning, we must lure people into our messages through expressions that are catchy, easy to follow, and introduce our central theme. In the middle, we must get people to take a deeper, more reflective look at our theme as we use media to express meaning from various vantage points, so that people can reach a greater realization of our central theme—or idea. At the end, we want to trigger the thoughts and emotions that move people to action by allowing them to experientially reminisce on the themes that have already been conceived and developed, thus confirming and reinforcing the meaning that's been established in their minds.

CASE STUDY 6B

Viaduct Furniture

Address: http://www.viaduct.co.uk
Client: Viaduct Furniture Ltd.
Experience Designer: Alex Griffin

The future wave of furniture.

Viaduct Furniture Ltd. is an interior retailer located in London, England which specializes in elegant, modern designer furnishings. When James Mair, Viaduct's founder, hired Deepend (now defunct) to create an online presence, he was absolutely determined that Viaduct online reflect the high-quality designs that Viaduct the store is known for internationally.

The underlying conceptual direction was to create an experience that captures the essence of the curves and shapes of the products. They also wanted to have a dynamic and interesting environment for thier products, yet one that would not detract from a focus on the products themselves. This was achieved by a very understaned design that uses flowing lines and simple animation to bend people's attention toward the products as the content focus. Three simple navigational sections are presented which foster easy visual orientation and focus. When a person makes a selection, the entire environment modulates and shifts to a new center of energy. Then entire experience has a sense of unfolding just like when entering the store.

The goal was to be elegant and creative, yet not frivolous. Instead of loading in a combersum array of bit-map images to show product selection, for example, Deepend chose to presents line art images of Viaducts products for faster loading. The fact that the execution is *just plain cool* is a biproduct of trying to be responsible with bandwidth. If a particular product looks interesting, people click on a line art representation to see further details and photographic images of a product. When asked about thier unique solution, Design Director Alex Griffin stated:

"Viaduct has a long history of experience in the area of designer furniture. As such, the design of the site was bold in its use of shapes and animation to create an atmosphere for the user, rather than a list of products that would have said nothing about the character and personality of the company."

Read our interview with Alex Griffin from de-construct.com online at: http://www.trainofthoughts.com

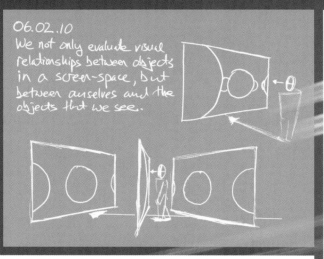

06.02.10

We not only evaluate visual relationships between objects in a screen-space, but between ourselves and the objects that we see.

06.02.10 We must draw minds closer through design modulation.

As a sequence of notions unfolds, what's happening is that we're drawing people deeper into an understanding of our ideas. Drawing people into an idea can have sensory parallels. As people approach understanding, an idea becomes bigger in their minds. In the same way, as people approach each succeeding notion in a message, the presence that the accompanying media elements assume in the screen-space becomes larger as well.

When people attend to a stimulus, what they're really doing is redirecting their foveal focus from another stimulus—perceived or remembered—to the peripheral stimulus that has somehow caught their attention. The cause of a shift in foveal focus is usually some form of movement—although it could also be some other stimulus, such as a sound. People's focus must be captured by the design of the screen-space and then shifted through time via modulation. What this does is reinforce the proximity relationship between person and media—a process that is essential in building emotional equity in an online experience.

According to Reeves and Nass, animation is one of the most effective tools for modulating a person's focus. They say, "The cadence of motion and rest is a critical part of a successful presentation."

06.02.11 It's important to understand that this doesn't mean that constant motion is good.

In fact, the opposite is true. Reeves and Nass add, "Motion can prepare a person to attend and learn, but conversely, motion can interfere if it interrupts a critical segment." Unnecessary peripheral motion should be banished from the experience if it is not intended for people to switch their focus. Apart from content that contains motion by its very nature, such as video, motion should be restricted to shifting a person's focus from one notion to another. When motion is used in this way, attention immediately turns to the source of the motion. This reaction is the visual orientation process, which in a sense is working in a third dimension.

In music, modulation occurs when the composition is moved from the environment of one key signature to another. In a notion-flow, modulation occurs when we give people the sense of moving from one screen-space environment to another.

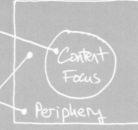

06.02.12
Animation day here.
It helps clarify the
message.

Only use animation
here to redirect focus
to the next notion.

Note:

When we simulate the condition of putting
a person in a close proximity relationship
with a stimulus, we can create dramatic
configurations that are more intimate,
personal, intense, and exciting. People will
often have strong positive reactions when
we do this appropriately.

"Navigation" is a poor term, and, as outlined in Chapter Four, is a component of the same failed paradigm that brought terms such as "architecture", "site", and "page" into cybernetic sciences. Although usability consultants denounce the use of animation in "navigation," I dismiss this view because I feel that it's the result of the limitations imposed by the outmoded paradigm of information architecture. I will, however, qualify this assertion by stating that it's perceptually *appropriate* implementations of motion in navigation that will be experientially effective. There are many examples of motion in navigation that don't aid in the visual orienting process, and these are often not helpful.

Navigation isn't just a mechanism that provides utility within a notion-flow. It provides a mechanism through which strong emotional momentum can be established for a Web experience. There're many benefits to doing this, while having been overlooked by many usability experts, that haven't been overlooked by others such as Dr. Reeves and Dr. Nass. According to them:

"Motion alerts people to pay attention. This is especially true for movement that might harm us. Consequently, objects that move toward us or loom in front of our faces will get the most attention—and quickly. When people are exposed to motion, particularly motion that is a visual surprise, they focus on the source of the motion and stop all other unnecessary activities. This reaction is called a visual orienting response, and it is more than just a mental reaction... Visual orientations can also produce physical changes in the body [that] prepare the body to process the *consequences of motion.*"

The ramifications for the formulation of dynamic navigation have not even begun to be fathomed. It's the task of those who develop this next generation of online resources to bring what has until now been known as "navigation" to the next level.

06.02.12 As we move people deeper into our ideas, the way that the screen-space needs to be utilized changes.
Because the functional volume of a presentation is oriented to more granular information, the spatial grid can modulate to accommodate this finer level of detail.

Animation is one of the keys to helping people keep their orientation as this transition from one grid to another occurs. Altering the grid in this way is what Barratt referes to as *grid flexure*. As we have the sense of drawing nearer to media elements in terms of proximity, they tend to become more emotionally engaging. This is especially true when the edges of some elements become cropped, resulting in a dramatic configuration that intensifies the sense of a close proximity relationship with the viewer.

06.03 <small>Summary</small>

It's clear that the current Web media design status quo won't carry us through the twenty-first century. We need to quickly make a break with the electronic document paradigm because we'll never be able to make electronic documents behave as well as their counterparts in the physical world. But neither flamboyantly excessive nor painfully austere design extremes have found acceptance as models for the future. Instead we need a new paradigm for electronic media that takes advantage of the inherent capabilities of not only *perceptually* dynamic online media, but also media that's *conceptually* dynamic (see Chapters Three and Four).

Furthermore, we must begin to establish visual relationships in our screen-space environments that better assist people in maintaining a continual flow of perceptual concentration on the ideas our messages carry. The way media work together synergistically is really the key to succeeding in our effort to convey meaning with elegance, clarity, and creativity. By properly balancing the presentation of our media in consideration of perceptual needs, we'll develop Web experiences that effectively draw people into our messages not only perceptually, but also cognitively and emotionally. As always, our aim is to artfully guide *people* into comprehension of our online messages.

GALLERY 06

club john frieda™
registration

sheer blonde®
the commercial
behind the scenes
where to buy
club john frieda
contact

join now — it's free!

JOHN FRIEDA
london · paris · new york

06.01.01 — www.johnfrieda.com
White space and strong centers of energy are utilized to help people
comprehend the visual organization of this elegant online resource.

06.01.02 — http://www.jump-tomorrow.com
In jump-tomorrow.com, the curving lines of the road maps and screen
elements create visual interest while effectively connecting multiple
centers of energy.

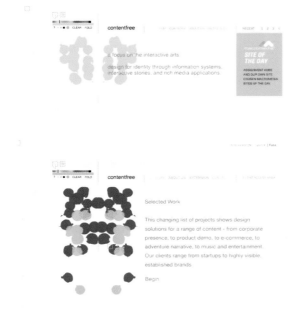

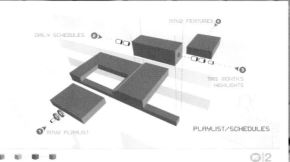

http://www.mtv2.co.uk/

Mtv2.com exemplifies design modulation by drawing people deeper into the conceptual three-dimensional environment and providing a sense of progression between spatial environments.

06.02.10 – http://www.contentfree.com/contentfree.htm

This online resource has an interesting array of spatial and tonal variations on its overall navigational theme.

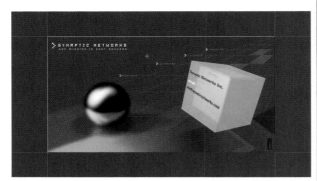

06.01.11 – http://www.e-axis.com/clients/syn/main_flash.htm

In this example of a screen-space grid, the eye is drawn from left to right, beginning with the large three-dimensional ball and then moving into the distance where navigational options are arrayed.

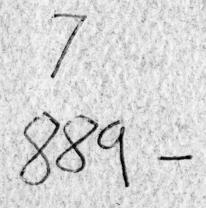

PART TWO

USING SPEED TO SUCCEED WITH EXPERIENCE DESIGN

INTRODUCTION
To Part Two

i2.00 Process Confusion

It's great to have a solid conceptual foundation for Web experience design. It's equally important, however, to have a solid conceptual foundation for bringing online resources into meaningful existence through effective process. This is an obvious statement. What's not so obvious, however, is the underlying reason why organizations have so much trouble with process.

The answer is that most organizations don't have an adequate *concept* of what good process is, and they therefore lack insight regarding what process is meant to accomplish. Some turn to books to find answers, but most books don't help much because they represent rehashings of the same old ideas, wherein, process is viewed merely as a series of linear phases composed of tasks that must be "checked off" to consider a project completed. While process certainly leads to a completed project, when we *fixate* on deadlines and task lists, we tend to stray from an orientation to the *value* that we're trying to build into our online resources.

DON'T get me wrong—being on time and on budget are important. Being on target, however, is equally important. Although most organizations wouldn't argue this point, tragically, the process that they typically employ is almost sure to keep their projects off target (not to mention overdue and overbudget). Especially when they adopt the bandwagon process that "everyone else seems to be using" without ever really reasoning through the established "best practices," they fall into the trap of status quo that leads not to online effectiveness, but to online mediocrity.

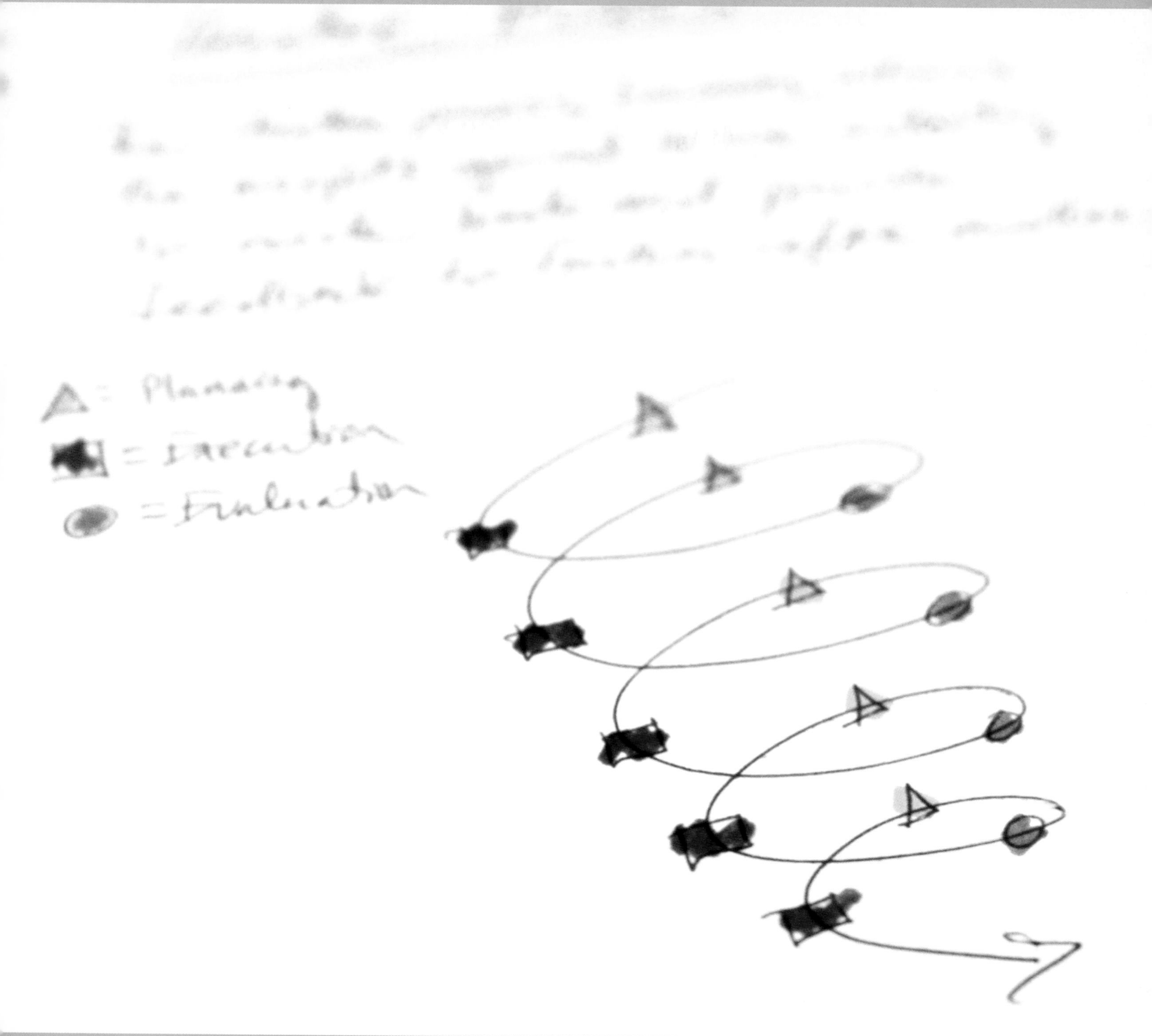

△ = Planning

▨ = Execution

⬤ = Evaluation

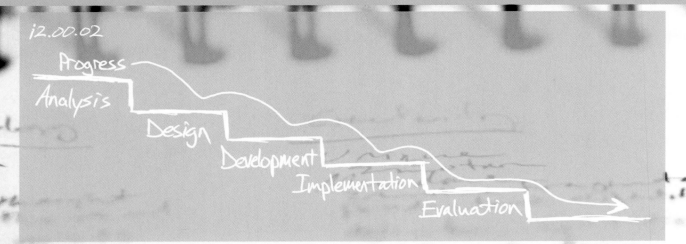

i2.00.02

Progress
Analysis
Design
Development
Implementation
Evaluation

i2.00.01 Without vision, process serves only to fill project team member's schedules with marginal meetings and activities.

This burns most budgets at a rate that makes it almost impossible to see a project through to an effective outcome. Although tasks are getting "checked off" as being completed, this often creates a false sense of having accomplished objectives. It's important to remember that objectives aren't accomplished if a project is completed, but only if the results of the completed project meet the expectations of all stakeholders, including patrons, sponsors, and all concerned parties within the organization itself. Because of inherent deficiencies in the typical four- or five-phased process, by the time organizations realize that the project is straying seriously off course, it's too late to do anything to correct the situation because the project's resources and time allotment have been largely expended.

The problem is that most organizations suffer from a lack of exposure to innovative thinking regarding process.

i2.00.02 The typical process is composed of four or five phases that linearly sequence activities such as analysis, design, development, implementation, and evaluation (ADDIE), when in fact the core of these activities must be much more integral to be effective.

The fact is that almost every process being used to produce online resources today is based on the ADDIE model, which arguably is an outgrowth of the *Instructional System Design (ISD)* model developed by Florida State University in the 1970s. It doesn't matter how an organization wants to *spin* their "unique" process. They all share the same roots and similar components—analysis, design, development, implementation, and evaluation. Just because everyone uses it, however, doesn't make it effective.

The problem with processes that are based on ADDIE is that they present a *waterfall* of activities in which insights can flow into the next phase but never back "upstream" into the activities of previous phases. In other words, design insights gained in the development phase are mute because the design phase is over and done with. Because the entire design budget (and in many cases part of the development budget) is usually expended in the design phase, it's usually too costly to go back and make fundamental changes to the design during the development phase. The same can be said for the evaluation phase. Budgets are expended in the early phases of the process and by the time a broad range of stakeholders have evaluated the project and given feedback, it's too late to do much in response. The insights gained from stakeholder evaluation should be able to flow upstream and be leveraged to make the end result better. The ADDIE process doesn't allow for this.

Rather than following this *waterfall method*, it's much better to *iteratively* zero in on a solution by completing progressively refined cycles of planning, execution, and evaluation.

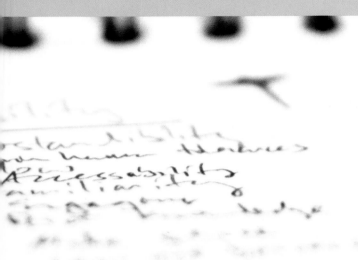

i2.00.03 I feel a need for SPEED.

Owing much to what I learned regarding processes from Dr. Michael Allen and others during my tenure at Allen Interactions (they have a process known as SAVVY), I've developed a process model that I call SPEED (S>PEE>D):

> Strategy
> Planning
> Execution
> Evaluation
> Deployment

The emphasis of the SPEED model is that of *iteratively* formulating effective Web experiences. Even though there are five letters in the acronym and five corresponding words, the PEE portion of the process (I know, I know) is iterative and its components are contained in what I call the *Iterative Execution* phase. The five components of the process break down into three phases as follows:

> Phase I: Strategy Formulation
> Phase II: Iterative Execution (cycles of planning, execution, and evaluation)
> Phase III: Deployment

i2.00.04 *Train of Thoughts* is a book about concepts, and this extends into the discussion in Part Two regarding process.

Part Two isn't intended to be exhaustive in its presentation of the mechanics of the SPEED process. That would take much more space than I'm allotted in this work. Instead, it's intended to comprehensively touch on all the bases of this process to serve as a catalyst for innovative thinking. I've tried to provide some fundamental insights while leaving enough flexibility for situational adaptation. The point isn't to provide a panacea but to stimulate thinking and growth that will hopefully lead readers to a progressively greater vision for process. I deal with these subjects in the remaining chapters:

> Chapter Seven deals with Phase I—Strategy Formulation
> Chapter Eight deals with Phase II—Iterative Execution
> Chapter Nine deals with Phase III—Deployment
> Chapter Ten deals with the creative aspects of Iterative Execution

My goal is to create some waves without tipping an organization's boat. I'm aware that changing the status quo doesn't happen overnight, and I'm also well aware that there are a wide range of perspectives and insights that many readers will bring to this debate. My goal in writing this, therefore, *isn't* to set myself up as a *process answer-man*, but instead—and as is the obligation of any serious student—to be a catalyst for further, more stimulating debate, discussion, and progress within the community of Web enterprises.

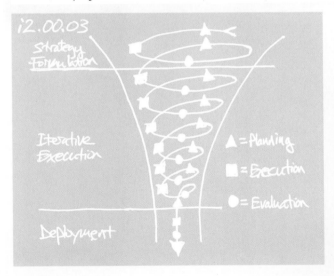

CHAPTER 07

"A work of art is a solution to a problem."

—Krome Barratt

Strategy Formulation—
Reconciling Stakeholder Needs

Although there are many important steps in a process, perhaps the most crucial are those that take place during the first phase, which is *strategy formulation*. Without an *accurate* understanding of what problems a Web enterprise is trying to solve for its patrons, its sponsors, and itself, moving on to the iterative execution phases will be less than effective and could lead to total disaster.

Unfortunately for many Web enterprises, the people involved in the formulation of online resources often expend the lion's share of their time, budget, and energy working toward the completion of tasks that don't truly support the underlying business objectives. This is the result of following directives handed down by executives and, in some cases, experience designers who have the power to control the direction that a Web enterprise takes, yet who move forward with little more than unqualified personal insight. I call this the *Foolishness of Unqualified Wisdom Syndrome.*

To be effective, it's crucial that we instead base the iterative execution phase on the legitimate research, analysis, and reconciliation of all stakeholder needs.

07.00.02 We need something from outside our own experience to spark our insight in a way that wouldn't occur to us otherwise. The search for this spark is known as *horizontal thinking* and is where we get the notion of "thinking outside the box." Picture it in geological terms. If you're interested in mining for gold, you generally don't start in your own backyard. You search across the horizontal "plane" of the earth until you find a place that seems like it might have potential. You then begin digging. If you have no luck, you search for another place and dig again—taking into consideration the lessons that were learned in the previous attempt. The process continues iteratively until you zero in on the right location and begin digging vertically until you strike it rich!

In the same way, the key to being successful in the endeavor to develop effective Web experiences is to look for minds to mine that are beyond the fences of the project war room. We must access the conceptual frameworks of external stakeholders and experts in search of the analogies, metaphors, and crazy ideas that will inevitably be uncovered and that will provide the inspiration crucial to developing a competitive advantage.

Horizontal thinking is the complement to vertical thinking and can lead us to more innovative starting points from which our logical minds can reason through digging. This doesn't mean that merely any whim should be elevated above the intuition of internal stakeholders, but it can provide them with food for thought in the quest to expand the potential of their logical reasoning.

07.00.01 The problem with our own intuition is that we don't know what we don't know.
Although most people in business pride themselves on having a good sense of logic and deductive reasoning, this confidence can often be a rather deceptive trap. Most people, indeed, do have a good grasp on logic—or what is otherwise known as *vertical thinking.* Krome Barratt, however, points out how the mere use of vertical thinking can lead to trouble:

"[The critical] flaw in vertical thinking is that it proceeds from the known to the unknown [… and] can carry false assumptions. Consequently it is possible, even likely, that [...] observations may have built-in bias that is all the more confining because it is unconscious. History reveals that while vertical thinking can bring our full intellectual powers to bear upon a problem and thus to consolidate a position, it is chance [or inspiration] that causes us to stumble upon it in the first place."

This is the reason that so many online resources fall short of expectations. Internal stakeholders tenaciously defend the direction in which their initial intuition led them in. When evidence turns up that doesn't support the initial direction, in many cases, it's either dismissed or explained away. The ironic thing is that for almost any situation where projects are misguided in this way, there are usually one, two, or more individuals who knew better but who were either stifled or ignored because those in control had their agenda and wanted to stick to it. It's for this reason that bringing in outside consultants is often helpful. They are often in the best position to rise above these political barriers, and in some cases remove them.

07.00.03 When we begin looking for inspiration from within the organization, we quickly find ourselves in a defensive position. Rosenfeld and Morville are right on target when they state that "...designing successful sites is an incredible challenge."[1] I disagree, however, that the task is made easier by "brainstorming mission and vision." As logical as this may seem, we're still digging in our own backyards. This is the point when agenda setting begins and when things often begin to get off track with a Web enterprise.

The problem is that organizations usually have ideas regarding what they want to do with a Web enterprise that aren't rooted in what their patrons or sponsors actually need to get done as a result of interacting with the organization's online resource.

Rather, I believe that the process should begin more like a scientific investigation. The organization should form a *hypothesis* regarding the needs that it feels its patrons and sponsors have, and then speculate regarding actions that could be taken to fulfill those needs. The aim is always either to initially provide or to further increase value for these external stakeholders. To do this, the organization should take an investigative role as it begins researching various external stakeholders in a quest for either validation or, more likely, their modification and expansion of its hypothesis.

But what if the external stakeholder needs that research uncovers don't align with or otherwise contradict the needs or the objectives of the organization?

07.00.04 An organization's objectives are important and should be met, but meeting these objectives must be the natural by-product of serving the needs of its patrons and its sponsors.
If accomplishing the organization's goals isn't an extension of serving external stakeholders, then the organization should reconsider going forward with the Web enterprise. Making sure that the goals of the organization and its constituents can find common ground is the responsibility of everyone in an organization who is accountable for the success of the Web enterprise.

This statement isn't meant to dissuade people from engaging in a Web enterprise. It's only meant to encourage an organization to evaluate and reevaluate what the nature and scope of its project should be based on: the research and analysis of *all* stakeholders. If this effort overturns an initial hypothesis, this is good news! This means that the process has helped prevent the development of an off-target online resource that could lead to financial and public-relations catastrophes.

[1] *Information Architecture for the World Wide Web*

07.00.05 It's important to reconcile internal and external stakeholder needs and then develop a plan that will address and satisfy them. Krome Barratt gave us this formula to define the degree to which a solution is elegant:

"[the] elegance of solution = multiplicity of variables / simplicity of [the] organization"

This means that we can estimate the effectiveness that a proposed strategy will have by finding common ground between the various stakeholder needs. The more ways that we find common ground, the fewer buckets we'll need to try and fill (which is what he means by "simplicity"), and the more elegant and effective the solution will be.[2]

Although the process of researching and reconciling stakeholder needs will often infuse an organization with the excitement that accompanies a vision that is both elevated and substantiated, it's conceivable that there's a certain critical mass of needs-commonality below which it's unlikely that a project will be successful. In these situations where all stakeholder needs don't have enough in common, it's better for an organization to pull back and reevaluate its business objectives before moving forward with a project. It's the responsibility of those involved in a Web enterprise's strategy for-mulation to know not only when and how to move forward but also when and how to pull back. The only way this can be determined successfully is through comprehensive and appropriate research.

[2] Simplicity of organization refers to functional efficiency and should not be confused with aesthetic functionalism. I'm an advocate of aesthetic Constructivism and Expressionism, which should be apparent from reading Chapters Five and Six.

07.01 Researching Stakeholder Needs

As mentioned in 07.00.03, strategy formulation mustn't get bogged down with what often ends up being the ethereal mishmash of mission and vision discussions. These sessions often amount to nothing more than executive/project leader "glad handing" and are usually both a waste of time and an impediment to true progress toward providing value to external stakeholders. Instead, a hypothesis that makes speculations regarding external stakeholder needs must be quickly established and then investigated.

07.01.01 Querying internal stakeholders can help us develop a working hypothesis.

The difference between a hypothesis and a mission/vision statement is that much time usually goes into the latter, whereas very little time goes into the former. The more time and resources that an organization invests in this initial activity, the more an investment is made, and the more defensive people will be when these initial ideas are challenged.

Nonetheless, an organization must still have some basis for its initial hypothesis. It must begin, therefore, by asking questions of itself, but this should not be a protracted process. The following are examples of questions that can help formulate an initial hypothesis:

> What are our business objectives for the Web enterprise?
> What are the the "givens" that we should consider?
> How is our Web enterprise currently faring compared to other Web enterprises in its category?
> Who are the primary audiences being served?
> What problems do we perceive that patrons and sponsors would like to solve as a result of embracing our Web enterprise?
> What problems are we trying to solve for ourselves?
> What are the implications of not going forward with the project?
> What are the criteria for deeming the project a success?

If key internal stakeholders are polled with a short list of questions such as these, an initial working hypothesis can in most cases be developed quickly.

07.01.02 A hypothesis is never a plan but always the basis for what should be a thorough investigation.

A hypothesis looks something like this:

"We speculate that if we did x, y would result."

What follows this speculation is the investigation that's necessary to qualify the hypothesis as being true or false. In the likely event that a hypothesis turns out to be false (even if it's partly false, it's still false), the goal becomes to try and reformulate a hypothesis that has at least the potential of being true and then investigate that.

Instead of formulating reasonable hypotheses and then investigating their validity with very little time and resources at risk, what often happens instead is that initial hunches are acted upon and developed to a significant degree. When project leaders feel that their vision has been sufficiently actualized, they endeavor to validate their designs through either *focus groups* or through *usability studies*.

In focus groups, subjects are banded together into groups that discuss the pros and cons of a given suite of design options. If you remember the dynamics of group-think discussed in Chapter One, you'll remember how the social dynamics and pressures of these types of situation make it almost impossible to arrive at any substantive conclusions regarding what the individuals of the group actually thought. In other words, an artificial norm is produced that would not likely reflect the norm if individual anonymous surveys were employed instead.

In usability studies, subjects that supposedly constitute a random sample from the population of a target audience are put in a room and are monitored in various ways to determine which design (or aspects thereof) is most effective. But what are the results?

07.01.03 Although I believe that the idea of stakeholder investigation is most strongly championed by usability experts (and this is commendable), I believe that usability studies are often both misguided and untimely.

As outlined in Part One, these studies are often so focused on issues of simplicity and practicality that in most cases they ignore the broader social, emotional, perceptual, and comprehension issues.

Nonetheless, I agree with the usability folks on one point. It's important to conduct studies as early in the process as possible. But I emphasize the need to validate not just design but the strategy behind the design. Waiting until the design is completed is bad enough. When Web enterprises wait until later stages of the typical ADDIE design phase, however, matters almost couldn't get worse. A too narrowly focused line of inquiry, combined with the untimeliness of stakeholder involvement, leads to unfortunate consequences, which include:

> Because significant capital and human resources have been expended getting to this point, drastically departing from one of the initial designs would make the initial effort seem like a sunk investment—and it often is! Project managers are reluctant to face their superiors with news such as this, so they try to put the best spin they can on the results.[3]
> Subjects are often put in the position of choosing between the lesser of two or more evils, much like voters who feel that none of the candidates in an election are worthy of their votes. Votes don't necessarily reflect their true feelings.
> The heuristics that are used to judge the quality of the Web experience are often very subjective and can be interpreted to prove any point that those who control the project want to make.
> Comprehension of online messages is not generally tested.
> Executive management is often sheltered from the reality of usability study findings and are very "put out" several months later when the Web enterprise isn't performing as desired.

Again, I recognize that usability experts also recommend against conducting usability studies late in the game. I still think, however, that the way most usability studies play out, an overly substantial investment has been made in the work being presented when these studies are generally conducted. The investment in the work that's been done therefore serves as a limiting factor and restricts the possibilities for further innovation.

[3] Just a little side note. Project leaders usually know several months in advance that a project is destined for failure. It's usually at this stage that they put out their résumés. They can accept other opportunities before the failures become evident and their reputations are sullied. After they've left an organization, they can blame those who remain by saying, "They didn't follow my advice."

07.01.04 The purpose of an investigation isn't to validate assumptions but to arrive at the truth.

In light of this, it's important that the people within an organization who are responsible for a Web enterprise put themselves in the most objective situation possible. The only way I know of achieving this is to avoid starting with an agenda but rather start with some fundamental hypothesis with which to launch an investigation into stakeholder needs.

Rather than conducting usability studies, I advocate the practice of conducting *validation studies* before any design has occurred at all. In other words, not only should stakeholder validation occur within each iteration of a *planning, execution,* and *evaluation* cycle within the *iterative execution phase*, as mentioned in the introduction to Part Two of this book, but stakeholder validation should also be conducted within the *strategy formulation phase*. This is the point when it's not too late for findings to do significant good.

[4] For our purposes, controlling the conversation isn't about convincing those we are surveying to do or think anything, but merely to ensure that they disclose their real needs, attitudes, and beliefs by asking good questions and then listening.

07.01.05 The objective of querying external stakeholders in the strategy formulation phase of our process is to identify what their *real* needs are versus what an organization *perceives* these stakeholder needs to be.

Its purpose is also to get their opinions regarding the best ways to try to meet those needs through an online resource. When these are determined, we are in the best possible position to conduct further investigation into possible solutions.

With so much resting on the success of this investigative process, it's important that we understand how to ask good questions. Consider this quote by Roy Chitwood, a noted professional sales consultant and speaker:

"The way to control[4] a conversation is by listening, and the only way to know what the other person is thinking is when they are talking."

Our tendency as humans is to attempt to validate our credibility by showing others how smart we are by talking. The fact is that the success of our investigation hinges on our ability to ask effective questions, listen for important information, and then develop a solution based on real expressed needs.

The *question* becomes that of determining how we formulate a series of questions that will uncover the other party's true needs, attitudes, and beliefs.

According to Chitwood, there are two types of questions: *fact-finding* and *feeling-finding*.

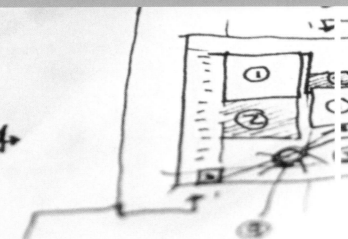

07.01.07 Feeling-finding questions help us understand people's attitudes and beliefs.

Here are some examples of feeling-finding questions:

> Why do you suppose that is?
> Where do you think this course of action will eventually lead?
> How does that make you feel?
> What, if anything, makes you feel optimistic about the potential for improvement?
> How do you think this project will make a difference?

Through these questions, root problems are often revealed. Through probing feeling-finding questions, we may uncover certain attitudes that could lead us to asking fact-finding questions that we might not otherwise have thought to ask.

For example, a project committee may have initially planned to add more features to an online inventory-management system to improve accuracy and speed in fulfillment. Attitudes uncovered with feeling-finding questions, however, could lead us to understand that the inaccuracies and inefficiencies have nothing to do with the system lacking features, but everything to do with a lack of understanding on the part of customers regarding the role of existing features. In this case, what is needed is training, not feature expansion.

07.01.06 Fact-finding questions help us understand what a person understands his or her own situation and needs to be.

Here are some examples of fact-finding questions that we ask both internal and external stakeholders:

> What are the problems with the current online inventory system?
> What criteria would you use to judge the value of improvements to this online resource?
> What are some examples of situations when you had to leave an online session without having your needs satisfied?
> What's your wish list for the new intranet?

This obviously isn't an exhaustive list, but these types of questions help us quickly get to the bottom of stakeholder needs. It's not that we assume that external stakeholders understand their own needs. They often don't; they misdiagnose the cause of their problems and therefore, are in search of the wrong cure. It's the responsibility of those formulating strategy to learn how to make determinations regarding the true meaning, implications, and ramifications of all stakeholder responses to these types of questions. If they're properly interpreted, fact-finding questions can provide not only valuable information but also springboards from which to probe deeper into attitudes and beliefs.

07.01.08 Use one of three ways to pose your questions—as *open*, *reflective*, or as *directive* questions.

Open questions begin with "Who," "What," "When," "Where," "Why," or "How." If you're trying to ask good open-ended questions, avoid questions that begin with "Do," "Don't," "Shouldn't," "Couldn't," and similar words.

Reflective questions accomplish two things. First, they show the other party that we as investigators are engaged in the listening process. Second, they get the other party to dig deeper into the implications of the original answer. Here's an example of how a reflective question is used in an interchange:

Interviewer: (Open question) What do you personally understand the root of your inventory problems to be?

Subject: We can't seem to get updated information on our intranet fast enough. People in the procurement departments of our client base don't seem to get it."

Interviewer: (Reflective follow-up question) Get it?

Subject: No one seems to understand the system. I've heard that it has some pretty nice features, but people get so frustrated trying to figure out how to use those features that they never get beyond the basics. Everyone who uses the system is practically a beginner!

Directive questions must be used with caution. The other party could feel pushed if he or she feels that the investigator hasn't gotten a good enough understanding of the situation yet. Directive questions are good, however, at summing things up and narrowing the focus of what might otherwise be an overly broad conversation:

"If we could streamline the way that people interact with the system by making it communicate in a way that's easy to interpret and understand, and then develop an online training module that could certify people on the system, they'd probably be much happier and effective with the existing features, right?

07.01.09 Time directive questions carefully.

Asking directive questions at the beginning of an inquiry is often presumptuous. This practice gives the indication that the person conducting the investigation isn't really interested in doing anything more than pushing an agenda. Asked at the end of an inquiry, however, this type of question can give the sincere impression that the investigator has truly been listening.

At this stage of an interview, after asking a spectrum of unassuming fact and feeling questions, an investigator uses directive questions to test a hypothesis. It's very likely that the preceding questions will already have nullified the hypothesis in the investigator's mind. If so, a skilled investigator will be able to reformulate a hypothesis or two "on the fly." This can lead to a very energetic dialogue that resembles a brainstorming session.

07.01.10 The objective of our investigation isn't to sell external stakeholders on the advantages of a planned online resource but to get them to suggest problems and possible solutions.

The goal is to unearth the *real* criteria that will determine the acceptance of an online resource as valuable in the marketplace.

As seen in 07.01.08, if a key influencer in the project leadership is a *feature-geek*, the revelation that the project should be more focused on experience design and training than on adding more features may be heavily resisted. This is the defensiveness I mentioned earlier that's the result of internal politics and agenda-setting based on ulterior motives versus actual external stakeholder evaluation.

07.01.11 The research component of the strategy formulation phase is often skipped because it's viewed as presenting an unessential and costly delay to the progress of an online resource's development. "We don't have the time, and we can't afford to do it" is a commonly expressed sentiment by those on an executive committee. As the saying goes, and as many unfortunate Web enterprises have learned the hard way: "They can't afford *not* to do it."

Here's a key insight that can make research much more contracted and less costly.

Our methods of conducting research have, in many cases, not kept pace with the affordances of new technology. Not only can we use technology within the context of our Web enterprises to add value to our online resources, but we can also use technology to improve the cost-to-benefit ratio of the research that contributes to the planning of our online resources. Ward Hanson supports this view:

"Companies [should] use the digital capabilities of the Net to better understand and track their market environments. [...] Research is showing that substituting low-cost online market research for costly physical surveys and demonstrations can provide accurate data at a fraction of the cost. This allows lower cost research that saves money and allows more in-depth studies."

07.01.12 The most commonly used traditional research methods can be qualitatively enhanced while minimizing costs via the input substitution of online digital equivalents such as these:

> Surveys—These are much more convenient, accurate, cost effective, and time efficient when conducted online.

> One-on-one interviews—Intelligent systems can interactively formulate meaningful dialogues of questions and answers. They can also help compile data into meaningful summaries that bypass the lengthy process of people having to sort through and categorize responses.

> Focus groups—Online message boards can take away the burdens of time and place that accompany focus group sessions. The cost can be minimized through various bartering strategies with key constituents of a target population. Online message boards also can remove inhibitions that people may otherwise have about contributing their true feelings about a subject. This can *help* to curb the consequences of group-think (see 01.02.05).

> Direct observation—Key indicators of the quality of a person's experience while interacting with an online resource (whether the organization's or a competitor's) can to some degree be monitored automatically through the innovative use of online technology.

Please hear me; I'm NOT suggesting that all human-to-human research interactions should be replaced by mediated alternatives.

I do think that the use of mediated alternatives versus conventional research can vastly reduce the cost and time requirements. The results of this automated research can help an organization identify areas that warrant direct interactions. These sessions can be much more effective because they can be refined based on what has been learned through preliminary research online. Taken together, these forms of research can put an organization in the best possible position to go forward with enlightened analysis that will eventually help determine an appropriate course of action.

The importance of these tools is so significant that one of the main endeavors of my Web strategy and design consulting firm involves creating these tools.

Questions that we ask ourselves to find these patterns include

> What are the similarities in terms of expressed, implied, or observed problems or needs?
> Are there similarities in progressions or chains of events that lead to either successful or unsuccessful outcomes?
> Are there similarities in terms of expressed or implied solutions that would satisfy needs?
> Do people with similar requirements have similar profiles?
> Are there many or few categories for what would be considered major issues? For minor issues?
> Are there similarities in terms of people's comprehension of what our Web enterprise is trying to offer them and why?
> Is there congruence between what the organization states it's trying to accomplish for its external stakeholders and what these stakeholders express that they need the online resource to accomplish for them?
> Are there similarities in what people understand the value proposition of the Web enterprise to be?

Once these patterns are found, we must attempt to leverage the inherent value that exists when people tend to either do or think about things in a similar fashion. The objective is to reconcile what the organization *imagined* external stakeholder needs to be with what the research states these needs are. Once this reconciliation is accomplished and needs are fully substantiated, the task becomes that of determining the best way to serve these needs. This, however, can be determined only by examining the competitive landscape.

07.02   Analysis—The Interpretation and Reconciliation of Research Findings

Once the initial research has been conducted, the task becomes that of trying to determine "what it all means" and what the implications of that meaning are. Once meaning is established, a systematic investigation into the solutions offered by other competing Web enterprises should determine how, or even if, these needs are being addressed by other organizations. The goal is to find opportunities for developing competitive advantages over other Web enterprises. Needs must then be prioritized to maximize the benefits to all stakeholders. The aim here is to find congruencies between stakeholder needs in order to maximize the strength of the cost-to-benefit ratio of any planned course of action.

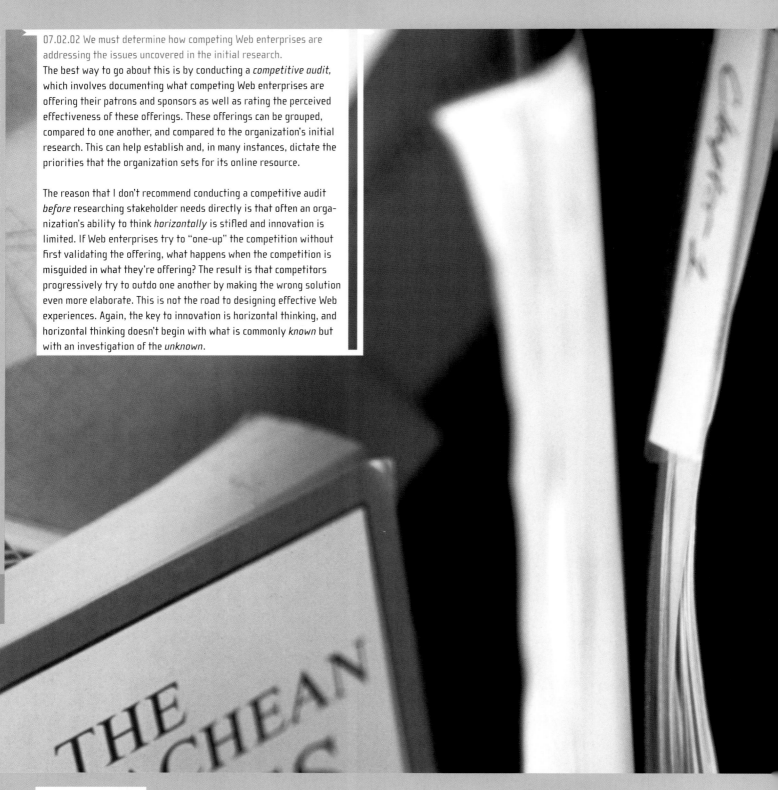

07.02.02 We must determine how competing Web enterprises are addressing the issues uncovered in the initial research.

The best way to go about this is by conducting a *competitive audit*, which involves documenting what competing Web enterprises are offering their patrons and sponsors as well as rating the perceived effectiveness of these offerings. These offerings can be grouped, compared to one another, and compared to the organization's initial research. This can help establish and, in many instances, dictate the priorities that the organization sets for its online resource.

The reason that I don't recommend conducting a competitive audit *before* researching stakeholder needs directly is that often an organization's ability to think *horizontally* is stifled and innovation is limited. If Web enterprises try to "one-up" the competition without first validating the offering, what happens when the competition is misguided in what they're offering? The result is that competitors progressively try to outdo one another by making the wrong solution even more elaborate. This is not the road to designing effective Web experiences. Again, the key to innovation is horizontal thinking, and horizontal thinking doesn't begin with what is commonly *known* but with an investigation of the *unknown*.

07.02.03 Once the full spectrum of stakeholder needs has been identified, it's important to determine which stakeholders benefit from possible courses of action.

Patrons may desire the ability to do x, but if x doesn't either directly or indirectly benefit the Web enterprise, it's not likely to be an advisable course of action. In another scenario, if the course of action benefits both the Web enterprise and its patrons but doesn't in some way align with the sponsor's needs, the course of action—especially in situations where the revenue model is based on sponsorship—is unlikely to be advisable. Ward Hanson comments on this point:

"To be sustainable, [serving external stakeholder's needs] must be matched with benefits to the firm. Improvement-based benefits from the Web are the impacts that lead to internal savings, increased marketing effectiveness, and changes in consumer attitudes. Important examples are lower costs, improved image, higher customer loyalty, and enhanced use of the products offered by companies."

These don't necessarily need to be direct benefits. For example, they don't need to always lead to an immediate sale or in some other way generate revenue from customers—although they might.

Once commonality of benefit has been established, the work of prioritization can follow.

07.02.04 When an organization's needs are compared with those of its patrons and sponsors, *seven zones of priority* can be established. Figure 07.02.04 shows how these seven zones are established and how they relate to one another.

The large circles each represent the set of needs corresponding to of the three groups of stakeholders. The overlapping of these three circles creates the seven zones. The dots within the circles represent possible courses of action. The more dots that are placed in a zone, the larger that zone's area becomes. The size of each zone's area visually indicates the degree to which the relationship among a Web enterprise, its patrons, and its sponsors is healthy. The priority on size proceeds from Zones One to Seven, in that order. The more expansive Zone One's area is, the more healthy the overall relationship is, because all stakeholders benefit. If the combined area of Zones One through Four is substantially more than the combined area of Zones Five, Six, and Seven, it's more likely that the Web enterprise presents a sustainable business model. If the reverse is true, this indicates a high degree of incongruence in stakeholder needs.

Zone 1—All stakeholders directly benefit.

Zone 2—The organization and its patrons directly benefit.

Zone 3—Patrons and sponsors directly benefit.

Zone 4—The organization and its sponsors directly benefit.

Zone 5—Only the patrons directly benefit.

Zone 6—Only the sponsors directly benefit.

Zone 7—Only the organization directly benefits.

Again, in prioritizing possible courses of action, it's extremely important that the combined area of Zones One through Four be substantially greater than that of Zones Five through Seven. with the most importance being placed on the area of Zone One. The initial research and competitive audit should be used to establish an agenda that creates this condition.

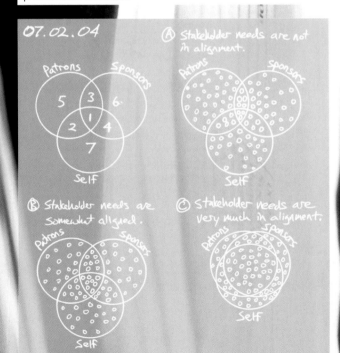

07.02.04

Ⓐ Stakeholder needs are not in alignment.

Ⓑ Stakeholder needs are somewhat aligned.

Ⓒ Stakeholder needs are very much in alignment.

07.02.05 After the initial prioritization is complete, it's important to determine which courses of action the organization is presently in the best position to address with its Web enterprise.

Any number of circumstances could dictate this readiness, from financial parameters to parameters placed on the Web enterprise based on corporate mission and values. It's often fruitless to spread resources thin by attempting to change everything at once, anyway. Therefore, the elimination of a few possibilities is acceptable as long as there are enough viable possibilities left to make a significant enough contribution to the fulfillment of all stakeholder needs.

07.02.06 After priorities have been whittled down, it's important to form more hypotheses and then subject them to further external stakeholder evaluation.

This is the second round of stakeholder validation—and we're still in the strategy formulation stage! No design has occurred. The role of this round of validation studies is to basically state and ask the following of ourselves:

"We've listened to what you've expressed your needs to be, and here is what we've understood you to say. Is that correct? If not, where have we misunderstood? Based on your concurrence that we've understood what you've expressed your needs to be (if, indeed, the subject does concur), here are some ways that we believe we could successfully fulfill these needs. Do you agree that these stated courses of action have the potential of successfully fulfilling your needs if well executed?"

Based on the results of this validation study, an organization may choose either to move forward or to drop back and reevaluate its findings to reprioritize. Once an agenda has been firmly established, it's time to "flesh out" and refine these general priorities into specific strategies that can be planned for and executed. The distinction between the proposed course of action and a specific strategy can be seen in figure 07.02.06.

Figure 07.02.06

Problem	The inventory on the intranet isn't updated on a timely basis.
Hypothesis	If we enhance the feature set of the online inventory management system so that people in our customer's procurement departments have more options, we believe that the system will be updated in a more timely fashion. Do you believe that this is correct?
Research results	The real reason there's a delay in the process is that most people in the client base don't understand how to use the online procurement system because they're confused by its interface.
Proposed course of action	Modify the way that the system interacts with people so that it more effectively communicates meaning.
Reformulated hypothesis	If we make the system more understandable and enjoyable for the people interacting with it, we believe that the system will be updated in a more timely fashion. Is this your understanding?
Specific strategy based on validated hypothesis	Let's develop flowpaths for the procurement personnel that use a series of notions to mimic the way that the procurement process happens between two people when orders are placed by phone.

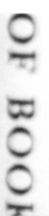

07.02.07 After research has uncovered valid starting points through *horizontal thinking*, *vertical thinking* can be employed to arrive at specific strategies.

Logical reasoning has a much better chance at being on target when the possible starting points have been validated and/or expanded through research. Krome Barratt gives this three-stage model for vertical thinking:

Stage 1:
> Define the problem
> Simplify definition of the problem
> State criteria of success
> Put criteria into a hierarchy
> Define critical criterion of success

Stage 2:
> Redefine the problem from Stage 1 findings
> Define the parameters
> Reconsider the criteria of success and their hierarchy

Stage 3:
> Subject findings to critical examination
> State the activity
> Why is it necessary?
> How is it to be performed?
> Can it be eliminated?
> Can it be combined with another activity?
> Can it be done at a different time?
> Can it be done at a different place?
> What is the hierarchic significance?
> Repeat the procedure for each emergent detail, as for the whole.

07.02.08 A good barometer for the value of a finalized strategy is to examine the degree to which it furthers three specific causes.

According to Dr. Ward Hanson, the online strategies that will be the most effective will invariably hinge on their abilities to deliver better *price*, *assortment*, *convenience*, and *entertainment*. I would add to this list *understandability*, as well as *social*, *emotional*, and *aesthetic appeal*. Hanson proposes that three factors weigh into the degree to which a Web enterprise can deliver these benefits:

> Input substitution
> Clearer communication
> Digital convergence

07.02.09 The cost of producing physical objects such as catalogs, banks, stores, and mail is always greater than producing their online equivalents.

In Hanson's terms, atoms are more costly than bits. Input substitution is a principle that states that when a new resource in business is discovered that contributes to a completed product or service in a more economic way than an established resource, that new resource will be substituted for the established resource. Competition within the marketplace is what forces this principle to be adhered to. If one competitor begins to substitute a cheaper new input for an older, more costly input, other competitors must follow if at all possible or be left behind. As a result, competitors are driven to be the first to innovate so that they can stay one step ahead. In most cases, this is a good thing and leads to innovations that add value and bring progress to the marketplace.

According to Gordon Moore, a cofounder of Intel Corporation, the efficiencies of digital technology will perpetually double every eighteen months. This is known as *Moore's Law* and is what powers the input substitution that Dr. Hanson suggests provides the "basic economic force that [...] guarantees the importance of online [resources]."

This means that the cost of computer processing is continually falling because the technology is getting drastically more efficient on an ongoing basis. The same cannot be said of trees, bricks, and mortar. When an organization offers online resources as substitutes for physical alternatives, as long as these online resources are effective (and that's the catch), they reduce the cost of doing business and strengthen competitive position in the marketplace.

07.02.10 If an organization isn't careful, however, its efforts to practice input substitution will backfire.

This happens all the time, unfortunately. Organizations reason for example that customer service representatives are more expensive than online or telephone *self-help* systems. Therefore they rush into a misguided input substitution strategy while drastically reducing staff. The trouble is that, from the perspective of patrons, the automated systems that they're substituting don't provide viable alternatives to real, accessible customer service agents. The reason organizations get away with this practice is that every other competitor is doing the same thing. Consequently, patrons don't have any alternatives but to take the abuse of being taken for granted.

As I've stated, most online resources are less than effective, and when this type of misguided input substitution occurs, it serves only to cut people off from *any* viable means of gaining the customer service that they desperately need. An organization should be sure that its research is indicating that the input substitution will benefit external stakeholders as much as if not more than it will benefit the organization. If not, the so-called *strategy* will serve only to disenfranchise an organization from the people who are its lifeblood.

What's the moral of the story (and I'm speaking to executive-level individuals here)? Don't underestimate the need to invest appropriately in designing effective Web experiences. Don't be like the Web enterprise offering an online customer loyalty program which I'm familiar with; it nickel-and-dimed itself into over twenty million dollars worth of sunk investment. The Web enterprise persisted in following its own intuition and engaged in successive initiatives that added failure upon failure until finally the parent organization abandoned the entire Web enterprise.

The opportunity that exists for organizations that must apply input substitution via the Web is to bring significant innovation to the substituted online alternative in order to ensure the effectiveness of the solution. This will lead to a competitive advantage and higher patron satisfaction.

07.02.11 The hallmark of an effective online strategy is that it makes it easier for an organization to understand its patrons and for its patrons to understand the organization.

As was discussed at length in Part One of this book, strategies that aim to make communication clearer have a competitive advantage because people know what to do, as well as why, how, and when to do it. To a great degree, this clearer communication will have to do with personalization. Hanson notes that:

"Keith (1960) was one of the first marketers to observe that [technological] development initially caused a 'depersonalizing' of business. Mass production ruled, and the power of standardization dominated. Over time, technological change has moved steadily back toward focusing on the individual."

The most ideal situation in communication is the model wherein an expert individual, serving as a guide for a second individual, identifies his or her unique needs and then nurtures that person into comprehension of the organization's solutions to those needs. The end result is generally to invoke that second individual to take some course of action. Our online resources must come ever closer to approximating this human-to-human model. The organizations that accomplish this goal will be the most successful in the online marketplace and, since the marketplace is going online because of input substitution, in the marketplace, period.

07.02.12 Strategies that leverage the convergence of digital mediums and resources are effective because this type of consolidation increases *both* efficiency and value.

The mantra of this generation is to kill as many birds with one stone as possible. As an example, the average businessperson who lugs around a phone, personal digital assistant (PDA), pager, PC, and audio player is keenly interested in new, hybrid products that wrap all these things into one. Why spend ten times as much for an array of items that would require a "Bat-belt" to carry, when a simple, palm-sized alternative works even better because everything's integrated?

In the same way, strategies that bring convergence of traditionally disparate resources will go a long way toward winning patrons. According to Hanson:

"Digital convergence is the merging of industries, technologies, and content which used to be separate, but now overlap. The three most important converging industries are computing, communications, and media content."

One problem facing marketers is that business practices are converging more slowly than technology. The Web enterprise that's first to help other organizations "get with it" within a certain category will win a high degree of both market share and long-term loyalty. This should be part of any good online strategy.

07.03 Summary

Strategy formulation is an extremely crucial phase in the process of designing effective Web experiences. If the project is pointed in the wrong direction, it will always arrive at the wrong destination, no matter how well executed it is. The key to developing effective Web strategy is not to rely solely on the intuition of *internal* stakeholders, but instead to explore other, more innovative starting points that are based on the horizontal thinking that's inspired by the research of *external* stakeholders, as well as other sources that might be less conventional. If these inquiries into stakeholder needs ask the right types of questions of the right types of people, a Web enterprise puts itself in the best position to understand what it really means to get people to do the right things at the right times.

If an organization can learn to recognize and interpret the patterns in research findings and then capitalize on their congruencies, it has put itself in a good position to develop a prioritized list of possible courses of action that are likely to benefit all stakeholders. When these priorities are in order, an organization can use vertical thinking to arrive at the specific strategies that will most likely fulfill its objectives of either developing a new online resource or enhancing an existing one.

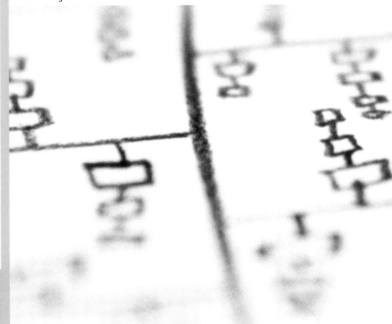

CHAPTER 08

> "[A common problem with organizations developing websites is that] design and production storm ahead without any unifying principle to guide the site's development."
>
> —Louis Rosenfeld & Peter Morville

Iterative Execution—
Exploring Cycles of Planning, Execution, and Evaluation

If the efforts in which a Web enterprise engages are to meet or exceed stakeholder expectations, the unifying principle that *must* guide the design and development of a particular online resource is simple. The principle must be to foster the resource's evolution in such ways that when complete patrons are successfully guided into comprehension of the Web enterprise's online messages; this with the aim of leading them into response interactions with the organization itself, or with its sponsors when appropriate.

While the agenda that our strategy formulation phase yielded gives the needed *guidelines* for success, these guidelines must now be used in the iterative execution phase to determine what our online messages should probably convey, how they most likely should be composed, and how our procedural models should most likely be programmed to properly combine individual notions to form effective personalized notion-flows. We must then execute the plans that we've formulated (which involves design and development) in such a way that we expend the *least* amount of time and resources that are necessary to test the validity of a given iteration. We then repeat these iterative cycles until we zero in on a final execution that's ready for deployment.

The way that we evaluate the degree to which what we've executed is on-target is through *validation studies*. These employ a sufficiently thorough sampling of stakeholders to identify areas that warrant further refinement.

In more simple terms—in the strategy formulation phase, we found out what external stakeholders wanted us to provide them with, and we created an agenda that specifies what we're going to try to accomplish for them. In the iterative execution phase, our job is to

> Plan how to give it to them
> Take a stab at the project as quickly and inexpensively as possible
> Find out how effective we were in our attempt through validation
> Note areas of weakness and repeat

In a sense, our iterative execution phase is itself an *Interactive Narrowing Process* (see 04.03.04), whereby we progressively zero in on the most effective execution of a strategic objective through successive cycles of *planning*, *execution*, and *evaluation*.

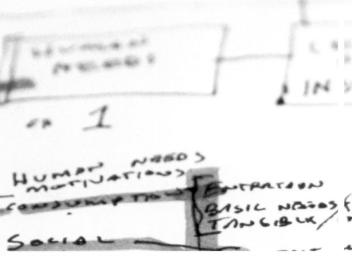

08.00.01 A major indicator of the success of our iterative execution phase is the degree to which what we've created can be considered to be an implementation of 'soft' technology.

According to Dr. Donald Norman, "Hard technology refers to those systems that put technology first with inflexible, hard, rigid requirements for [people]." He proposes that "The correct approach is to develop soft technology that starts with the needs of [people], not with the requirements of technology."

Dr. Norman is correct, and starting with the needs of people is reminiscent of our discussion in Chapter One. But how is this done?

The answer is that we must begin by designing to the specifications of a person's *comprehension* needs in each moment of an idea's presentation and then build toward the particulars of each notion's *technological* execution from there (see Chapter Three). In days gone by, this would've been a luxury that was hard for most organizations to afford. Today, however, because of the excellent technological tools that are available as well as the ever-increasing availability of skilled designers and developers, this approach *can* be very practical and effective if the process is properly managed.

I place only one other qualification on this optimism. The leadership of the teams that are executing the formulation of these notions as well as the programming of their governing control systems must know precisely how to lead patrons through the three stages of online communication: *attract, inform,* and *invoke.*

08.00.02 The thing that will circumvent the incorporation of 'flexibility' in our execution is the rigid practice of approaching experience design as if it were an exercise in developing architectural blueprints.

It's time to begin moving away from the information blueprint as a viable mechanism to govern the formulation of information flows. As outlined in the 04.00 series of notions, this approach may have somewhat served a purpose in its time. That time is now passing, and the practice of information architecture is becoming a liability rather than an asset to effective process.

I stated this in Chapter Four, but it bears repeating. Not only does the process of designing information architecture reduce a solution to the lowest common denominator for each given audience, but it's also the wrong area of a project's execution to emphasize in the first place. Rather than drain time and resources investing in a watered-down compromise that attempts and usually fails to help people *access* appropriate information, a higher rate of return will almost *always* be attained by investing in making the presentation of ideas and concepts through sequences of notions as valuable and viable as possible. That step, combined with innovative flowstems that intelligently sequence appropriate notions based on people's feedback, will always outperform the generalized solutions that are derived from the practices of information architecture and their constraining information blueprints (see Chapter Four).

08.00.03 If we're going to do something substantive with process and not merely go through the motions, we're going to have to actually work with both internal and external stakeholders during each and every cycle of iterative execution.

In Chapter Seven, we learned that if we try to formulate strategy in a vacuum, we'll point ourselves in wrong directions. What's more, if we try to *execute* in a vacuum, we'll inevitably become enamored with our initial iterations and will most likely find ways of protecting our earliest ideas. The result is that we'll have inflicted our patrons, our sponsors, our organizations, and ourselves with the maladies that accompany the foolishness of unqualified wisdom syndrome, discussed in 07.00.

Please don't be fooled by the false security blanket that *user case scenarios* provide. They are brief summaries of various members in a target population that speculate on how a member of that population will intuitively accomplish various tasks online. Although these are sometimes based on real research, which might make them more helpful, they're most often based on the unqualified logic of those who are designing and/or developing the online resource. As with any conclusions that are deduced by traveling from the known into the unknown (see 07.00.01), these scenarios can often blind a project team into thinking that one direction or another has been validated with a given audience when actually it hasn't been.

08.00.04 Because solutions that are effective almost always require several informed iterations, resources must not be squandered on the initial cycle of execution.

Because it seems to be so blatantly ineffective, it's almost hard to believe that the process that I'm about to explain is in reality common industry practice. The approach that most organizations take during an initial execution is to put as many resources as possible on the task of creating as many design options as possible. These are then reviewed and the "best direction" is chosen. Since the individuals or teams working on these creations want to be viewed as having been successful with their respective attempts, generally huge amounts of the budget are expended as each works tirelessly to achieve the best result. Are these efforts really contributing to an effective solution? Rarely.

The reason is that each separate initiative is working in parallel. When several initial design ideas are being worked on concurrently, none of the separate initiatives is benefiting from the lessons learned of a prior iteration. Consequently, each team can be making the same mistakes, which could have been avoided if an iterative execution process had been employed instead. Since the budget's burn-rate is greater when more teams are working on designs in parallel, the net effect is that the entire team is working together to flush the budget down the toilet as quickly and efficiently as possible! By the time everyone figures out where each initiative is off target, it's often too late to make a solid effort in a better direction. Interestingly, this entire doomed process happens with the best intentions.

Nonetheless, there *are* instances when budget and human resources aren't the problem, but time is a big problem. In cases like these, it's might be *okay* to play the numbers game (to work on several design ideas concurrently) to ensure against falling short of ideas within a given timeframe. This isn't optimal, however, and the underlying thinking, which is a primary component of *true* design, cannot be fully undertaken in these circumstances.

08.00.05 Another practice that's a huge time and money pit is that of creating prototypes and mockups in a medium other than the one in which the project will be delivered.

When either an information or visual designer develops mockups in page layout, image editing, or other applications that aren't specifically designed to deliver content on the Web, time and money are wasted. The reason is twofold. First, if and when a design is ultimately approved, it will need to be completely *re-created* in an application that can deliver content for the Web. Second, in this re-creation process, there will invariably be variations between the prototype and the final presentation. These might include pagination differences (how words and other media elements flow) as well as technical problems that weren't anticipated and that could all but nullify the validity of either a part or the entirety of the design.

The practice of designing print prototypes of online resources doesn't exist because it's what's best for the project. The reason it exists is because designers are most familiar with the print medium and with applications that support the print medium. At this point in the evolution of the Web design and development community, the labor force still has many members who don't have specialized training in Web design and development. It's composed of those with print design and broadcast media backgrounds. Even the vocational institutions that teach Web design don't have a cogent philosophy for interactive multimedia. Their instructions are generally adaptations of principles taught in the print medium. As someone who has worked extensively with top-notch college interns and grads, I've seen that their education has often not prepared them for dealing with the technical execution issues that ultimately define a project's success.

In light of this, it's clear that the Web design community must begin to be trained to effectively and efficiently leverage Web applications to create prototypes in the delivery medium.[1]

[1] Two notable organizations that provide this type of specialized training include Allen Interactions (www.alleninteractions.com), which offers classes in Minneapolis, Chicago, and Tampa; and Sterling Ledet & Associates (www.ledet.com), which offers classes in Atlanta, Chicago, Minneapolis, and San Diego.

08.00.06 The mission of each iterative cycle is to increasingly align execution with the direction that validation studies indicate will most effectively satisfy patrons' needs, interests, and expectations. It's time that the practice of putting all the time and budgetary eggs in the proverbial "one basket" is done away with. This basket is what is typically known as the "design phase." This practice constitutes a huge hit-or-miss gamble with the project's very viability. Once this phase has been completed, there's no going back. As mentioned in the introduction to Part Two, processes that are based on linear phases that don't loop back on themselves are sometimes referred to as *Waterfall* methods. Picture water flowing down a staircase where each stair is a phase in the process. Once each phase has been passed, there's no going back. After all, water doesn't flow uphill!

Rather than blowing the whole budgetary "wad" in one all-encompassing design cycle, it's much better to do quick-and-dirty passes that progressively become more polished as design directions are validated. These begin with stick-figure-level passes and, throughout the iterative execution phase, work themselves into whatever final form is appropriate for the project. By getting things off to a quick iterative start in what is referred to as *rapid prototyping*, there will be time, budget, and energy to have several positive *mid-mortems* instead of one big, negative *post-mortem.* In a mid-mortem, the team can still say "Whew! I'm sure glad we caught this before we spent any more resources on it." In post-mortems—which tend to be finger-pointing sessions in which people try to salvage their jobs—the sentiments are more like "Why the hell did we do that? Who authorized that design direction?!?"

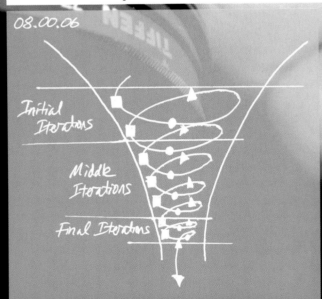

08.00.06

Initial Iterations

Middle Iterations

Final Iterations

08.00.07 The cycles within the iterative execution phase are not meant to amble on forever.
Rather, they wrap themselves up (no pun intended) as they proceed through three general stages of maturity:

> Initial iterations—These are ideas in their *infancy*, where we paint with broad strokes to plan general directions for their lives.
> Middle iterations—These are ideas in their *adolescence*, where we discipline them until they become more refined while they're still moldable and adaptable.
> Final iterations—These are ideas in their pre-adulthood, where our sculpting is more focused and granular as we fine-tune them for life on their own in the World Wide Web.

The sections in this chapter that follow explore how the nature of our iterations evolve during the *planning, execution,* and *evaluation* stages of our idea's design and developmental maturity that occur within the *iterative execution* phase.

08.00.08 As mentioned in 08.00.05, the key to succeeding in iterative execution, and especially rapid prototyping, is to be expert at designing and developing in the delivery medium.

If experience designers can't design and develop in the delivery medium, the entire process becomes more expensive and slows down. The only prequel to this practice would be the even quicker and dirtier practice of using sketchbook or whiteboard exercises to facilitate either group or individual brainstorming.

Interestingly, the best way to make these *early* iterative attempts meaningful isn't by being locked away in a room somewhere. The best way to create these rapid prototypes is by sitting right next to a person in the target audience whose input the team is seeking.

Figure 08.00.08 is a role-play that illustrates how a designer and a subject might interact as they try to design a notion that would answer one of the agenda items that was formulated in the strategy phase. By interacting with a *real* patron in this situation, the *real* issues can often be interactively zeroed in. This can save immense amounts of resources that would otherwise be spent working out and following "hunches" that ultimately would have proven out to be misdirections. I've seen five-minute sessions like this avoid the expenditure of days of effort and thousands of dollars.

I want to clarify the value of rapid prototyping sessions in which stakeholders are involved. These are not validation sessions but collaborative execution sessions. When it's time to *validate* the work, this type of interaction between experience designers and stakeholders is not valuable and can lead to confusion.

Figure 08.00.08

Designer: In our research, we determined that people such as you had trouble understanding what our online resource was attempting to communicate at this stage of the presentation. We were told that if we improved this communication problem, people would complete their transactions more frequently. How do you see this situation?

Subject: I agree. My eye is drawn to all these buttons over here (subject points to a part of the screen). Looking at the screen, I had no idea that what I was supposed to do was focus on this section of the screen (pointing again). It makes me very confused.

Designer: Makes you confused?

Subject: Yes, because this part of the screen is so prominent (pointing at the screen again), it's really distracting. Why do these elements need to exist on the screen here if you don't want me to pay attention to them?

Designer: Good question. That doesn't make much sense, does it? I guess we thought that it was important to keep this particular part of the marketing message as prominent as possible at all times. How about if we reduced the size of this like so (Designer works in the application to transform the situation right before the subject's eyes) and then moved this part here, to the center?

Subject: That helps a little (watching intently), but I think that it would be better if you just got rid of it. I've already "bitten" the marketing message bait at this stage of the game. Why do I need to be constantly reminded of it? It would be as if I were at a store and told the clerk that I wanted to buy the item and clerk kept telling me how good of an idea it would be if I bought the item. I'd think that the clerk was dense!

Designer: I see your point. Let's remove it and redistribute the elements on the screen-space like this. Let's see how this notion would fit with representative examples of notions that would come before and to see if they flow together well. (They try the interaction.)

Subject: That's better. The only thing is that I would only expect to see this notion if I made one particular choice on the screen-space that came just before this one.

Designer: Interesting. What if we made a rule for the system that presented only this notion if you made that particular choice?

Subject: That would be great.

Designer: What should we do at this stage to make the interaction flow well for each of the other possibilities? ...

08.00.09 After fundamental issues are worked out as in the role-play from the previous figure, subsequent iterations can focus on improving the aesthetics of the interaction.

While some argue that people can't possibly know if the interaction is going to work or not unless the final execution is evaluated, time and tide have proven that rapid prototyping is a major contributor to keeping a project on track in terms of timeframe, budget, scope, and the value of the end result.

The rapid prototyping role of iterative design is foundational to the success of the iterative execution phase of our process. It's also somewhat of a landmark practice. The reason is that in the past, paper-based prototypes and storyboards were used instead. One of the chief weaknesses of these practices is that there is usually a huge separation between when these artifacts are generated and when an attempt is made to actually transfer the ideas they present into the delivery medium. Because of the fluidity of project dynamics, in most cases by the time paper-based prototypes and storyboards are converted to the delivery platform the ideas they represent are obsolete. What's more, these mechanisms are based on the fiction of what people *might* do when interacting with the online resource, whereas prototypes created in the delivery medium are based on the realities of how functionalities actually play themselves out.

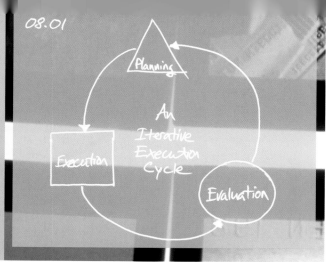

08.01

An Iterative Execution Cycle

Planning
Execution
Evaluation

08.01 Initial Iterations—Painting with Broad Strokes

In the first couple rounds of iterative execution, we're consumed with the task of fleshing out concepts for our online messages as well as their correlating notion-flows. Our prime concern is designing online interactions that communicate effectively and guide people into comprehension of the online messages that are the most interesting and beneficial to them. The best approach to this is to identify *real-life* interactions that are effective and then find methods of mimicking these real-life dialogues through online approximations.

The way that the planning, execution, and evaluation stages of each cycle play out in this effort are as follows:

> Planning—We need to discover the best approach to fulfilling the requirements discovered in the strategy formulation phase.
> Execution—After we have some initial ideas that seem to have the potential of being viable, we take a stab at designing and developing a rudimentary version of the notion flow.
> Evaluation—We determine through validation studies how the prototype performs when put to the test.

08.01.01 We must discover the variations regarding how real-life equivalents of online interactions occur.

The best way to go about creating meaningful interactivity isn't by beginning with screen-space design but by observing and charting the interaction of two important people. The first person is a representative patron. The second person is a representative professional who's an expert at serving the needs of people in the area in which he or she operates:

> In a hospitality business, this person might be a guest services manager from a hotel who's well versed in the various issues that come up with guests. This person could also be a chef or the host of a fine restaurant.
> In the automotive industry, it could be a sales or service rep who's known for high levels of customer satisfaction.
> In a financial services business, it could be a well-respected financial advisor.

The key question is this: What do these professional representatives do that makes them so successful at serving people's needs? The key task is to discover their secrets and then emulate their ways of interacting with people. This usually happens through observation in the field, not through studies in lab environments. The best approach is to shadow these experts for a day or two and quietly document how they and their patrons interact. I'm certain that the unifying factor in every observable situation that will be most common is this: These experts know how to give people the right information at the right times to get them to "do the right things at the right times," as Dr. Allen would say.

Isn't it interesting that those who are most successful at meeting the needs of the people they serve are the most successful in business? In effect, they take care of themselves by taking care of others. This is a virtuous cycle. The Web enterprises that take this approach within a given market space will be the most effective. The best that a mediated interaction can hope to achieve is to re-create this successful process, add to it an encyclopedic, institutional memory, and scale it to satisfy the needs of multitudes.

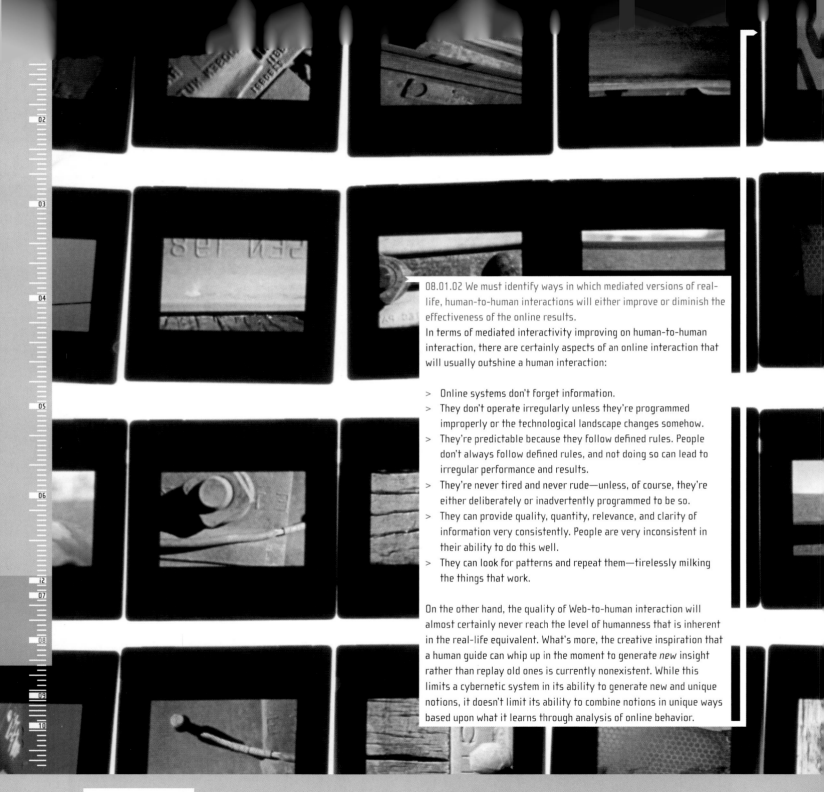

08.01.02 We must identify ways in which mediated versions of real-life, human-to-human interactions will either improve or diminish the effectiveness of the online results.

In terms of mediated interactivity improving on human-to-human interaction, there are certainly aspects of an online interaction that will usually outshine a human interaction:

> Online systems don't forget information.
> They don't operate irregularly unless they're programmed improperly or the technological landscape changes somehow.
> They're predictable because they follow defined rules. People don't always follow defined rules, and not doing so can lead to irregular performance and results.
> They're never tired and never rude—unless, of course, they're either deliberately or inadvertently programmed to be so.
> They can provide quality, quantity, relevance, and clarity of information very consistently. People are very inconsistent in their ability to do this well.
> They can look for patterns and repeat them—tirelessly milking the things that work.

On the other hand, the quality of Web-to-human interaction will almost certainly never reach the level of humanness that is inherent in the real-life equivalent. What's more, the creative inspiration that a human guide can whip up in the moment to generate *new* insight rather than replay old ones is currently nonexistent. While this limits a cybernetic system in its ability to generate new and unique notions, it doesn't limit its ability to combine notions in unique ways based upon what it learns through analysis of online behavior.

08.01.03 Based on what we've learned through observation and interview, as well as on what we know we must accomplish for all stakeholders, we must develop a plan of action for a flowstems' design and development.

The next step after observation and documentation (mind maps rather than reports) is to look for patterns. Find the "cowpaths" that people travel consistently and create baseline rules that mimic these patterns of behavior. Remember that flowpaths lead people through messages in such a way that they present ideas with a beginning, middle, and end. Some of the ideas we might communicate online are

> Hey, Mr. Customer, we have a great idea! Why don't you buy a product from us online!
> This machine can be disassembled in six easy steps.
> When you vote for Billy John Doe, you're voting for two chickens in every oven.
> A vacation at our resort will satisfy all your family's needs.
> Our cosmetic surgeons are the most reliable in the state.
> Our phone directory listings are more up-to-date than other leading directories.
> As a particle accelerates through space, it decelerates through time, and vice versa.

The challenge becomes to discover what thoughts need to be comprehended by the various people in an online population at each stage of the three-part communication process (see Chapter Two) and then figure out a way to make those thoughts sink in.

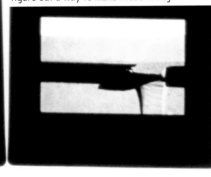

08.01.04 We must develop a rudimentary prototype for each notion in a possibilities pool that might come into play within a notion-flows. The goal of this stage of iterative execution isn't to make things look pretty. It's to get the fundamental notions down so that they can be validated. What we're trying to do through the development of notions in *initial* iterations is answer the question "What needs to happen at this moment? At this next moment? And at this next moment?" We therefore must formulate each notion in as bare-bones a fashion as possible while still getting the thought across. This will undoubtedly involve copywriting but may (and probably should) also involve quick-and-dirty digital photography, sketches, crude keyframe animation, and/or recorded speech as needed. The gradualness of this process depends on the scope of the online resource, the number of experience designers/developers involved, and the number of audience sets and subsets that the resource is intended to serve.

Although resources that are expended *refining* ideas at this stage are wasted, early refinement is still the most common industry practice. Designers often want instant gratification, so they put the cart before the horse. Unfortunately, the creativity that they think they're applying to their notions is often not creativity at all. It's not productive originality. It's shooting from the hip. The result, unless there's a fortunate accident, is that whatever comes out will most likely be a rehashing of what's been done and seen before. Yawn.

Why do designers do this? In many cases it's because they really don't know what else to do. Feeling that they have their hands tied and must somehow be showing their viability as members of the project team, they fill their time with meaningless exercises that in the end almost ruin the possibility that creative results will ever be achieved because budget is wasted (see Chapter Ten).

08.01.05 We must develop the rules and procedures for the system that will manage the notion-flow.

After initial notions are formulated, we need to figure out what the rules and procedures will be that govern how they're strung together into notion-flows that will travel down flowpaths into people's minds. For those who are familiar with programming, this amounts to a conglomeration of conditional evaluations. Web media applications with authoring capabilities can easily be put to work at this early stage of iterative execution. Let's say, for example:

> We have a three-stage communication model—attract, inform, and invoke (see Chapter Two).
> Next, let's assume that there's a minimum of one notion needed for the attract stage of an online message, with a possibility of two needed based on people's individual needs. We'll assume we have a pool of nine possible notions that can be drawn upon for these segments of our flowpath.
> The inform stage will go through three notions at a minimum but could go through as many as seven. The pool of possibilities has three hundred notions that are designed to initially populate the pool of possibilities. There are so many because we're assuming this is an e-commerce application with one hundred products, each with three notions that take three different approaches to showing how the product fulfills a set of needs.
> We'll plan on typically having two notions in the invoke stage but will allow for more if necessary. The pool of possibilities here will be ten notions.

After we know how to address people's comprehension needs in various moments along their flowpaths, the task becomes that of translating our representative human experts' reasoning into cybernetic form that prescribes notion-flows that mimic the expert's performance. Once in this form, the notions and procedures programmed into our flowstems can be tested in the medium in which the end product will be delivered. Only this will provide an accurate picture of a solution's strength to move people into response interactions.

08.01.06 We must identify a realistic and manageable set of variations for each notion to support the unique cognitive and emotional needs of various individuals within an audience segment.

As mentioned in Chapter Three (but which bears repeating), because people are different and their conceptual frameworks are different, they often must veer away from the normative flowpath. There are several possible reasons; here are two:

> They may need supporting evidence for a point that's being presented before they'll believe the presentation to be factual.
> They may not have a baseline of knowledge that the majority of the other people following the flowpath may have.

To minimize the burden of providing an inordinate number of variations of notion-flows for a given flowpath, the possibilities pools that corresponds with a flowpath should themselves be tailored to a specific audience subset.

If a person is going to a window manufacturer's online resource, the notion-flow that's encountered should be different, depending on whether that person is a consumer, an architect, a builder, or a distributor. When we present an architect with an array of information that's generalized for multiple audiences, we violate our Q-Q-R-C rules that govern polite communication (see 03.02). Even when we do tailor a possibilities pool for a given audience such as architects, within that architectural audience set there will inevitably be variations on what should be taken into consideration when dynamically sequencing an individual's notion-flow.

For example, let's say that a particular architect is new to a product line. That person should be "talked to" in a different way than an architect who has been a customer for years. That's how it would work in real life. Why shouldn't it work that way online? Can you imagine this scenario:

"Hey Earn, we've got a new tutorial for how to install the V45 casement windows! Would you like to go through it with me?!"

"What're you talking about, Herb? I've been installing that window for three years—and you've been selling them to me! Why would you ask me if I wanted to go through a tutorial? Do you think I'm stupid or something? Show some respect."

In real life, people feel slighted if others don't recognize their fundamental characteristics after several interactions. As a result, we work toward maintaining basic familiarity. We must also strive to do this for the people that our Web enterprises interact with online.

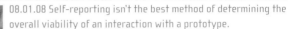

08.01.07 We must measure our success in achieving our goals for this iteration of execution through another round of validation studies. The first cycle of iterative execution should conclude with a validation study. Since there were two validation studies in our strategy formulation phase, this means that the first validation study in iterative execution will be our third validation study overall. Depending on how many iterations a particular flowpath requires before moving into deployment, there are *n* possible validation studies in iterative execution.[2] These are referred to as *formative evaluations* because feedback from these studies should serve to further *form* or refine the end product.

The best way to conduct these studies isn't by handholding people through an interaction. In other words, it shouldn't feel *collaborative*, as in the rapid prototyping sessions. That practice taints the study and clouds the results. Instead we must allow our subjects to go through the prototype on their own after reviewing a brief disclaimer. This disclaimer explains the rudimentary nature of the prototype and expresses that no attempt has been made toward visual or other refinement.

The subject is then given a set of consecutive tasks to complete through the prototype. The only valid way of conducting these studies is to have subjects interact with the prototype electronically, and hopefully within the context of a Web browser. If not, it will be harder to interpret the results.

[2] In the deployment phase, there's one more validation study, validation study *n+1*, which serves as a *summative* evaluation because it *sums up* the effectiveness of the project, but the feedback doesn't directly impact the current project.

08.01.08 Self-reporting isn't the best method of determining the overall viability of an interaction with a prototype.

Reeves and Nass discuss this issue at length in *The Media Equation*. They explain that while it may *seem* that the purpose of a study is to find out what a subject *thinks* about an experience, accurate insights into the impact that an online resource really has are often difficult to attain by merely asking his or her thoughts and opinions. Certainly asking people for their thoughts and opinions is part of a validation study, but it's not necessarily the most important part. The reason is that people tend to have trouble reporting their true attitudes and feelings as well as what they've truly gained from an experience. There are several reasons for this, which include

> Their feedback is based on their *perception* of the experience rather than the events of the experience. In light of this, self-reporting is useful only when the objective is to get information about people's *perceptions*.
> They misunderstand what they're being asked to respond to. They give what they *believe* to be the correct answer, but it is the correct answer, in a sense, to the wrong question.
> They may have a hidden agenda and try to impose it on the research results by coloring their answers.
> They may be trying to second-guess the agenda behind the study.
> They may be the type of people who don't like to give negative feedback or vice versa.

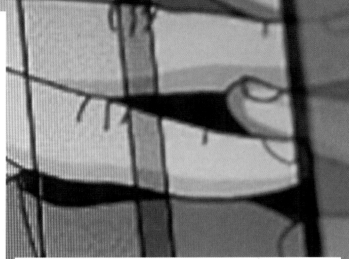

08.01.09 There are many possible strategies to gain more accurate information than can be arrived at through self-reporting.

Some strategies relate to watching what people do and listening to their undirected verbal commentary *during* their actual interaction with an online resource. This is much more effective than waiting until afterward to make inquiries. The reason it's important to monitor behavior in the moment is that people tend to blur these moments into less than helpful generalizations after the fact. These generalizations also are the result of reflective thinking, which requires self-analysis. Self-analysis—or second-guessing—almost always obscures the facts that researchers are after.

Another type of strategy involves getting people to respond in the moment to one stimulus when in reality the objective is to measure the auxiliary impact of another stimulus.

Let's say that our goal is to understand which clip in a pool of audio clips is the most psychologically engaging. Instead of asking the subject how engaging he or she thought the clip was after the fact, the subject is asked, while listening to the audio clip, to click a button every time a flash of the color red appears within the screen-space. The idea is that the more engaging the audio clip, the slower the response time to the red flash will be in milliseconds because the person becomes engrossed in the content of the clip and is therefore more distracted from the task of clicking. If the object is to see if a person was more engaged in one clip out of a group of possibilities, the average response times can be compared. The clip that yields the slowest average response time is the one that most engaged the person psychologically. Note that the subject has no idea what the purpose of the study is and therefore can't second-guess what a good response would be. The results are both objective and reliable.

I'll offer one final type of alternative to self-reporting, and that's simply to quiz a person's knowledge after the fact. If the Web experience is about information, verify his or her ability to integrate the new information into long-term memory. This can be verified immediately after the experience but can also be verified days and weeks after the fact to assess the longevity of the new information.

08.01.10 Web-based evaluation applications can make validation studies accessible, cost-effective, and accurate.

The goal of a validation study is to confirm or disaffirm the effectiveness of a particular flowstem's ability to both anticipate a person's flowpath and deliver an appropriate notion flow along that flowpath. Depending on the nature of the project, a list of criteria for success needs to be established, and the performance of the flowstem must be measured against it.

> Some of these criteria will relate to a subject's ability to easily accomplish the various tasks that were given.
> Some may measure time-related issues such as how long a person took to accomplish the task.
> Others may measure how long that person's interaction could be extended through providing valuable resources that enticed him or her to extend an interaction.
> Furthermore, some may measure how much money was spent or how many items were purchased.

The common thread in all of these cases is that they involve statistics. All of these statistics can be measured electronically behind the scenes and can be compiled into reports. It becomes very cost effective to actually develop a Web-based *validation apparatus*, if you will, that lays on top of the prototype. It integrates with the prototype to such a high degree that statistics can be extracted, compiled, and evaluated on a broader scale and at a cost that's almost always much lower than would be the case when tracking these statistics manually.

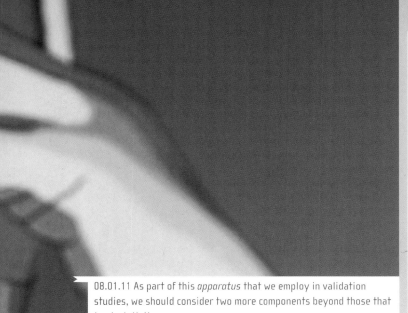

08.01.11 As part of this *apparatus* that we employ in validation studies, we should consider two more components beyond those that track statistics.

The first is a mechanism, as described in 08.01.09, that *allows* for subjects to make comments at any time during their journey along a flowpath. Again, comments are especially helpful when they can be recorded in the moments in which a person stumbles upon the aspects of the online resource that instigate these comments.

The next is a knowledge-testing mechanism that can be employed at the end of an online interaction, as described in 08.01.09, with a flowstem to evaluate comprehension of various online messages.

Again, the innovative use of technologies such as these make validation studies more accessible and therefore more valuable because they're much more likely to be employed throughout the iterative execution phase of our process. The results become the fuel for the planning stage of the next iteration. These tools are so important that one of the primary activities that I'm involved with is developing tools that fulfill these purposes.

08.02 Middle Iterations—Discipline and Refinement

When we leave the initial iteration stage of iterative execution, we've successfully taken the guidelines from the strategy formulation phase and converted them into a network of viable, although rudimentary, notions and flowpaths that we've confirmed through validation studies and that will lead to successful outcomes for all stakeholders. We've attempted to avoid investing unnecessary time and resources into activities such as substantial graphical execution, which have a high likelihood of being discarded in subsequent iterations. We don't care if we must discard things that have been quickly and inexpensively formulated. It's harder to discard work that was costly and time-consuming because we have more at stake both practically and emotionally.

At the beginning of middle iterations, the planning stage amounts to what I've referred to as a "mid-mortem." This is an assessment and planning meeting that will govern further content, interface, and cybernetic execution. Unlike initial iterations, the objective of middle iterations is to move the project to a *deployable state of refinement*. It's in this phase that we gradually yet progressively begin to invest the time and resources necessary to arrive at an emotionally engaging, aesthetically gratifying solution.

Even while progressively doing this, however, we test the ice before we step on it. In keeping with this, each cycle of middle iteration ends with evaluation, using the same integrated validation study application employed in initial iterations. What's driving this careful consideration of our every step is that we never want to move so far forward with an iteration that it would be cost-prohibitive to abandon the progress within that iteration if it became apparent in a validation study that the work was moving off target.

08.02.01 Here's the good news: Because our process mandates that prototypes be created in the delivery medium, the project team doesn't have to start over during middle iterations!

The reason that this is significant is that a working model now exists of the entire online resource. All the logic and programming that's been executed thus far can be carried forward into *middle* iterations for further refinement. If your executed programming code has been *bootstrapped* up to this stage, now is the time to make it neat and pretty. If not, the problems will only get worse (see the 09.01 series).

The significance of this is that our process doesn't have separate *design* and *development* phases. As a notion is being iteratively designed in the delivery medium, it's also being iteratively developed by default. This is significant because there's almost zero risk of designing something that in the end won't work. In the twenty-first century, a separation between design and development is an artificial separation that makes no economic sense.

08.02.02 Initial iterations draw to a close and middle iterations begin when an overall conceptual vision is fully grasped.

This vision pertains to how the online resource will accomplish the goals set in the strategy formulation phase. There are several lessons that should have been learned in the initial iterations:

> How to best represent thoughts/concepts/ideas for various types of individuals within an audience set or subset
> How to determine the level of personalization that will be required for a given audience subset
> How to determine the scope of the content that must be created to satisfy various types of needs
> How to best tell the story of each online message
> How to protract and contract a message based on people's interactive feedback

Once the information has been gathered from validation studies in initial iterations, the planning stages in the middle iterations will generate courses of action that will progressively bring various flowpaths to life. As mentioned, the goal is to begin moving execution toward a deployable state of refinement.

08.02.03 While we've learned during initial iterations how to best represent thoughts in each notion, now the work becomes that of honing the execution to reflect an artfulness—a thoughtfulness that represents the true, golden character of the organization behind the online resource.

> Strategy formulation told us *what* objectives needed to be accomplished through interaction with the Web enterprise.
> Initial iterations revealed *how* to best interact with people to accomplish these objectives.
> Middle iterations let us refine the precise *manner* in which we design our Web experiences to actualize these objectives.

Our aim isn't to overwhelm people with an *overly* sensory presentation but to find a balanced appropriateness that will engage the senses yet will not overstimulate them. In the end, the manner in which we design our Web experiences must support the continual flow of appropriate notions that drive people to a comprehension of and a response to our online messages.

08.02.04 Through our research and validation exercises, we've determined the degree to which notion-flows should be personalized. In his book *Principles of Internet Marketing,* Ward Hanson explains an important concept for understanding the benefit of personalization. He writes about a distinction between what are known as *search goods* and *experience goods.* Hanson frames this discussion in terms of product selection, but the principle applies to consumption of anything online. He writes:

> "Search goods are products and services that are easy for a consumer to evaluate."
> "Experience goods tend to be difficult to understand and evaluate."

Search goods are predictable items such as a nationally recognized soft drink brand or a pair of name-brand jeans. Experience goods are more difficult to evaluate because they may involve products or services whose quality is a matter of personal taste. These could include resorts, restaurants, decorative items, or anything else for which people's opinions vary. Hanson continues:

"Experience goods are especially hard to judge when there is a complex mixture of variety and quality attributes. Personalization techniques can assist consumers in choosing among experience goods. In almost all cases, consumers benefit from reducing their uncertainty about experience goods. An accurate personalization system with an effective way of matching [products and services] to tastes can eliminate many unpleasant consumption experiences."

It's essential that either our strategy formulation or initial iterations reveal the degree to which the information, products, services, or diversions that our Web enterprise aims to help people consume involves experience goods. The reason is that this helps us determine the scope of the project during middle iterations. The more irregular the response of a population is to what the online resource provides, the more valuable the personalization of the experience will be.

08.02.05 Danger! Beware of preexisting content.
Once the degree to which notion flows must be personalized in order to accomodate individual flowpaths is determined, the temptation becomes to try to "fill in the blanks" on the flowpath as quickly and as cost-effectively as possible. While these are good goals, if the end result is to be truly effective, an online resource mustn't become an organization's dumping ground for content that's been developed for other types of print, broadcast, or presentation projects. The insight that's been gained through research and evaluation will be squandered if the online resource merely serves as a framework for preexisting content.

While organizations are often enamored with the various things that it feels it must communicate, outsiders don't often find these communications to be very helpful (see Spotlight On Dr. Michael Allen in Chapter Three). It's not that valuable information can't be exhumed from these materials; it can be. The point is that the Web enterprise should be doing the exhuming and not the people trying to interact with its online resources.

Once exhumed and compartmentalized into agile notions, our flow-stems can intelligently prescribe these nuggets at times and in ways that are appropriate to individual people.

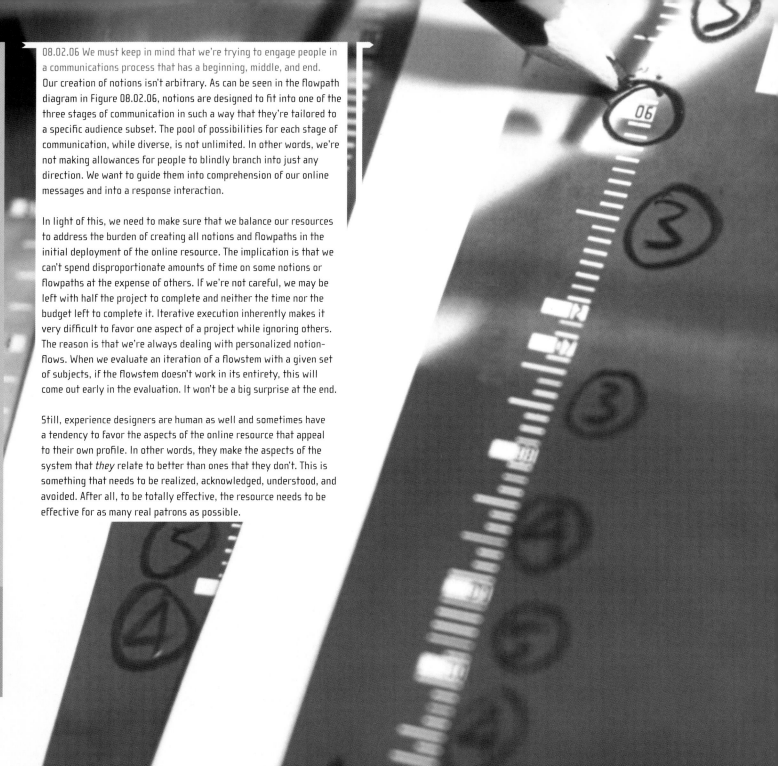

08.02.06 We must keep in mind that we're trying to engage people in a communications process that has a beginning, middle, and end. Our creation of notions isn't arbitrary. As can be seen in the flowpath diagram in Figure 08.02.06, notions are designed to fit into one of the three stages of communication in such a way that they're tailored to a specific audience subset. The pool of possibilities for each stage of communication, while diverse, is not unlimited. In other words, we're not making allowances for people to blindly branch into just any direction. We want to guide them into comprehension of our online messages and into a response interaction.

In light of this, we need to make sure that we balance our resources to address the burden of creating all notions and flowpaths in the initial deployment of the online resource. The implication is that we can't spend disproportionate amounts of time on some notions or flowpaths at the expense of others. If we're not careful, we may be left with half the project to complete and neither the time nor the budget left to complete it. Iterative execution inherently makes it very difficult to favor one aspect of a project while ignoring others. The reason is that we're always dealing with personalized notion-flows. When we evaluate an iteration of a flowstem with a given set of subjects, if the flowstem doesn't work in its entirety, this will come out early in the evaluation. It won't be a big surprise at the end.

Still, experience designers are human as well and sometimes have a tendency to favor the aspects of the online resource that appeal to their own profile. In other words, they make the aspects of the system that *they* relate to better than ones that they don't. This is something that needs to be realized, acknowledged, understood, and avoided. After all, to be totally effective, the resource needs to be effective for as many real patrons as possible.

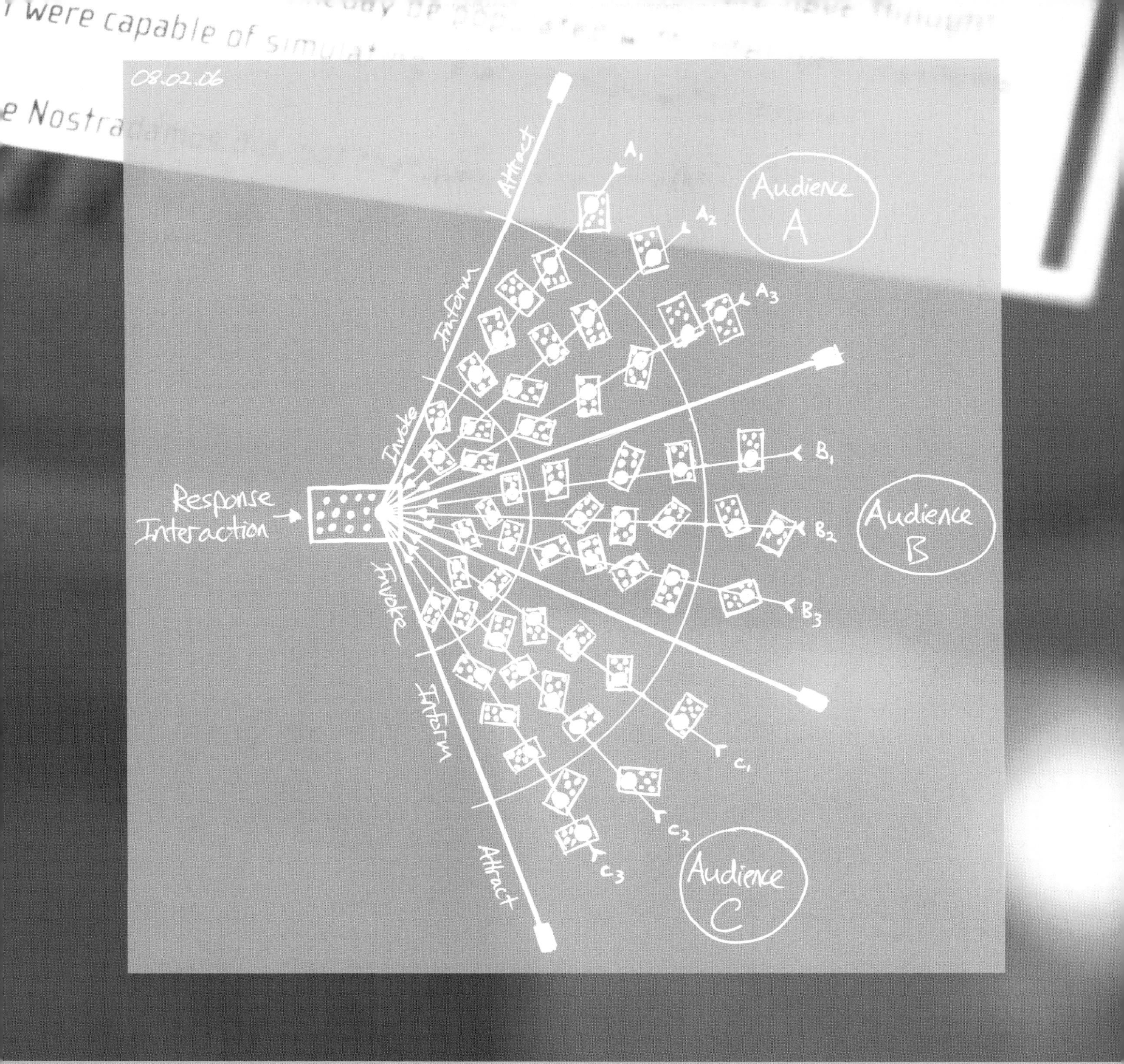
08.02.06
Attract
Inform
Invoke
Response
Interaction
Invoke
Inform
Attract
A_1
A_2
A_3
B_1
B_2
B_3
C_1
C_2
C_3
Audience A
Audience B
Audience C

08.02.07 We must have sufficient diversity in a possibilities pool to allow for the flexibility in scope that various people will require. The other caution I'll offer is to not deceive yourself into being overly optimistic about how frequently people will stick to a baseline notion flow. The danger is that the time and energy won't be put into the divergent notions that are necessary to help certain people over psychological hurdles. The beauty of the SPEED process (see i2.00.03) is that it takes the needs of many different types of people into consideration. If the creation of alternate notions isn't followed through, the online resource will not create optimum flow experiences for anyone else but those who fall inside the norm of the target audience. The greater the diversity of notions in each pool of possibilities that correspond with a segment of an audience flowpath, the more a person will identify with the content and have a sense that the presentation was unique. As mentioned in Chapter One, this "unique to me" aspect of our flowstems is a powerful force that causes people to make emotional connections with Web enterprises.

Understand that resource limitations will prevent *every* possible notion to be developed for *any and all* situations—at least initially. The beauty of flowstems, however, is that they're very organic and can grow over time. If a person has trouble comprehending a notion or fails to see the appropriateness of it in a given flowpath, that person's feedback can be used to create both new notions as well as new procedural insight in the intelligent system that manages the notion-flows. In this way, others will benefit from this new notion and won't get stuck in the same disconnect.

08.03 Final Iterations—Fine Tuning

When we move to the final level of iterations, an online resource *looks* as if it were ready for deployment. While the result of initial iterations is something that looks more like what the software development community might view as an *alpha* version of the resource, the result of the middle iterations is something that looks more like a *beta*. The result of final iteration is to move it more toward a *gamma*, or final version.

The work in final iterations is more granular and localized. Instead of having one big project to complete, we have several miniprojects that we're working to refine. Certain notions, as well as primary aspects of the flowstems, may need virtually no refinement at all. Other notions or procedural routines (see 04.02.06) may not quite be adequate yet.

What we're left with is what amounts to a contractor's *punch-down list*. This is an arbitrary list of things that need to be refined and validated before the entire resource is ready to be deployed for general online consumption. By systematically working through these issues, a project becomes ready to enter into the *deployment* phase.

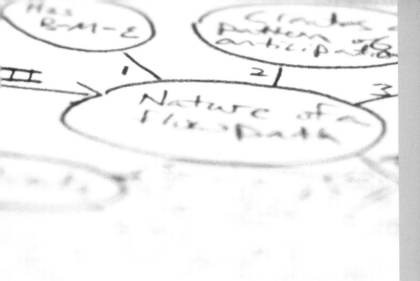

08.03.01 Some will wonder why I'm not including a 'production' stage or phase at the end of the iterative execution phase.

The reason is that with modern online authoring tools, optimum development strategies are so modular, and so driven by the externalized warehousing of information on databases, that there's really no need, in my opinion, for production—which is a fix-all/step-and-repeat stage or phase. The project gets iteratively improved over the course of each iterative execution cycle until it's ready for deployment. Regarding the quality of rapid prototypes, quality has been assured all along the way. Regarding the comprehensive needs of each audience set and subset, they have also been iteratively addressed all throughout iterative execution.

In other words, we haven't procrastinated and pushed off any major component of the project until the end. The reason is that when we don't consider our content comprehensively as we iteratively execute, some new consideration will inevitably manifest itself down the road, casting a shadow on the overall execution. Instead, as I've said, we have a project that's not only on time and on budget but also one that begins and stays on target.

08.04 Summary

In this chapter we addressed the *iterative execution* phase of the SPEED process. We learned the role of *planning, execution,* and *evaluation* at each of the three stages of iterative execution—*initial, middle,* and *final.* We learned how to procedurally design and develop an online resource in a way that is continually informed by stakeholder feedback. In this way, the chance that a project will in some way be off target is greatly minimized. Also, because design and development happen concurrently, there's little chance that what is designed will not be technically feasible.

The creative process wasn't specifically addressed here because it warrants special consideration that would have been out of balance with the rest of the content presented in this chapter. Because creative process is a very important topic, however, Chapter Ten has been dedicated to its exploration. Before we get to that, however, we'll finish off our high-level exploration of the three-phased SPEED process with an examination of issues related to the third and final phase—*deployment.*

In Chapter Nine, we'll learn how to properly deploy online resources by bringing them through quality assurance, by considering issues related to releasing them, by summatively evaluating them, and by integrating them with content management systems.

CHAPTER 09

Deployment—
The Real Work of the Final Phase in a Project

If a project team has made it this far with the SPEED process, things may not yet be perfect, but they should be pretty darn close. If instead it chose to follow the traditional *ADDIE* process spoken of in the i2.00 series, they generally are up to their eyeballs in trouble by now. The last phase in a *non*-iterative approach is usually the phase in a project's life cycle when *it* all hits the fan. If a project following the ADDIE process appears on the *surface* to be holding together, everyone involved is afraid to breathe lest the house of cards come crashing down. Because iterative validation-study procedures haven't been employed up to this point, there's a really, *really* good chance that everyone is by now living in denial.

By following the SPEED process, on the other hand, the middle phase where cycles of *planning, execution,* and *evaluation* occurred—called iterative execution—has helped the project team avert disaster. The reason is that the deployment phase is really only a *final* deployment phase. The validation studies conducted in each of the iterative execution cycles served as minideployments that have continually tested the waters to ensure that the project has stayed on target. By making stakeholder evaluation an integral part of execution, the evaluations have helped *form* the end product, not merely judge it. That's why they're called *formative* evaluations (see 08.01.07).

When following SPEED, the online resource is at this phase nearly complete. Now it must pass through quality assurance (QA), be released for general consumption, enter into summative evaluation, and then into an organic existence in which its content and the procedures governing notion-flows are continually managed and updated.

Jesse

erry@newriders.com

erry@newriders.com

erry@newriders.com

einman

erry@newriders.com

of Thoughts final cover files

message on 12/11/01.

John just captured the photograph
quickly can you get the

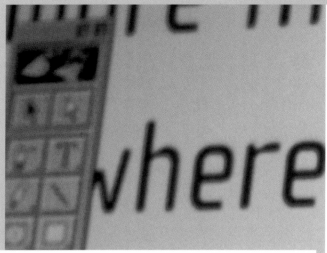

09.01 Quality Assurance

Note that the heading for this series isn't quality *control*, or quality *insurance*. It's quality assurance. Many people view quality assurance as quality control. The two are very different. Let me explain.

When quality is viewed as a *control phase* at the end of a project life cycle in which shoddy work is rescued, work suffers. Often people do sloppy work because they think that in the end some magic team of people will swoop down from heaven like guardian angels and *fix* everything. This is a costly presumption, yet one that's all too common. When it's taken for granted that things will get resolved in the end, it leads to contempt for good design and development.

On the other hand, when quality is viewed as a fundamentally integral design and development methodology in which issues are addressed in the moment, major problems can be greatly reduced. In the moment when problems first arise, minds are sharpest to resolve them. In essence, quality is assured through intelligent design, great process, and a solid work ethic that deals with bugs and other types of issues as they come up along the way.

09.01.01 Quality work is *prequalified* work.

The quality has been continually qualified throughout the iterative execution phase. By exercising good work habits, a project team will minimize its need to exercise crisis management skills. The bottom line is that the cost of fixing problems at the end of a project life cycle is always more than would be the case if problems were solved in the moment. The difficulties with end-time fixes are these:

> In the end, someone—whether it is you or someone else—will need to reacclimate to the situation. This can involve quite a bit of time—especially when it comes to issues with programming. The more complex the code is, the more time it will take to reacclimate oneself.
> It's harder to isolate problems in complex systems. Much time can be spent on wild goose chases trying to figure out which aspects of a complex program aren't running properly.[1] If problems are dealt with in the moment, however, this is much less likely to be the case. Combine this issue with the acclimation problem explained above, and a problem that would have taken a few minutes or hours to fix in the moment could now take hours, days, or even longer.
> Late in the game, fixing one problem can lead to causing other problems. When this occurs, developers get that sinking feeling that they're in the process of living a nightmare.
> Fixing problems at the end can cause much unnecessary stress. There's more pressure, and insecurities tend to come out in ugly ways—especially from project leaders. If the viability of a project is in question, no one will "sleep easy" until the problem's solved.

The moral to this story is twofold. Lesson number one—get really, really, really, smart people who employ solid methods to design programming logic. Lesson number two—make sure these people don't procrastinate in terms of artfully fixing problems. If not, you'll pay for it later and lose profitability and credibility. Actually, there's a third lesson—use modular systems.

[1] The *factorial* principle states that for every degree of complexity in a thing, the number of interdependencies grows in proportion to the multiplication of its consecutive integers. If there are 7 components, there would be $1 \times 2 \times 3 \times 4 \times 5 \times 6 \times 7$, or 5040 possible interdependencies. In factorial notation, this is represented as "7!".

Align

Align Objects:

Distribute Objects:

09.01.02 By utilizing modular development methods, problems remain largely isolated.

In *non*modular development environments, when one mistake is made in one situation, that mistake is propagated through duplication. Imagine, for example, that a graphical interface treatment was actually hardcoded into every screen-space in which products in an online product catalog were presented. (It often is.) If that design needed to be updated, someone would need to make the change over and over again for every product in the catalog! To avert this fiasco, methods such as cascading style sheets and templates are used. It doesn't stop here, however; perhaps the greatest application of modular design relates to how notions and flowstems are programmed to operate. Although this can be done in conventional Web authoring environments that are primarily based on HTML/JavaScript, more modern authoring environments are making the modular capabilities of online resources much more sophisticated and substantial.

09.01.03 When conventional Web programming languages are stretched to include the capabilities offered by modern Web authoring technologies, they rarely succeed in providing effective Web experiences because quality can never be *assured*.

HTML, DHTML, Java, and JavaScript will always fail you if you try to get too fancy with them. Keep it simple, or you'll pay the price.

Some of you are thinking, "Now wait a second! I thought you said that effective Web experiences needed to be dynamic and emotionally engaging to be effective."

My response is that they do need to be. Deductive reasoning should lead to only one conclusion, which is that conventional Web programming languages for front-end presentation should be relegated to a very peripheral, supporting role for more effective, modern authoring technologies. As of the publication date of this book, there's only one viable, universally compatible authoring environment that's both an effective development environment as well as one that offers the affordances needed to produce dynamic and emotionally engaging online resources. That technology is Flash by Macromedia.

09.01.04 Macromedia Flash succeeds where others struggle because it's a self-contained technology that, for the most part, supplants conventional technologies like HTML, Java, and JavaScript, and moves them to a very utilitarian, peripheral role.

DHTML technology, for example, is really only a *renovation* of the seriously outdated HTML technolgy and must rely on variables that simply can't be predicted to the degree that will consistently assure quality for almost all members of an online population.

When Flash is employed, on the other hand, quality can be assured on a very consistent basis. Although some usability experts dread the use of Flash because it relies on a plug-in (which is a small program that supplements the capabilities of a Web browser), their concerns are outdated. It's now common knowledge that most systems on the Web utilize the Flash Player plug-in. Its ubiquity has largely grown because developers of browser software and operating systems alike have realized that Flash presents an essential technology. Most, therefore, now automatically include the Flash Player plug-in with their software. If you doubt the validity of its ubiquity, go to Macromedia.com and read the statistics.

Although few Web enterprises are properly leveraging Flash technology to do the right things for people online, Flash is the first doorway through which Web enterprises have been able to lead people into effective Web experiences. You'll learn that even if we *didn't* factor in Flash's presentation and interactivity capabilities, it would still be worth employing because of its efficiency in working with database and middleware technologies to deliver personalized content over the Internet. When Web enterprises finally catch on that Flash isn't merely a tool to develop "cool" intros but is the most substantial authoring tool available for native Web applications, there should be a revolution in the way online resources are designed and developed. Just a note—I personally would like to be one of the leaders of that revolution.

Vertical Align Top

09.01.05 Notwithstanding iterative prequalification (read pre-quality-ification), work should be checked to assure quality, but only minor issues should be uncovered.

As stated earlier, quality should be controlled throughout iterative execution. Everyone involved in the project is responsible for quality. In the deployment phase, however, it's appropriate to quality-assure a final product. Despite the best efforts, a detail here or there will inevitably fall between the cracks.

These are not major problems but minor oversights. Think along the lines of a final pass of proofreading on a book. We're looking for typos, presentational artifacts, or minor performance inefficiencies that could be tightened up a bit. This should not be an inordinately time-consuming or costly stage of the deployment phase. It is, however, the responsibility of the project team to do due diligence and conduct quality assurance.

09.01.06 Some third party distant from the project team should oversee and manage quality assurance.

The reason that minor oversights occur is usually that the very capable team involved in execution is simply too close to the project to catch them. It's for this reason that a separate person or group of people—preferably from outside the organization—conduct quality assurance. If this isn't possible, it's usually best to take as long a sabbatical from the project as possible—in effect to wipe the cognitive slate clean. This practice, although not afforded in many situations because of deadlines, is the only second-best approach to quality assurance that there is. If the team conducts quality assurance themselves without taking a break from the project, the quality assurance is questionable at best.

09.02 Release

Call it *publication*, *broadcast*, *dissemination*, or simply *release*, this is the point at which a Web enterprise brings its new or improved online resource to the target population and its various constituencies. This is the big payoff for the project team: when it can bask in the satisfaction of a job well done—or not.

The activities in this stage of the deployment phase are to move the online resource to a hosting environment and then configure it to leverage technologies that will ensure its ability to handle the loads that will be placed upon it. Since these activities are of a technical nature, they're beyond the scope of this book. Check out one of the many books published by O'Reilly for a better understanding of this complex subject.

The release stage of the deployment phase does, however, include an activity that is within the scope of our discussion. This activity is known as *traffic building*, and because *exposure* is a prime component of traffic building, we'll touch on it briefly.

Traffic building relates to the beginning of our three-stage communication process.

Before we can attract an audience, we must *expose* it to our messages. Traffic building is therefore the first step in the *attract* stage of our online communication because it involves exposure. It's important to understand that a pattern of anticipation is initiated through exposure and that people have certain expectations regarding what the Web enterprise will deliver. It's therefore very important to make sure that people's expectations are not violated in an unfavorable way when they first engage the Web enterprise (see Chapter Four). Because getting and keeping Web traffic is one of the most challenging problems facing Web enterprises today, it's important that we put our best foot forward when we do get the opportunity to expose people to our online messages.

Ward Hanson provides a good list of ways that people first gain exposure to our online messages:

"Advertising, links, user habits, word of mouth, search engines, directories, and surf engines are all ways to shape and build Web traffic. Traffic building tools are critical to the success of any online marketing effort."

This idea is reminiscent of Part One of this book, but it bears repeating. Hanson continues:

"Effective traffic building requires both creativity and discipline. Creativity is needed to stand out from the crowd and attract attention. At the same time, measurement and testing can make traffic building a scientific and rigorous process."

Hanson's book *Principles of Internet Marketing* serves as a good introduction to some of these measurement and testing processes.

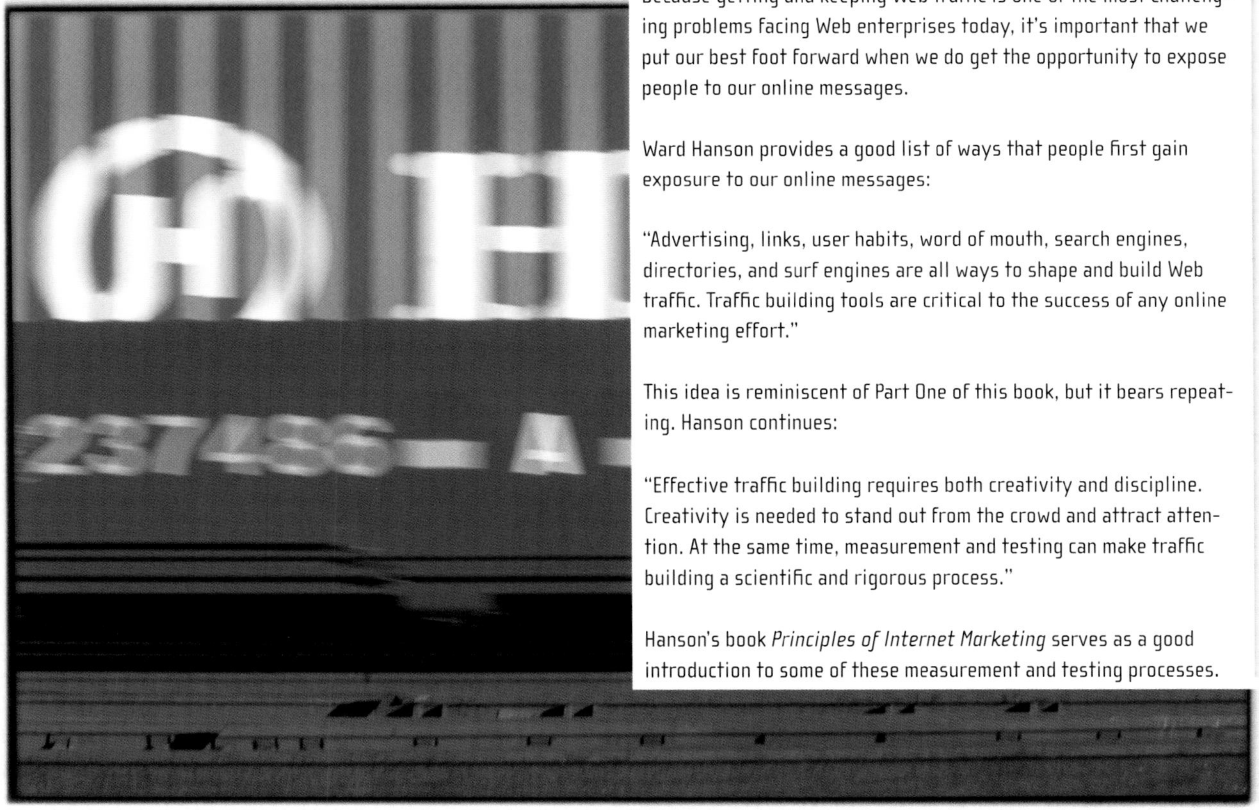

09.02.02 Acquiring traffic is expensive, so retaining traffic is essential to the profitability of a Web enterprise.

Because of the seemingly limitless number of options on the Web, it's challenging to attract people to a particular online resource. According to Hanson, because this is such a challenging proposition, it becomes extremely important to retain people as patrons after they've interacted with a Web enterprise on one occasion. In a nutshell, we want to ensure repeat business. The reason that this is so important versus merely attempting to continually attract new patrons is that site loyalty greatly lowers the cost of maintaining traffic. Hanson substantiates this in his text:

"A simple calculation shows the benefits of loyalty. Assume a website has an initial base of 50,000 active users and wants to grow to 100,000 active users. It decides to initiate an online banner ad campaign that costs $20 per thousand impressions (CPM) and has a click-through rate (CTR) of 2 percent. If each click-through is a new visitor, it costs the site ($20/1000) x 2% = $1.00 per new visitor. The site decides to buy 1 million banner impressions each month until its goal is reached.

"The cost of growing to 100,000 users per month rises rapidly if retention rates are low. At 100 percent retention, all new visitors become loyal users. With complete loyalty, it takes 2.5 months and $70,000 to reach the 100,000 user mark. The lower the retention rate, the higher the expenditures and the longer the time needed to reach the goal. With low retention rates, an increasing amount of the new users just replace defections.

"User loyalty means that far lower levels of advertising are needed to keep the 100,000-user level once it is achieved. With a 90 percent retention rate, 10,000 new users must be attracted each month to offset losses. More new users must be attracted each year than are in the active user base."

As can be seen in the bottom line, really delivering effective Web experiences is the key to achieving an effective business model. This is why it's so crucial that we engage people socially and emotionally through the creative, interactive communication of appropriate online messages (see Part One).

09.02.03 Traffic building activities involve on- and offline initiatives.

The primary online initiatives are these:

> Domain name—Choosing a URL (or Web address) that's easy to guess and easy to remember. Beware of getting so creative with this that no one will easily be able to remember or spell it.
> Portal presence—Using one of the main search or directory portal resources such as *Google, Yahoo!,* or *AltaVista* to gain exposure. It's essential that care be taken to properly classify a Web enterprise or component online resource with keywords, meta tags, descriptors, and categories. The ability to *hook* people with twenty-five words or less becomes paramount on portals.
> Buzz—Creating publicity through traditional public relations, promotions, and word of mouth. Free media coverage is also very important, so the ability to write a good press release is absolutely essential.
> Online ads—Although only a very few people click through on online ads, the number of people who do is very predictable. As the challenge of finding more effective ways to advertise online is reached, this will become an increasingly more effective source of Web traffic. Before this will ever happen, however, an advertising method that doesn't interrupt a person's continual flow of concentration on the message at hand must be determined (see 04.00.10).

Offline initiatives include traditional advertising such as television, radio, print, and billboard advertising.

09.02.04 Because building buzz is an important part of generating traffic, it's an important part of deployment plans as well.

Ward Hanson outlines research in sociology and marketing that focuses on how word of mouth motivates a pool of potential adopters into trial of the online resources offered by Web enterprises:

"An adoption path starts with a pool of potential users [and tracks their] conversion into loyal users, occasional switching users, or nonusers. Each of these groups of service users is a possible source of information to individuals who haven't tried the service."

Avenues of word of mouth online include:

> Email
> Usenet groups
> Email listservs
> Online forums
> Online media coverage

Keep in mind that word of mouth isn't necessarily positive. It used to be said that if someone has a good experience with a store or a restaurant, he or she would tell three people. If that person had a bad experience, on the other hand, ten people would be told. Multiply that by a hundred on the Web, and maybe we approach the possible up-and-down sides to word of mouth. According to Hanson:

"Word of mouth follows many of the same dynamics as Metcalfe's Law...As the personal value of a network grows with network size, and the community value grows even faster, companies are eager to create the impression that the network [segment being marketed] is rapidly growing.

"Expectations matter when an investment in a network makes sense for a user if the network reaches a critical mass. [...] A user will find it valuable to belong to a network if the value of the network exceeds the cost. As long as everyone believes a network will be large, consumers will join and the network will be large. But if consumers think that the network will be small, only the highest-value users will join, and the network will remain small. When expectations matter so much, consumers want to pick winners and to feel good about their choices. Celebrity endorsements, media stories, and a general "buzz" around a product all create the impression that many other consumers are also making the same choice. A big challenge for many companies is to make the endorsements convincing and believable."

09.03 Summative Evaluation (n+1)

"Summative evaluation is the collection and interpretation of data to determine the value of [a resource]." —Reynolds and Iwinski, *Multimedia Training*

Because there are an indefinite number of cycles in iterative execution, we say that there are n validation studies. Whatever number n is at the close of the iterative execution phase, the final validation study, which is a summative evaluation and which is conducted in the deployment phase, becomes $n + 1$. This is a significant study because its scope includes not only tracking feedback and statistics from patrons but also attempting to quantify return on investment. Because this is something that can take considerable time, the summative evaluation could extend for quite some time as well.

09.03.01 Patron satisfaction is one of the two most important measures of Web effectiveness.

"Online quality can result in a price premium, expanded sales, and an increase in customer satisfaction." —Dr. Ward Hanson

This quote directly relates to the patron retention issues discussed in 09.02.02. The aim of this portion of the summative evaluation is to verify that the online resource, which has now gone through several cycles of iterative validation, has indeed held true to the end.

Those following the SPEED process should find that the statistical averages uncovered in the original research, validation studies, and the summative evaluation are very similar. There simply should be no surprises. Although there are obviously many ways to measure patron satisfaction, one of the most relevant is the quality and quantity of response interactions that were achieved through well-formulated notion-flows.

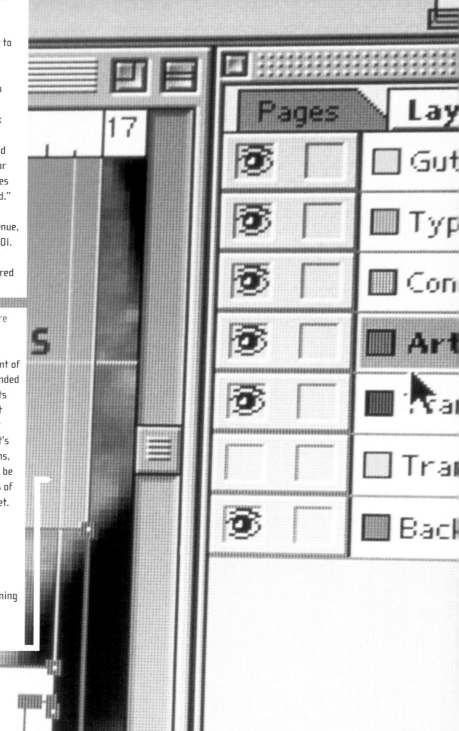

09.03.02 Return on investment (ROI) is the other chief indicator of Web effectiveness.

This isn't only a measure of the revenue that a Web enterprise generates, but also of the efficiency and accuracy that's brought to the transaction process. Again, Hanson shares these insights:

"The importance of online sales goes beyond the profits made on the sales themselves. It completes the cycle of online commerce and makes the entire process accountable. By being able to track marketing efforts all the way from initial contact to complete sale, the process can be precisely evaluated for effectiveness and profitability. A reliable return on investment can be calculated for sponsorships, banner ads, and prospect fees. Effective approaches can be expanded, and unprofitable efforts spotted and eliminated."

For Web enterprises that are not concerned with generating revenue, per se, other mechanisms will need to be employed to measure ROI. In e-learning applications, it could be measured in test scores or worker productivity improvements. In politics, it could be measured through increased votes or other indications of acceptance.

09.03.03 Summative evaluation becomes a catalyst for both future and immediate postproject changes, additions, and deletions, depending on their scope.

While feedback and statistics won't affect the further development of the online resource within the current project, changes can be funded through maintenance budgets that are allocated for improvements until the next major release of the online resource. It's important to understand that there must be a definite ending to the current project; otherwise projects could amble on forever. Feedback that's significant enough to warrant the consideration of major additions, subtractions, or modifications to the online resource will need to be folded into the next major project. Feedback that uncovers issues of a more minor nature can be handled under the maintenance budget. These issues include:

> Bug fixes
> Additions of notions to the pool of possibilities for a given flowpath segment
> Additions and improvements to the rules or procedures governing the flowstems
> Minor interface modifications
> Minor content corrections

09.04 Content Management

To be effective, an online experience must be successful for a person on more than one occasion. To build relationships, which is where return on investment thrives, the value of the online resource must continue to build over time. For this to become reality, it's essential that a content management strategy be developed in iterative execution, and then maintained after an online resource is deployed.

09.04.01 The driving force behind a content management strategy is the feedback and statistics that are maintained by the same 'apparatus' that's helped to conduct the validation studies in iterative execution (see 08.01.09).

This tool overlays our online resource and is ever present. The feedback and statistics maintained by it can be used to determine good opportunities to develop notions that would either replace or else supplement those that are already available.

As an example, let's say that a person is moving along a flowpath and comes to a notion in a flow that the flowstem decides is appropriate for a given person and situation. The only problem is that in this particular situation, there's a disconnect. The person isn't effectively informed and optimum flow is interrupted. If our feedback apparatus reports that there's a problem, the content maintenance team has an opportunity to come up with a notion, interactive or otherwise, to satisfy the new need. The procedures and rules for the flowstem can be updated to take new criteria into account when dosing out notions and can avert a "disconnect" the next time a person with this particular set of circumstances comes along.

This is why I refer to these systems as being organic because the people who maintain them in this way continually inject them with life in unpredictable, yet outstanding and beneficial ways. They are an important aspect of our virtual value activities online.

09.04.02 When at all possible, information must be separated from the authoring code.

In many cases, content cannot be separated from programming code because a notion presents a unique interaction that isn't patternable. In many other cases, however, information *should* be read into a template, because the instructions that define the environment and the manner in which the information is communicated *is* patternable.

One of the advantages of using Flash as the front-end environment for notion-flow sequencing is that it's much more efficient and effective when it merges data from a database with the programming instructions that make up the visual display of that information in a screen-space. HTML-based resources must query the database, access an HTML file, merge the data with the HTML file, transmit it over the Web, and then render it on the screen. The Flash solution, on the other hand, removes latency issues (delays) to a large degree. Whereas data from a database that's combined with HTML must be combined every time a new query is made on the database (see figure), Flash loads the instructions for rendering the content once, and must pull data in only on subsequent queries. This fact, combined with the inherent smaller file sizes that Flash enjoys when properly executed, makes an online Flash resource far superior to anything that can be done in traditional Web programming languages.

09.04.03 The key to an effective content management strategy is making it easy for people with even low-level development skills to update the system.

In instances when content can be managed by a database (which is increasingly becoming the norm), a benefit to the practice of separating content from code is that those who manage the content may only need to have administrative-level skills. This can lower the cost of maintenance and can make it more likely that content will be updated regularly. This certainly can be a good thing, and is often a very good thing. There are, however, pitfalls that must be avoided.

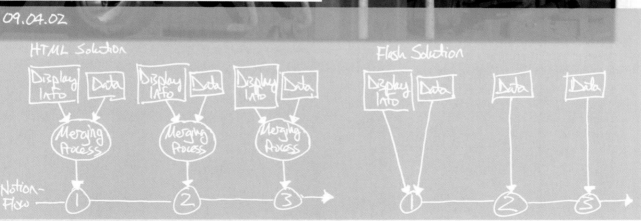

09.04.02

HTML Solution

Flash Solution

Notion-Flow

09.04.04 Even when information is separated from code, creative expression of ideas will always require creative human effort.

Again, we want to move away from the present, where the Web is a dumping ground for information developed for other mediums. In light of this, don't be tempted to make the task of flowing text or graphics into a template *merely* an administrative function. It's not. The words and other media elements that flow into a predetermined format must still be treated with care and precision. Even text carries with it a tone of voice, and that tone of voice must be on target for a given audience set or subset. When content is stored in a database and flowed into a template of any kind, the tendency can be to put creativity on autopilot. This must be avoided at all costs because the result will be monotonous communication.

09.05 Summary

In this chapter we touched on the third phase of our three-phased process, *deployment*, which was preceded by *strategy formulation* and *iterative execution.* We learned that quality is something that is controlled throughout the iterative execution phase and is only veri-fied in the final quality assurance stage of the deployment phase. We learned that building traffic is an integral part of the communication process and that patron satisfaction and return on investment are the two primary concentrations of summative evaluation. Finally, we learned that content management mechanisms must be put in place to ensure the viability of an online resource over time.

By following the SPEED process through to the end, we've done all we can to ensure that an online resource is within scope, within budget, on time, and on target.

In Chapter Ten, which is a parenthetical addition to the iterative execution process covered in Chapter Eight, we'll take one final look at the subject of artfulness in *creative* execution.

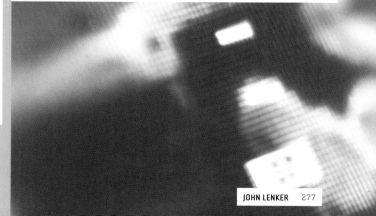

CHAPTER 10

Beauty is in the eye of the mouse-holder.

—The Author

Artfulness in Creative Execution—
Doing Due Diligence

Why are so many attempts to apply creativity to online resources ineffective? Why are so few concepts—even those with really serious creative potential—rarely artfully realized?

The reason is that the creative process is often misunderstood, rushed, or altogether ignored. Additionally, experience designers often emphasize the wrong sorts of things. When they attempt to make the wrong aspects of their presentations interesting, this is generally an indication that they lack insight regarding the real role of creativity in Web experience design (see Chapters Five and Six). As a result, even potentially *good* concepts remain unrefined, undisciplined, and pedestrian.[1] The opposites of pedestrian efforts are the inspired and skilled efforts of talented people. Because the practice of good process *governs* skilled effort, the *solution* to most creative confusion is the combination of accomplished people and a really great creative process.

To be ultimately successful in creative concepting and artful execution, designers must practice due diligence by iteratively executing their creative concepts. Solid design principles, as well as the qualification that comes through stakeholder validation, must govern each cycle of planning, execution, and evaluation. But what are the steps that go into planning? What's involved in creative execution? What are the proper methods of validating creativity?

These are the issues that we'll explore in this chapter.

[1] Their efforts often remain pedestrian because project leaders don't make allowances for a proper creative design and development process.

NEITHER HUMANITY

OR CREATIVITY CAN BE

10.00.01 To arrive at artfully executed expressions of genuine creativity, the entire creative process must continually be zeroing in on solutions that are both productive and original.

For a concept to have the quality of being *productive*, it must be *appropriate* for the audience and the need. For a concept to be *original*, it must be the result of diligent research, understanding, and interesting departures from the familiar. We'll deal with the appropriateness issue in the remainder of this notion. We'll deal with the *originality* issue in the next.

Appropriateness is in essence a social construct, and, as mentioned throughout Part One of this book, is governed by four principles of polite and helpful communication which are: *quality*, *quantity*, *relevance*, and *clarity* (Q-Q-R-C). Isn't it interesting that beyond the emotional role that aesthetics and creativity are often understood to play, there's a strong social role as well? What are the implications?

Well, for one thing, it means that to be successful in mainstream online communications,[2] creativity can't be viewed as an outlet for an *artist's* self-expression but rather as an essential conduit for a *patron's* self-resonance. Remember that one of the keys to success with experience design is to properly reinforce the social, emotional, and intellectual identities of the people interacting with a Web enterprise. When experiences are oriented more toward the designer than to the audience—and informed designers know this—the result is that online messages are difficult for audiences to easily interpret.

Far from being polite and helpful, this is rude and inconsiderate behavior because it forces people to reflect on unproductive aspects of the design in order to decipher meaning.[3] Ironically, this is the same problem that occurs with the boring text-based solutions that leading usability gurus are pushing. Both practices, although in different ways, present perceptual as well as interpretive problems that the people within an online audience must grapple with.

Instead, appropriate communication must be like a helping hand of friendship that's extended to indirectly communicate the message:

"I'm here for you. I'm understandable, embraceable, worthwhile, and enjoyable for you to interact with. I'll make you a deal. If you spend the next few moments with me, I'll enrich you in ways that far exceed the investment of time and effort that you're making in me."

Yep, to be successful, our expressions of creativity in mainstream communications must indirectly convey all of that information. The good news is that when creativity is on target, it communicates this message almost instantly.

10.00.02 The other component of creativity, which is originality, can only be arrived at by three means—through accident, through epiphany, or through horizontal thinking.

Since by definition neither accidents nor epiphany can be planned, it's best to rely on horizontal thinking—which can lead to wonderful accidents and epiphanies! As mentioned in 07.00.02, this horizontal thinking takes us to starting points that are not mundane. Vertical thinking, which is logical, deductive/inductive reasoning (07.00.01), can then be used to help us comprehensively uncover the unique possibilities that horizontal thinking has helped us to newly discover.

The key to the success of these original starting points is this. These possibilities must be unique enough to be interesting, but they must not be such a great conceptual departure from what is known and understood by the audience that they require great difficulty in bridging the conceptual gap (see 03.00.09). The unique creative concept must still branch out of something already present in people's conceptual framework. Remember that while on the one hand people get bored when they're forced to absorb things that are mundane because they've become too familiar, on the other they get frustrated if they're compelled to absorb things that are too great a stretch from that which is already familiar. The trick is to find the *appropriate* balance.

[2] Please note that I make a distinction between mainstream communication and expressions of fine art. Obviously expressions of fine art are founded upon both the artist's identity and perspectives.

[3] While usability experts express some of the same sentiments, often their solution is to limit creative expression almost to the point of extinguishing its benefit.

10.00.03 Although arriving at a genuinely creative solution to an experience design problem isn't difficult work, it is nonetheless reached by working *toward* a valid solution.

Far from being hard work, the creative process can be both extremely enjoyable and rewarding. The point, however, is that it *is* still work—work that takes time, energy, talent, and dedication. What's more, arriving at solutions that are truly creative is not the result of aimless, haphazard work. Ask anyone who's acknowledged as a successful designer or artist, such as Hillman Curtis. It doesn't matter what the genre, those who are successful base their success on specific processes that they know and follow, and that provide them with consistent results. Therefore I contend that, although *genuine* creativity often arrives via epiphany or accident, it can most *reliably* be arrived at by faithfully following an effective process.

While more than one process can be effective, the process that I recommend for the creative aspects of Web experience design is both a symbiotic parallel and a component microcosm of the larger SPEED process we've explored in Chapters Seven through nine. In essence, before moving on to a subsequent cycle of the iterative, creative-execution process, the creative team should first work to ensure that the work is conforming to the following appropriateness and originality principles:

> Creative development is being governed by the experiential needs of the people who will be interacting with the online resource.
> Creative direction isn't going in an arbitrary direction for expediency or ego's sake but instead, is developing based on meaningful rationale.
> Creative direction isn't slipping into an autopilot mode simply because the project must conform to an organization's other branding or advertising initiatives.
> Media are being crafted in such a way as to attract and hold the attention of the people in a particular audience set or subset.

Before we dive into the specifics of this process, let me reiterate two points. First, try really hard not to sell the process short by giving in to either your own or your management's impatience. Second, don't become enamored with early ideas. Instead, let the creative process outlined in the remainder of this chapter do its work. The results will be far better than would have been the case had you moved forward based on your initial concepts.

10.01 Zeroing In on Unique Yet Appropriate Concepts and Themes

The word "creative" is an adjective, and is therefore qualitative in nature. We have ideas to communicate, but *how* do we express them as online messages? What will the *qualities* of that expression be? Although many media designers want to dive right in to actually executing media, jumping into media design at this stage means that we're jumping the gun. If we want an expression of meaning through media to break the pattern of the mundane appropriately and uniquely, we must do a lot of preliminary groundwork. Through these efforts to discover effective creative expression, our goal is to arrive at the answers to questions such as these:

> We must set a tone. What will that tone be? Will it be serious, light-hearted, happy, sad, or somewhere in between?
> We must find a suitable level of emotional intensity. How intensely do we want to affect people emotionally?
> We must define a range of sensory dynamics. When and why will we modulate the amplitude and frequency of these dynamics?
> We must choose a repertoire of associative constructs. What associations will be most effective for an audience set or subset?
> We must choose a set of aesthetic characteristics. What determines what these characteristics will be?

The answers to these questions are rarely arrived at without considerable effort. Being too hasty with these decisions will almost always lead to unrefined, unskilled results. It's not that arriving at the answers to these questions must be hard work, but the answers must be arrived at through investigation and discovery, which do require time and effort. How do we approach this investigation and discovery? Where do we begin? What should our focus be?

10.01.01 We must attain project summary-statements from all stakeholders, including members of the experience design team. When mining for precious metals or stones, we must often move tons of earth before we uncover anything valuable. Similarly, in our search for effective creative tone, intensity, dynamics, constructs, and aesthetics, we must begin by excavating everything that's inside the minds of stakeholders in an effort to uncover anything of value. These initial exercises, however, rarely provide solutions to creative experience design. That's not the purpose of the exercise. Instead, these initial clues that we uncover lead us to other, previously unimagined starting points for further, more targeted investigation.

Although there are a variety of possible ways to get this initial mind-dump, I believe that the best way to proceed is to have members of the organization, the project team, audiences, and sponsors all write essays, which I call *project summary-statements*. The goal is to look for patterns of similarities as well as areas of divergence in perspective. Because these are mind-dump exercises, an emphasis should be placed on being exhaustive. Any little thing, although seemingly insignificant on the surface, may be of incredible value in the final analysis. Participants should write and write and write until they can say, like Forrest Gump, "That's all I have to say about that."

The summary-statements are basically people's responses to a short list of initial questions such as these:

> What do you understand the purpose of this project to be?
> What do you think that the organization needs to communicate through this online resource to reach its audiences effectively?
> How should people feel while interacting with the underlying online messages that this resource is communicating?
> What are some appropriate metaphors, analogies, or anecdotes that relate to the central themes or concepts that this online resource either is or should be communicating?
> What aspect of the proposed online resource, if any, has the potential of being meaningful to you or someone else?
> What are some of the content characteristics that you believe will aid people in comprehending our online messages?

Participants answer each of these questions in an electronic document of their own, taking as much space as is necessary to scrape out every corner of their conscious thought. The result of this project summary-statement is something that resembles an informal essay.

10.01.02 We must sift through summary-statements to understand people's conceptual constructs.

There are two primary benefits of generating project summary-statements from the full gamut of stakeholders. First, we get a varied picture of people's conceptual frameworks regarding the subject of the online resources. Second, by understanding what everyone else understands, we can set conceptual parameters so we don't create something that's either so familiar as to be boring, or so farfetched as to present a conceptual disconnect. The goal is to look for clues for appropriate creative inspiration.

After the project summary-statements have been gathered, the process of sifting through them proceeds as follows:

1. All summary-statements are compiled into one document. This document isn't a composite of all responses at this point. Instead, each respondent's statement is kept intact. The master document is then distributed to everyone who participated in the exercise.
2. Each respondent carefully reviews the other respondents' statement and highlights what each perceives as the key conceptual constructs.
3. Project team members meet to review and combine each unique conceptual construct into one master list.
4. This list is then prioritized, and the three to seven most heavily weighted constructs are isolated for further investigation and discovery.

Here are some examples of conceptual constructs that were used when designing this book:

> Emancipate people from the narrowness of usability and infuse them with the passion and understanding for a more artful vision.
> Merge principles of psychology, understandability, and creativity into a holistic experience design philosophy.
> Give people a sense that there's an open road when they design a Web experience and that their minds can be a gateway to a world of possibilities.
> Show people the importance of making concepts clear in the microcosm of the moment.
> Empower people to execute online resources that will help their patrons ascend into understanding by aligning content to people rather than forcing people to align with content.

10.01.03 After we isolate what we believe to be the most important constructs, we begin the first of several radiant-thinking exercises. Otherwise known as *mind-mapping* or *thought-ballooning*, we want to employ *radiant thinking* to get all of the most obvious conceptual associations related to each construct down on paper so that we can focus on what *isn't* obvious without constantly being distracted by what *is* obvious—and therefore pedestrian. In other words, our goal is to identify the known so that we can begin searching the unknown for conceptual starting points that, while unique, will not be completely foreign. Radiant thinking is a paper-and-pencil or whiteboard-based exercise that follows these steps:

1. We begin by placing one of our three to seven primary constructs in the center of the drawing surface. We then draw a circle around this central construct and ask ourselves this question: "Well, *what* is there to say about this construct?"
2. Each of the answers to this question is placed in a circle around the central circle. Arrows are then drawn to *radiate* out from the central circle to connect with each first-tier response that answers the "what" question.
3. For each of the first-tier responses, we ask: "*Why* is this true?" Again, arrows radiate out from the first-tier circles to connect to each of the second-tier circles. It's not that other questions can't be answered in this second tier, it's just that the *why* question seems tends to help get a critical mass of detail on the table.

4. Lastly, for each of the second-tier responses to the "why" question, we ask a "how," "where," or "when" question as appropriate. Arrows radiate out from the second-tier circles to connect to each of the third-tier circles.

This exercise should be completed on an individual basis, and then refined in a group setting. The result will be a master mind-map for each conceptual construct. Rather than uncovering anything truly original at this stage, we map our thoughts to find clarifications to our understanding of the central construct. In the end, we compile the most relevant aspects of our radiant-thinking exercise into a new, more refined project summary-statement for each of our three to five working conceptual constructs.

The results of this exercise should be incorporated with one of the broader validation studies that should be going on in iterative execution. The goal is to see whether all stakeholders validate the selection and accuracy of the conceptual constructs that have been determined. The primary question we're asking is this:

"From all we gathered, we've formulated these statements. Do these reflect what the project is really about?"

It's good to have both the original group of respondents as well as a fresh group of respondents evaluate the current list of statements.

SEPARATED, NOR CAN

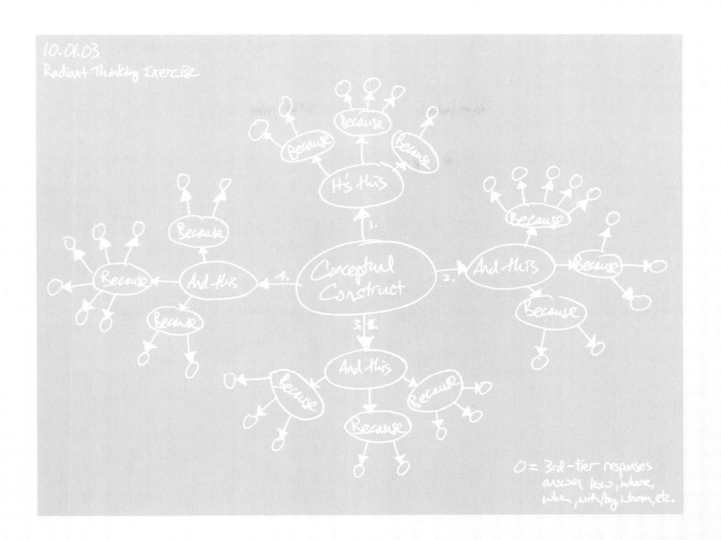

THEY BE CONTAINED. T

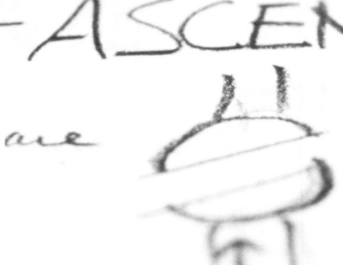

It's now safe to unfasten our seat belts and move freely about the cabin to look for interesting departures from the familiar. So far we've been employing vertical thinking to investigate these central concepts. As previously mentioned, vertical thinking is the logical, hierarchical thinking that basically seeks to document what's already familiar about a construct. It's now time to move on to horizontal thinking, which aims to explore associations with the current collective conceptual framework that haven't yet been commonly established. The goal is to come up with unique starting points for further investigation and discovery. In our efforts to think horizontally, we engage in two exercises:

The first is free association. We employ free association to release subconscious thoughts that relate to the thinking that's reflected in the project summary-statements. This is a fairly straightforward exercise. We write down a conceptual construct and, within a very limited timeframe such as sixty seconds, begin writing down everything that comes to mind related to that subject. The goal is to relax our conscious thinking to allow less familiar, subconscious thoughts to pass into our consciousness. This can be done most effectively within a group setting where individuals work on their own and then periodically share their associations with others. After the pans have been filled with the sand that free association yields, the sand then can be sifted with a group to separate the grains of gold. This process is repeated until a substantial base of meaningful associations is compiled to form substantial equity in a conceptual construct.

The second exercise is what Tom Monahan refers to as *Intergalactic Thinking*.[4] According to Monahan, intergalactic thinking is an attempt to search for "inobvious," seemingly farfetched, yet oddly appropriate new associations that can graft into the existing collective conceptual framework. What we're doing is trying to find ways of building conceptual bridges that are new and interesting for our audience members. In effect these bridges join a person's sense of need with what he or she perceive as an organization's ability to uniquely and effectively fulfill that need.

10.01.05 Intergalactic thinking is essentially a radiant-thinking exercise, but with a twist.

Instead of having one of our central concepts occupy the central circle as on pages 284-285, we instead place in that circle something that's not even in the same galaxy as the concept under current consideration. We then use the radiant-thinking questions to try to somehow meaningfully bridge back to the established conceptual framework. If this an underlying concept, for example:

"Watching pro football on Monday nights is an essential part of American male culture."

An intergalactic thinking exercise might begin with a central seed such as this:

"An intimidating grandmother wearing a flowered sundress."

The purpose of this exercise is to explore the galaxy of an old grandmother's sundress in search of a humorous tie-in to the central concept. The intention is to both gain and hold attention and make the key insight memorable because of its pattern-of-the-mundane-breaking strength.

Although this type of thinking may seemes farfetched, the greatest conceptual treasures can often be found where two galaxies of thought converge. Interestingly, since I began this book, I've seen a television commercial for the NFL that was based on the very concept of football players in sundresses! Talk about synchronicity.

[4] Read Tom Monahan's excellent book, *The Do-It-Yourself-Lobotomy: Open Your Mind To Creative Thinking*.

⁵This is not my original idea, but none of my colleagues can agree on what a source for this practice might be. Maybe Carmichael Lynch Advertising.

10.01.06 Based on the results of our free-association and intergalactic thinking exercises, we now zero in on a thematic label for each of our three to seven central concepts and embody them in what I refer to as *conceptual handles.*

A conceptual handle is a label that captures the essence of a concept and is easy to hold on to and springboard off of. It's a fabricated compound word, descriptive phrase, or some unique combination of hyphenated words that we develop to convey a concept's unique meaning. Like a person's nickname, its role is to sum up the conceptual construct's personality in a catchy way.[5]

Since the design team for this book followed this process, I'll share with you our list of conceptual handles and their meanings:

> Emancinfuse—To *emancipate* Web enterprises from the bondage that leading usability gurus have imposed and infuse them with a more holistic experience design philosophy.
> Printhesis—Represents the synthesis of the principles from psychology, understandability, and creativity that converge in my *notion-flow* philosophy.
> Mind-flow—Relates to the network of associations that our minds flow along in search of meaning.
> Micro-clarity—Relates to the balanced synthesis of media elements (which address people's psychological, conceptual, and aesthetic needs) required to meaningfully communicate a notion, which is the microcosm of an online message.
> Align-ascend—As we align notions with people's conceptual frameworks, they'll ascend into understanding.

You may scratch your head and wonder how these conceptual handles expressed themselves in the creative concepting of this book. The fact is that if you looked at my notebook, you'd not only see the visual influences, but you'd also see that some of the key conceptual insights, which you *may* have highlighted in this book, grew directly out of my exploration of these conceptual handles. You'd also note that there are many unique terms that I introduce throughout this book that grew out of my exploration of these handles. Again, these handles are meant to influence not only how media elements look, sound, and behave but also how we uniquely and appropriately express ideas.

10.01.07 We brainstorm to find synergy in the true meaning of our conceptual handles and then develop what should be *final* summary-statements for each.

This final radiant-thinking exercise is a group effort whose purpose is to define our conceptual handles as fully formed central concepts in their own right. This is usually a very exciting vertical thinking exercise for the experience design team in that it's a lot like getting to know a set of new friends. By following the steps in 10.01.03, with our conceptual handles occupying the center circle, we're prepared to get our arms around the true meaning of these concepts.

After the brainstorming exercise is completed, the information from the thought balloons is converted into an outline and simplified, and a one-paragraph summary-statement is written to define the conceptual handle. From this point on, we no longer refer to these as conceptual handles and summary-statements, but simply as *the concepts.* When reading over these final concepts, it should be apparent that the end result is of a much higher creative quality than would have otherwise been the case.

10.01.08 As in everything else in the SPEED process, we must not proceed from one iterative execution cycle to another until we get stakeholder feedback.

In this case, this feedback regards our newly reformulated concept statements. There are two goals of this final validation study regarding conceptual direction. The first is to ensure that the concepts really do communicate effectively to the patrons of the Web enterprise. The second is to verify that the final concepts haven't in some way inadvertently crossed a line regarding an organization's communications guidelines. If that has happened, we must adjust our concepts to reflect the overall organizational platform.

Since everything that the final concepts were based on flowed out of the input of all stakeholders, no disconnect should occur. However, because the nature of employing unique conceptual perspectives is "newness," it's important to make sure that the decision makers in the organization are comfortable with this newness. Most marketing executives will be cautious (as they should be) out of a concern that *any* creative departure from the familiar will be "off-brand." This is why it's so important that the design team take the time to lobby some of the more open-minded key influencers within the organization prior to any important presentations regarding creative direction. When resistance is encountered however, it's critical not to just roll over and play dead. You can believe in your ideas because you've put the right kind of thinking into them as a result of this process. Put some faith in these ideas, therefore, and take some calculated risks, my friend.

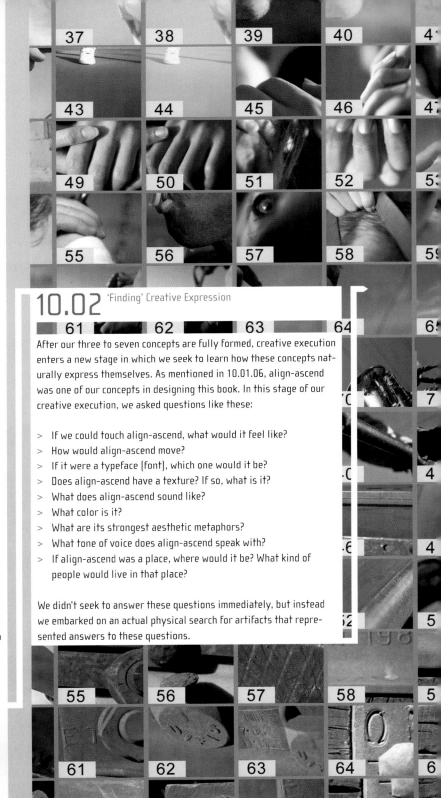

10.02 'Finding' Creative Expression

After our three to seven concepts are fully formed, creative execution enters a new stage in which we seek to learn how these concepts naturally express themselves. As mentioned in 10.01.06, align-ascend was one of our concepts in designing this book. In this stage of our creative execution, we asked questions like these:

> If we could touch align-ascend, what would it feel like?
> How would align-ascend move?
> If it were a typeface (font), which one would it be?
> Does align-ascend have a texture? If so, what is it?
> What does align-ascend sound like?
> What color is it?
> What are its strongest aesthetic metaphors?
> What tone of voice does align-ascend speak with?
> If align-ascend was a place, where would it be? What kind of people would live in that place?

We didn't seek to answer these questions immediately, but instead we embarked on an actual physical search for artifacts that represented answers to these questions.

10.02.02 Concept boards become the domains of imagination that each concept rules.

When we collect the objects, images, sketches, type samples, and other elements that seem to express facets of our concepts, we must put these items together in one place. This place is called a *concept board*. In the center of this concept board, we tape a typed copy of our conceptual handle and accompanying summary-statement. Around this piece of paper, we pin everything we gather. It's important to examine not only the relationships of the items within a board but also apparent relationships of items from one board to another. Since in the end the creative direction that our final media goes in is influenced by elements from all of these boards, it's important to find conceptual congruencies between all boards. It's not like one board is chosen over another in the end. We simply let each one communicate its substance to us, and then choose the elements that we feel communicate most effectively the meaning that our audiences expressed that they were after.

In the case of this book, the train metaphor seemed to dominate. The results can be seen not just in the train imagery (which was a very late afterthought), but in the way we've isolated each notion into boxes that, like cars on a train, are linked together in continual flow of meaning within the context of a concept. Each concept represents a new number sequence within a chapter. Each chapter represents an idea. The body of chapters represents the subject *Designing the Effective Web Experience.* What do trains and experience design have in common? The answer is nothing unless we can build a conceptual link between the two galaxies of thinking.

The goal of doing this was to take the approximately 100,000 words that ended up being written for this book and fold them into notions that would be easy to encode into long-term memory. If you have trouble remembering something you read, think of the train meta-phor. Break it down in your mind until you find the associations that you're looking for, resting there and waiting for you to rediscover them and, hopefully, to reflect on them to form even more unique and personal insights and meanings. When they come to you, I hope you'll email me (john@trainofthoughts.com) and share them with me (please reference notion numbers when doing so).

10.02.01 Sometimes we try to discover how our concepts express themselves by searching for treasure in dumpsters.

Okay, so maybe we didn't look in actual dumpsters (Steve might have, though; he climbed some telephone poles and almost got arrested for lying down on railroad tracks), but we did look in junk shops. We also looked at the world around us as well as in magazines and the Web. The point is to look for things that stand out as somehow relating to one of the three to five concepts. By examining a plastic pearl necklace, for example, I was reminded of the idea of beat and rest which eventually would work itself into Chapter Five. I saw the pearls as being the beats and the gaps between the pearls as being rests. After I saw this, I started noticing other things that had instances of a repeating stimulus with gaps in between. Some of the other things I noticed were a series of birds perched on a wire, power lines strung between power poles, and train cars linked together along a track.

Perhaps the greatest progress that we made in understanding how our concepts expressed themselves, however, was through a fun exploration of the corners in our own imaginations. The artifacts we discovered there expressed themselves as the sketches that you've been looking at throughout this book. These weren't sketches that were used to conceptualize a final creative execution but instead were little doodles and diagrams that often would capture the essence of a concept.

10.02.03 It's important to *allow* the concept boards to inspire us.
This requires alternating periods of pondering them and then forgetting about them. The reason it's important to forget about them for a while is that it gives our collective subconscious time to work. This can lead to some incredible revelations when we least expect them. These revelations are often stifled when we think too long and too hard. In regard to the periods of pondering, these periods don't necessarily need to involve external exercises. Sometimes sitting and staring is an extremely worthwhile exercise. This isn't an expression of laziness but a necessary activity because it produces a state of mind in which reflective thinking can occur. The point of reflective thinking is to restructure our knowledge to identify and reinforce appropriate associations and patterns both within and among our concept boards.

The point of the elements on our boards isn't to eventually work their way directly into our final execution of media. In other words, we don't directly scan in and use a texture we find (although we may do this). Instead, these elements serve as catalysts for further reflective thinking and inspiration.

10.02.04 The sketchbook—yes, real live paper—is the key to finding originality that's truly productive.
As stated earlier, as we ponder these boards, it's extremely important to have a sketchbook in hand. Often important realizations occur by examining what comes out almost unconsciously through our sketches. Although many people want to plow right into digital execution of final media elements, at this stage they're selling the process short if they do.

Sketchbooks are important tools because there's no consequence for making mistakes. We often document visions that we would dismiss if recording them meant working within the digital medium. In a sketchbook, however, there are no boundaries, no procedures, and no rules. I personally have never worked on a project where the final concept evolved out of anything *but* one of my doodles. Our sketchbooks are what bridge between the concept boards and what will end up being our initial forays into digital execution. In them, the influences of all of the various concepts merge in singular expressions of creative meaning. Here is where the *real* inspiration of our concepts becomes manifest. Eventually, the concept boards will be photographed for posterity and future reference. From now on, the sketchbook is what will translate into the digital medium.

THEY'RE BOTH EXPLO

10.02.05 There's definitely logic involved in making final experience design decisions.

The statements of concept on our boards, while arrived at via horizontal thinking, are themselves governed by vertical thinking. We went from the known in the first radiant-thinking exercise to the unknown of a horizontal thinking exercise, but now we've defined the unknown and we explore it logically. In other words, we're looking for things that fit into our fledgling conceptual frameworks, not things that stretch beyond them as in the intergalactic thinking exercise. By following the principles of inductive and deductive reasoning, we should arrive at an optimal expression of each concept on its respective concept board.

After the concept boards begin to fill up and the project team has had sufficient time to become inspired, various individuals within the group will begin to get hot on the trail of some really powerful ideas for execution. They'll start to hear, feel, see, and almost taste where the concepts beg—almost demand—to go in terms of actual electronic execution. If due diligence has been performed throughout this process, these won't just be hunches, but an inner-knowing of what the concept wants to be when it grows up. It's important to groom it and foster its growth until it reaches maturity. Before this can proceed *too* far, however...

10.02.06 The selection of a final creative direction must be based on qualified input from all stakeholders.

Here again, it's important not to storm *too* far ahead into digital execution without subjecting the concept boards, as well as the respective leading ideas that are emerging out of the boards, to validation studies. In addition to validating them, there's one other very important function of these validation exercises for the design team. By progressively involving stakeholders, especially internal stakeholders, and involving them frequently, there's almost no chance that anyone will have a significant disconnect with the creative direction in the end.

Moreover, internal stakeholders are more likely to grow in their enthusiasm for the project because they feel more enfranchised into the process—they'll feel like they were *part* of the solution, not merely recipients of it. They'll see the results of their input, and they'll be inclined to move forward instead of pulling back.

IVE WITH VARIETY.

10.03 Expressing Our Creative Concepts Through Digital Media

This is the stage of creative execution that aligns with the *middle* and *final* cycles of the iterative execution phase outlined in Chapter Eight. As stated earlier, SPEED's creative process is simultaneously both a parallel process and a component process of the overall SPEED system. The reason for this distinction is that in the *initial* cycles of iterative execution (while the team is working on how the online resource and its component online messages will creatively express themselves), the team must *also* be working on a parallel set of activities. These activities deal with uncovering what needs to happen and be communicated in a timely manner and why. They also relate to finding the scope of what the developmental issues will be.

Often two subsets of the overall project team work on the functional and the creative issues separately and in parallel during initial iterations, but with some cross-pollination of team members to maintain continuity. After initial iterations, however, the groups must merge back together. This is a necessity because, as I've said, we work in the delivery medium in such a manner that design and development commingle. Although functional prototypes are developed in the digital medium almost from the start, this is not the case for prototypes that contain the execution of creative media. The reason is that cycles of iterative execution related to functionality can happen more effectively and more frequently in the digital medium during initial iterations than cycles related to creative execution can. In most cases, several cycles of functional execution could happen digitally before concept boards are even started.

By definition, when concepts begin to express themselves in a digital media form, we *have* entered the stage of iterative execution that I call *middle* iterations. This is the stage of iterative execution where everyone should know where the project is going and why. In this stage, we're working toward a *deployable state of refinement.* This is the only safe time to begin experimenting with creative ideas in the digital medium because the thinking behind the execution of media has been allowed to take its course. Now meaningful expressions of the concept are brewing and almost bubbling over in the experience designers' minds. This is the first point in the process where working on creative digital execution won't lead to pedestrian results and wasted time, energy, and resources.

Our concepting exercises have flown us high into the skies of our imaginations. It's now time to jump out of the idea airplane and begin a free-fall back to the ground. As we get closer to *final* iterations, we can pull the rip cord and land softly on the firm ground of an innovative and artfully formed final execution.

TRA
DESIGN

JOHN C. LENKER

www.trainofthoughts.com

10.03.01 Making sketches come to life digitally requires artfulness.
Not everyone is cut out for this task because it really requires having a talent for *visualization*. People involved in formulating the aesthetics of an online resource must therefore be highly skilled at making intangible conceptual directions tangible, real, and artful. It's impossible to describe all the ways in which the ideas from the concept boards work themselves into the sketchbooks and then into the digital medium. It's a process that requires vision and talent. In one case, a photograph of a misty Scottish landscape at dawn will influence the way the media elements will work together to foster a certain *feeling*. Maybe a certain doodle will speak to the way that navigation must move to help people visually reorient to a succeeding screen-space. Maybe, as in the case of our *micro-clarity* concept, there's an example from some other medium that does a good job of making a complex system as easy to understand as one-two-three. This will influence the breakdown, pacing, and expression of thoughts in our notions.

When planning important evenings of conversation with friends, business colleagues, or significant others, it's important to choose both the people and the setting conducive to the objectives of the discussion. It's the same with our online resources, except that instead of living people we have mediated online messages, and instead of physical environments we have digital environments. We want to communicate the right things in the right ways and at the right times to lead people through the three stages of communication—attract, inform, and invoke—until they're quickened to enter into a response interaction with a Web enterprise. The psychological impact of aesthetics on comprehension shouldn't be underestimated.

The question then becomes, how do we use the concepts? The answer is twofold. First, the concepts must influence *how* we express our thoughts through both content and environmental media. Second, the concepts must inform how we modulate people from one notion to another. We want to guide people's senses both across and between our screen-spaces in such a way that the flowpaths are clearly defined and provide emotional impact.

10.03.02 We must realistically, not wishfully, address technical parameters and requirements.
Please take heed. The greatest ideas in the world will only frustrate people if they don't function as planned. The bottom line is that creativity must work itself out in ways that make sense for the technological landscape. This has to do with bandwidth, processor speed, and compatibility issues.

If you're using a DHTML/JavaScript-type scenario, be careful! Most implementations of dynamics will fail to achieve the desired results. If you employ a more modern online delivery tool such as the Flash Player, you have a much better chance at achieving the desired results. You can, however, do inappropriate things even with this technology, which might all but offset the value of employing the technology in the first place. Embedding too many poorly compressed bitmap images into the Flash files, for example, can cause lapses in the very optimum-flow experiences that we're trying to create. Not being efficient in terms of eliminating developmental redundancies is another example. What's more, causing Flash to perform an excessive number of calculations will tax some microprocessors and cause things such as dynamic navigation to plod along—not a good result.

The bottom line is that the principles of the notion-flow philosophy can be achieved in any environment. The question becomes—to what degree? To use another musical example, I've written some songs that I overproduced in the recording studio in an attempt to achieve a substantial emotional impact. What I've learned is that sometimes in our zeal to *manufacture* impact, we bury the innate power that the meanings of our messages hold. Sometimes a single instrument and a single voice provide more emotion, intensity, and impact than a roomful of musicians could ever achieve. In light of this, it's really important to understand the substance of an online resource's subject as well as the substance of its online messages. The job of experience design is to reveal the meanings of our thoughts, concepts, and ideas in their truest, purest form. When this is done well, our ideas will seem natural and inspiring to people—never boring or overmanufactured. One indication that our notions aren't conveying true meaning is if they seem to rely on window dressing to mask a lack of any genuine conceptual significance.

10.03.03 Selecting an authoring environment hinges on creative execution as much as anything else; creative direction should therefore play an integral role in determining that environment. The qualifying statements made in the previous notion notwithstanding, this isn't a mandate for *developers* to storm ahead and determine the delivery medium for the online resource without first considering the conceptual, perceptual, and emotional needs of its audience sets and subsets. It's often the case that the use of dynamic media elements is essential to the success of the project. Some would argue that this is true of every case. In light of this, it's essential that those responsible for the aesthetics of an online resource be integrally involved in the selection of the delivery medium.

10.03.04 The quality of execution is a determining factor regarding the effectiveness of a person's online experience.

It's important that experience designers spend just as much time ensuring that the quality of the final execution is as refined as the concept behind the execution itself. When a final execution is sloppy and subprofessional (both on and under the surface), this reflects on the quality of the underlying online messages themselves. As stated in Chapter Nine, the reality is that people make unconscious judgments about the professionalism of a Web enterprise within seconds of first interacting with it. Online resources that come across as being sub-professional can also call into question the Web enterprise's claims to quality in either product or service.

It's the responsibility of every member of the experience design team to ensure that the approach to everything from visual design to notion formulation, flowstem development, and artfulness in final execution is up to snuff. The bottom line is that the quality of the execution, just as the quality of the underlying ideas being communicated themselves, is a determining factor in the effectiveness of Web experiences.

10.04 Summary

In this final chapter, we explored a facet of the *iterative execution* phase whose focus is developing creative concepts that are both unique and appropriate. We've learned that by following a proven, deliberate process, we can discipline our creative expression through the skill and precision necessary to make an online resource stand out as being attractive, inspiring, and compelling. We also learned that by interweaving both vertical and horizontal methods of concept exploration based on stakeholder insights, we place ourselves in the position of being on target with our creative direction. Finally, by following through with artful execution, we've learned how to succeed in employing genuine creative expression as a strong asset in our efforts to design the effective Web experience.

INDEX

Solutions from experts you know and trust.

www.informit.com

New Riders has partnered with **InformIT.com** to bring technical information to your desktop. Drawing on New Riders authors and reviewers to provide additional information on topics you're interested in, **InformIT.com** has free, in-depth information you won't find anywhere else.

- Master the skills you need, when you need them

- Call on resources from some of the best minds in the industry

- Get answers when you need them, using InformIT's comprehensive library or live experts online

- Go above and beyond what you find in New Riders books, extending your knowledge

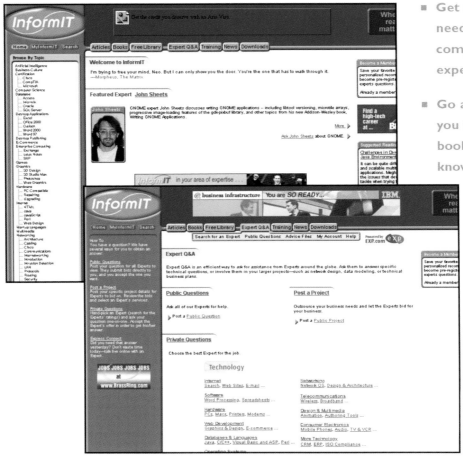

As an **InformIT** partner, **New Riders** has shared the wisdom and knowledge of our authors with you online. Visit **InformIT.com** to see

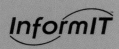

www.informit.com

www.newriders.com